**VOL 1**

— **KEEP UP YOUR** —

# Biblical Hebrew

**IN TWO MINUTES A DAY**

THE TWO MINUTES A DAY
BIBLICAL LANGUAGE SERIES
INCLUDES:

Keep Up Your Biblical Greek in Two Minutes a Day
Volume 1
365 Selections for Easy Review

Keep Up Your Biblical Greek in Two Minutes a Day
Volume 2
365 More Selections for Easy Review

Keep Up Your Biblical Hebrew in Two Minutes a Day
Volume 1
365 Selections for Easy Review

Keep Up Your Biblical Hebrew in Two Minutes a Day
Volume 2
365 More Selections for Easy Review

Keep Up Your Biblical Aramaic in Two Minutes a Day
365 Selections for Easy Review

VOL **1**

-------KEEP UP YOUR-------

# Biblical Hebrew

IN TWO MINUTES A DAY

365 SELECTIONS FOR EASY REVIEW

*Compiled and edited by*
*Jonathan G. Kline*

HENDRICKSON
PUBLISHERS

**Keep Up Your Biblical Hebrew in Two Minutes a Day, Volume 1**

© 2017 by Hendrickson Publishers Marketing, LLC
P. O. Box 3473
Peabody, Massachusetts 01961-3473
www.hendrickson.com

ISBN 978-1-68307-060-3

Book cover and jacket design by Maria Poulopoulos

*Printed in the United States of America*

*First Printing—November 2017*

## Library of Congress Cataloging-in-Publication Data

A catalog record for this title is available from the Library of Congress
Hendrickson Publishers Marketing, LLC ISBN 978-1-68307-060-3

# Contents

# Preface

*Keep Up Your Biblical Hebrew in Two Minutes a Day* has been specially designed to help you build on your previous study of Hebrew by reading a small amount of the Hebrew Bible in its original language every day in an easy, manageable, and spiritually enriching way. This book does not do away with the need to consult traditional textbooks and to review paradigms and the fundamentals of Hebrew grammar, which are essential tasks for developing an enduring ability to read and understand Hebrew well. Rather, this book complements such grammatical study by enabling you to build a robust vocabulary base and by encouraging you to work with the biblical text and review morphology and syntax in a largely inductive manner.

In order to help you reconnect with Hebrew in a direct and efficient way, this book contains no grammatical jargon or extraneous material—only verses from the Hebrew Bible, in Hebrew and English, carefully selected and presented (along with brief vocabulary entries) in a manner intended to facilitate rapid and enjoyable learning. The book is designed to be used on a daily basis (ideally), or in any case with some measure of consistency. The page for each day includes the following:

- one new vocabulary word, with transliteration and meanings, and two review words from earlier in the book

- the English text of a verse from the Hebrew Bible, with these three Hebrew words embedded in it, as they appear in the verse

- the Hebrew text of the verse, in full and then divided into phrases or clauses, with the corresponding English phrases or clauses next to them

To encourage you to spend a little time with Hebrew on a regular basis, each page is labeled with a day number (from 1 to 365), a date (from January 1 to December 31), and a week number (from Week 1 to Week 52). The book is thus designed so that you can work through it in a calendar year (whether starting on January 1 or any other date), though of course you need not use it according to this scheme. What is important, in any event, is not perfection or following a rigid schedule, but regular practice. There is no reason to feel bad if you miss a day or two, for example; the next time you have a chance to use the book, you can simply pick up where you left off, or skip to the page for the current date.

As the title *Keep Up Your Biblical Hebrew in Two Minutes a Day* indicates, spending at least two minutes with each day's page is recommended. Yet glancing at the page for a given day for even ten or fifteen seconds can still provide real benefits; and in any case this is better than not opening the book at all. Here are some suggestions for different ways you might wish to use this book, depending on how much time you have on a particular day:

**10 seconds to 1 minute.** *Activity:* Read the daily Bible verse in English, noticing the Hebrew words in parentheses. *Benefit:* You have read a Bible verse in English and have been quickly reminded of what a few Hebrew words mean and perhaps of an aspect or two of Hebrew grammar. *Alternate activity:* Look at the Hebrew word for the day and read its definitions. *Benefit:* You have been reminded of the basic range of meaning of a Hebrew word that occurs with a relatively high frequency in the Hebrew Bible.

**2 to 5 minutes.** *Activity:* Read the daily Bible verse in English, noticing the Hebrew words in parentheses. Next, look at the Hebrew word for the day and its meanings. Finally, read the Hebrew text as best you can, perhaps only in the phrase/clause section on the lower half of the page, simply ignoring what you don't understand (even if this is all or most of the words). *Benefit:* You have read a Bible verse in English and (as much as you are able) in Hebrew. You have been reminded of what at least a few, and perhaps many, Hebrew words mean, and perhaps also of certain principles of Hebrew morphology and syntax.

**10 to 20 minutes.** *Activity:* Every day of a given week, look at all seven pages for the present week, spending whatever amount of time you desire on each page (perhaps skimming some pages and spending more time on others). *Benefit:* After the week is over, you will likely have developed a deep familiarity with the week's biblical texts and a lasting knowledge of the week's vocabulary words. You will also have deepened your familiarity with various principles of Hebrew morphology and syntax.

As these suggestions indicate, although this book has been designed to provide substantial benefits if you use it for only two minutes a day, mulling over (and, as need be, puzzling through) its contents for longer periods of time can help you even further along the journey toward achieving a lasting mastery of Hebrew.

Another interesting and helpful way to use this book—one that is especially suited for more advanced users—is to review vocabulary by means of a "chain" method. For example, pick a day in the book, perhaps at random and preferably toward the end (say, Day 363), and read the page. Then, pick one of the two review words for the day (e.g., כְּסָא), go to the page on which that word is the new word for the day (Day 332), and read that page. Next, pick one of the review words on this new page (e.g., יָמִין), go to the page on which it is the new word for the day (Day 315), and read that page. You can repeat this process as many times as you want, until you reach (or get as close as possible to) the beginning of the book.

If the verse for a particular day is one that you would like to internalize or try to memorize in Hebrew, feel free to temporarily suspend your regular reading of a new page each day and instead spend several days, or perhaps even a week, reading the same page every day. By doing so, you may notice new things about the grammar or syntax of the verse, and at least some, if not all, of the verse will likely remain in your mind and heart for a long time to come. If you take the time to meditate on a verse in this way, you may also wish to look up the verse in a technical commentary or two to see what scholars have said about it; or you may choose to look up the verse in the index of an intermediate or advanced Hebrew grammar in order to learn about the morphology of the words the verse contains or about its syntax. Meditating on or memorizing even two or three Hebrew verses in this way over the course of a year can go a long way toward helping you internalize and become proficient in the language.

As the foregoing discussion indicates, the benefits you derive from using this book will obviously depend on how much time you spend with it and how often, the specific ways you choose to use it, your current level of Hebrew proficiency, and your ability to learn inductively. Nevertheless, I have done my best to design the book so that it can help you make substantial and enduring gains in learning even if you are able to use it for only short periods of time at most sittings and even if your Hebrew is at a rudimentary level when you begin.

## The Vocabulary

*Keep Up Your Biblical Hebrew in Two Minutes a Day* presents, one day at a time and in order of descending frequency, the 365 most frequently occurring words in the Hebrew Bible—that is, all the words that occur more than 120 times. This amounts to about two-thirds of the vocabulary that one typically learns in a first-year Hebrew class. If you master these 365 words, you will know the lexical form lying behind about two-thirds of the Hebrew words that the *Biblia Hebraica Stuttgartensia: A Reader's Edition* assumes knowledge of (i.e., the words that that volume does not gloss in its apparatus).

I created the initial list of 365 core review words for this book by comparing the main frequency list of vocabulary found in *The Vocabulary Guide to Biblical Hebrew*, by Miles V. Van Pelt and Gary D. Pratico (Zondervan) and a similar list generated using the computer program BibleWorks; I then made my own decisions regarding which words should be included in the list for this book and regarding each word's frequency. The frequency for a given word is found to the right of the gray box containing the word's gloss(es) and followed by an "x."

For readers who are in the beginning stages of their knowledge of Hebrew grammar and who are accustomed to using Strong's concordance in their study of the vocabulary of the Hebrew Bible, I have also included the Strong's number for each daily vocabulary word. These numbers are prefixed with an "S" and are found below the frequency numbers.

## The Glosses

I generated the initial list of glosses for the 365 core vocabulary words in this book by abridging the relevant entries in the public-domain Hebrew dictionary prepared by James Strong that accompanies the well-known concordances that go by his name. Although Strong produced his dictionary many years ago, his glosses provided a helpful basic list to which I then made a large number of modifications on the basis of my years of experience studying and teaching Hebrew in seminary and university settings, and also on the basis of consulting standard modern lexicons, especially William Holladay's *Concise Hebrew and Aramaic Lexicon of the Old Testament* (Eerdmans).

I have intentionally kept the glosses basic and brief so that you can quickly grasp a word's essential or most common meaning(s). The glosses are not exhaustive. For more comprehensive and nuanced glosses or definitions, please consult a standard Hebrew lexicon.

Likewise, and again to facilitate rapid and easy review, I have kept grammatical information in the glosses to an absolute minimum. For example, for verbal roots I have not indicated which stems a verb occurs in, nor therefore have I stated which meanings of a given verb are attested in which stems. (As a small help to the reader in this regard, however, I have normally used a semicolon, as opposed to a comma, to separate meanings attested in different stems.) Grammatical information of this nature can readily be found in standard lexicons and vocabulary guides, and I encourage you to consult such resources as much as you are able. Again, my primary goal has been simply to provide the most common meanings of the new vocabulary word for each day in a way that can be quickly understood.

## The Verses

In this book I have attempted to present an interesting and inspiring variety of verses from the Hebrew Bible, in terms of both content and grammar. The process by which I chose the verses was an organic and creative one that was guided by grammatical, theological, aesthetic, and—above all—pedagogical concerns. I have included verses from nearly every book of the Hebrew Bible and of varying lengths and difficulties. The verses contain content that is inspiring, comforting, challenging, and thought provoking. This allows you, if you wish, to use the book as a kind of daily devotional. Whether you think of the book in this way or not, my goal in creating it has been not only to help you improve your knowledge of Hebrew for its own sake, but also—and more importantly—to help you engage closely with, meditate on, wrestle with, be challenged by, and find solace and hope in the words of the biblical writers.

## The Phrases and Clauses

In breaking up each day's verse into phrases and/or clauses, I have done my best to help you see the correspondence between brief elements in the day's Hebrew text and English translation. Naturally, however, a one-to-one correspondence does not always exist (and in a technical sense never completely exists) between a Hebrew word, phrase, or clause and its English translation. For this reason, you may occasionally find the way that I have matched up parts of the Hebrew and English verses to be slightly forced. It goes without saying that the correspondences shown are not meant to be completely scientific or precise in every case; rather, they are a pedagogical tool intended to help you work through each day's verse little by little and in a short amount of time, in order to arrive at a basic understanding of the grammar and syntax of the Hebrew.

Correlatively, in an attempt to be sensitive to the unique content of each day's verse and to help you understand it as well as possible, I have sometimes divided syntactically or grammatically identical structures found in different verses in different ways. Such inconsistencies are intentional and, again, are always the result of my trying to present the parts of a given day's verse in the way that I thought would be most helpful, as well as in a way that makes the most sense in light of the specific English translation used for the day in question. By breaking up the verses in different ways, in fact, I hope to have made the point that there is no rigid or single system that one ought to use for analyzing a Hebrew sentence's grammar in order to achieve understanding.

## Highlighting and Bold Type

On each day's page (except on the first two days, when there are not two review words), there are three Hebrew words embedded in the full English verse at the top of the page, with the English equivalents marked in bold type. In keeping with the minimalist approach I have used for the glosses, I have kept the number of English words in bold type to a minimum, since this formatting is intended primarily to remind you of a word's basic meaning, not (as a rule) to convey syntactic information communicated by the word in question.

Because of the differences between the morphology and syntax of English (an Indo-European language) and of Hebrew (a Semitic language in which discrete lexical and syntactic information is often communicated by means of prefixes and suffixes), in certain cases there is no perfect way to use bold type and highlighting in order to show the correlation between words, phrases, or clauses in the two languages. Two of the most frequently occurring instances of this are when one of the day's three highlighted Hebrew words is either a construct form or a word with a pronominal suffix.

For example, the phrase אַנְשֵׁי יִשְׂרָאֵל, "the men of Israel," appears in 2 Sam 2:17, which is quoted on Day 26. The genitive relationship in this phrase is signaled most visibly in Hebrew by the fact that the first noun, אַנְשֵׁי (the so-called *nomen regens*), is in the construct state; thus, this word conveys the idea "the men of," and the word יִשְׂרָאֵל conveys the idea "Israel." Because the point of this book is to help you focus on the essential *lexical* information communicated by a given day's three highlighted words, however, in the English verse at the top of the page I have put only the word "men" in bold type in this and similar cases and have embedded the word אַנְשֵׁי in parentheses immediately after this word—the result being "the **men (אַנְשֵׁי)** of Israel." Although imperfect, this formatting seemed to me to be the best of the available alternatives, and I hope in any case that the main point is clear: namely, that the basic meaning of the word אַנְשֵׁי is "men."

On the other hand, because the section of phrases and clauses located at the bottom of the page is intended to highlight *syntax*, I have kept the "of" in such cases with the *nomen regens* when I have placed this word and the *nomen rectum* on different lines (e.g., "the men of" / אַנְשֵׁי // "Israel" / יִשְׂרָאֵל). Such small inconsistencies between the way the text is presented in the full English verse at the top of the page and in the section of phrases and clauses at the bottom are therefore intentional, and once again, my goal in all of this has been to help you understand the Hebrew as easily and efficiently as possible.

More awkward are the many cases found in this book that involve pronominal suffixes. Unlike many prefixes (e.g., בְּ, בַ, כְּ, לְ, and וְ), which I normally removed before embedding the Hebrew forms in the English text (since this could often be done without altering the morphology of the words in question), suffixes cannot usually be detached from the bases to which they are joined without turning the latter into nonsense forms. For this reason and for the sake of consistency, I decided to retain all suffixes on the Hebrew words that I embedded in the English verses, even though in some cases this results in a slightly odd presentation of the parallel between the relevant English and Hebrew words. This is not so striking when a form like "your **fathers (אֲבוֹתֵיכֶם)**" occurs (e.g., on Day 38), in which case the English pronoun reflecting the Hebrew pronominal suffix *precedes* the English word in question. But the situation is more pronounced in cases when the English pronoun *follows*: for example, in such phrases as "**with (אִתְּךָ)** you" (Day 131) and "**sent (שְׁלָחַנִי)** me" (Day 87). Again, I hope that this presentation of the information, albeit imperfect, is clear enough and achieves its goal of helping you learn the meaning of the Hebrew words in question.

Rarely it happened that removing a prefix (such as the preposition בְּ when spelled בַ, as in בִּימֵי in Ruth 1:1, quoted on Day 25) would have resulted in a form that looked erroneous because of the absence of a vowel under the first consonant (e.g., יְמֵי, as opposed to יְמֵי). In such cases, I therefore retained the prefix when embedding the word in the English verse text (thus, בִּימֵי).

A few final clarifications on my method of highlighting: When a finite verb form appears as one of the three marked words for the day, I have normally put the relevant English pronoun (if one is present) in bold type as a reminder of the fact that this information is encoded in the verb form (though admittedly this practice is slightly at odds with not highlighting grammatical information in connection with non-verbs). An exception to this, however, is that if a Hebrew personal pronoun accompanies a finite verbal form, I have not put the English pronoun in bold type—in order to draw your attention to the presence of the Hebrew pronoun. In addition, I have highlighted the conjunction *waw* on verb forms only when it functions "conversively" (i.e., in *wayyiqtol* and *weqatal* forms), though I have not put the corresponding "and" in English (if it is present) in bold type. In a similar vein, but slightly differently, I have not highlighted the preposition לְ when it is prefixed to an infinitive construct, but I have made the corresponding "to" in English (if one is present) bold.

Such details as the foregoing, which occasionally result in apparent inconsistencies in formatting, reflect the fact, again, that a one-to-one correspondence does not exist between Hebrew and English (or, of course, between any two languages). I have done my best to be as consistent as possible in how I have formatted the text, and I was always guided by what I thought would be most helpful to you, the reader. As with the way I have broken up the text into phrases and clauses, the bold type and highlighting are meant not to reflect a "scientific" analysis of the Hebrew text but simply to help you quickly understand what the words mean.

## Sources Used

The Hebrew text quoted in this book is taken from the Michigan-Claremont-Westminster Electronic Hebrew Bible, a popular electronic version that is based on the BHS and that has been revised by its creators on the basis of comparison with the Leningrad Codex. This electronic text is in the public domain and has been made available courtesy of the J. Alan Groves Center for Advanced Biblical Research. For ease of reading, I have removed the Masoretic accents and—for the same reason—in cases of Ketiv/Qere I have omitted the Ketiv form and included only the Qere.

The following English translations are used in this book: NRSV, ESV, NASB, NIV, CSB, and MLB. I chose these six translations because most of them are widely used, and I wanted to help provide a sense of different ways in which Hebrew can be rendered in English. Another reason I chose these particular translations is because most of them—especially the NASB, ESV, and NRSV—tend to be rather "literal" renderings; one indication of this is that their syntax often corresponds closely to that of the Hebrew, making it relatively easy to show which parts of the English text parallel which parts of the Hebrew text (a key feature of this book). The other translations used here—the NIV, CSB, and MLB—are often relatively literal but, in contrast to the NASB, ESV, and NRSV, they usually lie further toward the "dynamic equivalence" end of the translation spectrum. I hope that by seeing how each of these translations deals with a sampling of verses, you will grow in your familiarity with and appreciation of the translation philosophies that underlie them.

In addition to embedding three Hebrew words in each day's English translation, I have made a number of minor modifications to the punctuation and formatting of the translations for the sake of clarity and consistency of presentation. The most common changes include the following: the change of a comma or semicolon at the end of a verse to a period; the insertion of an opening or closing quotation mark when a quotation is carried on from the previous verse or carries on into the next verse; and the capitalization of a lowercase letter at the beginning of a verse. When a verse constitutes a complete quotation, I have removed the quotation marks at the beginning and end of the verse. I have also removed the italics from words in the NASB that mark English words that do not explicitly correspond to a word in the Hebrew.

For the most part, I have cited entire verses. Occasionally, however, in order to make all the text fit on the page for the day, it was necessary to omit material. Material omitted from the middle of a verse is always marked with ellipses, but material omitted from the beginning or end of a verse is generally not marked. Occasionally I have used ellipses at the end of a verse not to indicate omitted material but to signal that the text that has been quoted constitutes an incomplete sentence.

In a few instances, I have inserted one or more words in brackets in the English Bible translation to indicate a word (or more than one) that is present in the Hebrew but not reflected in the translation. On a greater number of occasions, I have inserted a more literal rendering in brackets, prefixing it with "lit."

Because both the English and Hebrew verses quoted in this book are presented in isolation, I encourage you, as often as you are able, to look at them in their original contexts in order to gain a better understanding of their meaning and how they function in the passages from which they have been excerpted. Please note that when the Hebrew and English verse numbers differ, the former is listed first and the latter second, in square brackets.

\* \* \* \* \*

I offer this book with empathy and in friendship to everyone who has spent countless hours studying Hebrew but who has experienced difficulty, principally on account of a lack of time, in keeping up with the language. May you receive encouragement, challenge, hope, joy, and peace from the time you spend with the biblical texts on these pages.

—Jonathan G. Kline, PhD

In the beginning God created the heavens **and (וְ)** the earth. (MLB)

| וְ | and, but | 50524x |
|---|---|---|
| *vĕ* | | |

בְּרֵאשִׁית בָּרָא אֱלֹהִים אֵת הַשָּׁמַיִם וְאֵת הָאָרֶץ:

| In the beginning | בְּרֵאשִׁית |
|---|---|
| God | אֱלֹהִים |
| created | בָּרָא |
| the heavens | אֵת הַשָּׁמַיִם |
| **and** the earth | וְאֵת הָאָרֶץ |

Lead me in your truth **and** (וְ) teach me, for you are the God of my salvation; for you I wait all **the** (הַ) day long. (ESV)

| | |
|---|---|
| הַ<br>*ha* | the              24058x |

וְ    ➤    DAY 1

הַדְרִיכֵנִי בַאֲמִתֶּךָ וְלַמְּדֵנִי כִּי־אַתָּה אֱלֹהֵי יִשְׁעִי אוֹתְךָ קִוִּיתִי כָּל־הַיּוֹם:

| | |
|---|---|
| Lead me | הַדְרִיכֵנִי |
| in your truth | בַאֲמִתֶּךָ |
| **and** teach me | וְלַמְּדֵנִי |
| for you | כִּי־אַתָּה |
| are the God of my salvation | אֱלֹהֵי יִשְׁעִי |
| for you I wait | אוֹתְךָ קִוִּיתִי |
| all **the** day long | כָּל־הַיּוֹם |

He had [lit., **And (וְ) to (לֹו)** him were] two wives: the name of one
was Hannah **and (וְ)** the name of **the (הַ)** other Peninnah; **and (וְ)**
Peninnah had children, **but (וְ)** Hannah had no children. (NASB)

| לְ | to, for, of | 20378x |
|----|-------------|--------|
| lĕ |  |  |

וְ  ➤  DAY 1          הַ  ➤  DAY 2

וְלֹו שְׁתֵּי נָשִׁים שֵׁם אַחַת חַנָּה וְשֵׁם הַשֵּׁנִית פְּנִנָּה וַיְהִי לִפְנִנָּה יְלָדִים
וּלְחַנָּה אֵין יְלָדִים:

| He had [lit., **And to** him were] two wives | וְלֹו שְׁתֵּי נָשִׁים |
|---|---|
| the name of one was Hannah | שֵׁם אַחַת חַנָּה |
| **and** the name of **the** other Peninnah | וְשֵׁם הַשֵּׁנִית פְּנִנָּה |
| **and** Peninnah had children | וַיְהִי לִפְנִנָּה יְלָדִים |
| **but** Hannah had no children | וּלְחַנָּה אֵין יְלָדִים |

**In** (בְּ) God we have boasted continually [lit., all **the** (הַ) day], and we will give thanks to your name forever [lit., **to** (לְ) eternity]. Selah. (NRSV)

| בְּ<br>bĕ | in, among, with | 15550x |
|---|---|---|

הַ  ➤  DAY 2     לְ  ➤  DAY 3

בֵּאלֹהִים הִלַּלְנוּ כָל־הַיּוֹם וְשִׁמְךָ לְעוֹלָם נוֹדֶה סֶלָה:

| **In** God | בֵּאלֹהִים |
|---|---|
| we have boasted | הִלַּלְנוּ |
| continually [lit., all **the** day] | כָל־הַיּוֹם |
| and we will give thanks to your name | וְשִׁמְךָ . . . נוֹדֶה |
| forever [lit., **to** eternity] | לְעוֹלָם |
| Selah | סֶלָה |

The Lord God took the man (אֶת־הָאָדָם) and placed him **in** (בְ)
the garden of Eden **to** (לְ) cultivate it and **to** (לְ) care for it. (MLB)

| אֶת | (definite direct object marker) | 10978x |
| ʾēt | | S853 |

לְ ➤ DAY 3          בְ ➤ DAY 4

וַיִּקַּח יְהוָה אֱלֹהִים אֶת־הָאָדָם וַיַּנִּחֵהוּ בְגַן־עֵדֶן לְעָבְדָהּ וּלְשָׁמְרָהּ׃

| The Lord God | יְהוָה אֱלֹהִים |
| took | וַיִּקַּח |
| the man | אֶת־הָאָדָם |
| and placed him | וַיַּנִּחֵהוּ |
| **in** the garden of Eden | בְגַן־עֵדֶן |
| **to** cultivate it | לְעָבְדָהּ |
| and **to** care for it | וּלְשָׁמְרָהּ |

For I will remove the names (אֶת־שְׁמֹות) of the Baals **from** (מִ) her mouth; they will no longer be remembered **by** (בְּ) their names. (CSB)

| מִן | from, out of | 7586x |
|---|---|---|
| *min* | | S4480 |

בְּ  ➤  DAY 4          אֵת  ➤  DAY 5

וַהֲסִרֹתִי אֶת־שְׁמֹות הַבְּעָלִים מִפִּיהָ וְלֹא־יִזָּכְרוּ עֹוד בִּשְׁמָם:

| For I will remove | וַהֲסִרֹתִי |
|---|---|
| the names of | אֶת־שְׁמֹות |
| the Baals | הַבְּעָלִים |
| **from** her mouth | מִפִּיהָ |
| they will no longer be remembered | וְלֹא־יִזָּכְרוּ עֹוד |
| **by** their names | בִּשְׁמָם |

You have been rebellious against the **LORD** (יְהוָה) ever since [lit., **from** (מִ) the day] I have known you (אֶתְכֶם). (NIV)

| | | |
|---|---|---|
| **יהוה** | Yahweh, LORD | 6828x |
| *YHWH, ădōnāy* | | S3068 |

**אֵת**  ➤  DAY 5            **מִן**  ➤  DAY 6

מַמְרִים הֱיִיתֶם עִם־יְהוָה מִיּוֹם דַּעְתִּי אֶתְכֶם:

| | |
|---|---|
| You have been | הֱיִיתֶם |
| rebellious | מַמְרִים |
| against the **LORD** | עִם־יְהוָה |
| ever since [lit., **from** the day] | מִיּוֹם |
| I have known | דַּעְתִּי |
| you | אֶתְכֶם |

The Egyptians will know that I am the **Lord** (יְהוָה) when I stretch out my hand **against** (עַל) Egypt and bring out the Israelites **from** (מִ) among them. (CSB)

| עַל | on, upon, over | 5777x |
|---|---|---|
| ʿal | | S5921 |

מִן  ➤  DAY 6      יהוה  ➤  DAY 7

וְיָדְעוּ מִצְרַיִם כִּי־אֲנִי יְהוָה בִּנְטֹתִי אֶת־יָדִי עַל־מִצְרָיִם וְהוֹצֵאתִי אֶת־בְּנֵי־יִשְׂרָאֵל מִתּוֹכָם:

| | |
|---|---|
| The Egyptians will know | וְיָדְעוּ מִצְרַיִם |
| that I am the **Lord** | כִּי־אֲנִי יְהוָה |
| when I stretch out | בִּנְטֹתִי |
| my hand | אֶת־יָדִי |
| **against** Egypt | עַל־מִצְרָיִם |
| and bring out | וְהוֹצֵאתִי |
| the Israelites | אֶת־בְּנֵי־יִשְׂרָאֵל |
| **from** among them | מִתּוֹכָם |

Then the **LORD** (יְהוָה) said **to** (אֵלַי) me, "You have seen well, for I am watching **over** (עַל) My word to perform it." (NASB)

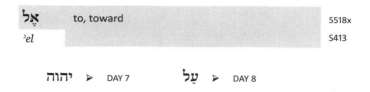

| אֵל | to, toward | 5518x |
| ʾel | | S413 |

יהוה ➤ DAY 7          עַל ➤ DAY 8

וַיֹּאמֶר יְהוָה אֵלַי הֵיטַבְתָּ לִרְאוֹת כִּי־שֹׁקֵד אֲנִי עַל־דְּבָרִי לַעֲשֹׂתוֹ׃

| Then the **LORD** said | וַיֹּאמֶר יְהוָה |
| **to** me | אֵלַי |
| You have seen well | הֵיטַבְתָּ לִרְאוֹת |
| for I am watching | כִּי־שֹׁקֵד אֲנִי |
| **over** My word | עַל־דְּבָרִי |
| to perform it | לַעֲשֹׂתוֹ |

God said **to** (אֶל) Noah, "This is the sign of the covenant **that** (אֲשֶׁר) I have established between me and all flesh **that** (אֲשֶׁר) is **on** (עַל) the earth." (NRSV)

| אֲשֶׁר | that, which, who | 5503x |
|---|---|---|
| ʾăšer | | S834 |

עַל    ▷    DAY 8      אֶל    ▷    DAY 9

וַיֹּאמֶר אֱלֹהִים אֶל־נֹחַ זֹאת אוֹת־הַבְּרִית אֲשֶׁר הֲקִמֹתִי בֵּינִי וּבֵין כָּל־
בָּשָׂר אֲשֶׁר עַל־הָאָרֶץ:

| God said | וַיֹּאמֶר אֱלֹהִים |
|---|---|
| **to** Noah | אֶל־נֹחַ |
| This | זֹאת |
| is the sign of the covenant | אוֹת־הַבְּרִית |
| **that** I have established | אֲשֶׁר הֲקִמֹתִי |
| between me | בֵּינִי |
| and all flesh | וּבֵין כָּל־בָּשָׂר |
| **that** is **on** the earth | אֲשֶׁר עַל־הָאָרֶץ |

Then David said **to** (אֶל) Joab and **to** (אֶל) **all** (כָּל־) the people
**who** (אֲשֶׁר) were with him, "Tear your clothes and put on
sackcloth and mourn before Abner." And King David followed the
bier. (ESV)

| | | |
|---|---|---|
| **כֹּל** | all, every | 5415x |
| *kōl* | | S3605 |

אֶל    ➤ DAY 9          אֲשֶׁר    ➤ DAY 10

וַיֹּאמֶר דָּוִד אֶל־יוֹאָב וְאֶל־כָּל־הָעָם אֲשֶׁר־אִתּוֹ קִרְעוּ בִגְדֵיכֶם וְחִגְרוּ
שַׂקִּים וְסִפְדוּ לִפְנֵי אַבְנֵר וְהַמֶּלֶךְ דָּוִד הֹלֵךְ אַחֲרֵי הַמִּטָּה:

| | |
|---|---|
| Then David said | וַיֹּאמֶר דָּוִד |
| **to** Joab | אֶל־יוֹאָב |
| and **to all** the people | וְאֶל־כָּל־הָעָם |
| **who** were with him | אֲשֶׁר־אִתּוֹ |
| Tear your clothes | קִרְעוּ בִגְדֵיכֶם |
| and put on sackcloth | וְחִגְרוּ שַׂקִּים |
| and mourn before Abner | וְסִפְדוּ לִפְנֵי אַבְנֵר |
| And King David | וְהַמֶּלֶךְ דָּוִד |
| followed the bier | הֹלֵךְ אַחֲרֵי הַמִּטָּה |

Speak to the people of Israel, **saying** (לֵאמֹר), "These are the living things **that** (אֲשֶׁר) you may eat among **all** (כָּל־) the animals **that** (אֲשֶׁר) are on the earth." (ESV)

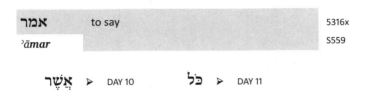

| אמר | to say | 5316x |
|---|---|---|
| ʾāmar | | S559 |

אֲשֶׁר   ➤   DAY 10      כֹּל   ➤   DAY 11

דַּבְּרוּ אֶל־בְּנֵי יִשְׂרָאֵל לֵאמֹר זֹאת הַחַיָּה אֲשֶׁר תֹּאכְלוּ מִכָּל־הַבְּהֵמָה אֲשֶׁר עַל־הָאָרֶץ:

| Speak | דַּבְּרוּ |
|---|---|
| to the people of Israel | אֶל־בְּנֵי יִשְׂרָאֵל |
| **saying** | לֵאמֹר |
| These are the living things | זֹאת הַחַיָּה |
| **that** you may eat | אֲשֶׁר תֹּאכְלוּ |
| among **all** the animals | מִכָּל־הַבְּהֵמָה |
| **that** are on the earth | אֲשֶׁר עַל־הָאָרֶץ |

So Moses **said** (וַיֹּאמֶר) to the LORD, "Why have you treated your servant so badly? Why have I **not** (לֹא) found favor in your sight, that you lay the burden of **all** (כָּל־) this people on me?" (NRSV)

| לֹא | no, not | 5188x |
|-----|---------|-------|
| lō' |  | S3808 |

כָּל ⊳ DAY 11          אמר ⊳ DAY 12

וַיֹּאמֶר מֹשֶׁה אֶל־יְהוָה לָמָה הֲרֵעֹתָ לְעַבְדֶּךָ וְלָמָּה לֹא־מָצָתִי חֵן בְּעֵינֶיךָ לָשׂוּם אֶת־מַשָּׂא כָּל־הָעָם הַזֶּה עָלָי׃

| So Moses **said** | וַיֹּאמֶר מֹשֶׁה |
|---|---|
| to the LORD | אֶל־יְהוָה |
| Why have you treated your servant so badly? | לָמָה הֲרֵעֹתָ לְעַבְדֶּךָ |
| Why have I **not** found favor | וְלָמָּה לֹא־מָצָתִי חֵן |
| in your sight | בְּעֵינֶיךָ |
| that you lay the burden of | לָשׂוּם אֶת־מַשָּׂא |
| **all** this people | כָּל־הָעָם הַזֶּה |
| on me? | עָלָי |

But Gideon **said** (וַיֹּאמֶר) to them, "I will **not** (לֹא) rule over you, and my **son** (בְּנִי) will **not** (לֹא) rule over you; the LORD will rule over you." (CSB)

| בֵּן | son | | 4941x |
|---|---|---|---|
| *bēn* | | | S1121 |

אמר   ➤   DAY 12       לֹא   ➤   DAY 13

וַיֹּאמֶר אֲלֵהֶם גִּדְעוֹן לֹא־אֶמְשֹׁל אֲנִי בָּכֶם וְלֹא־יִמְשֹׁל בְּנִי בָּכֶם יְהוָה
יִמְשֹׁל בָּכֶם:

| But Gideon **said** to them | וַיֹּאמֶר אֲלֵהֶם גִּדְעוֹן |
|---|---|
| I will **not** rule over you | לֹא־אֶמְשֹׁל אֲנִי בָּכֶם |
| and my **son** will **not** rule over you | וְלֹא־יִמְשֹׁל בְּנִי בָּכֶם |
| the LORD will rule over you | יְהוָה יִמְשֹׁל בָּכֶם |

And about the time of her death the women who stood by her said to her, "Do not be afraid, **for (כִּי)** you have given birth to a **son (בֵן)**." But she did **not (לֹא)** answer or [lit., and did **not (לֹא)**] pay attention. (NASB)

| כִּי<br>kî | because, for, that, indeed | 4487x<br>S3588 |
|---|---|---|

**לֹא**  ➤  DAY 13          **בֵן**  ➤  DAY 14

וּכְעֵת מוּתָהּ וַתְּדַבֵּרְנָה הַנִּצָּבוֹת עָלֶיהָ אַל־תִּירְאִי כִּי בֵן יָלָדְתְּ וְלֹא עָנְתָה וְלֹא־שָׁתָה לִבָּהּ:

| | |
|---|---|
| And about the time of her death | וּכְעֵת מוּתָהּ |
| the women who stood by her | הַנִּצָּבוֹת עָלֶיהָ |
| said to her | וַתְּדַבֵּרְנָה |
| Do not be afraid | אַל־תִּירְאִי |
| **for** you have given birth to a **son** | כִּי בֵן יָלָדְתְּ |
| But she did **not** answer | וְלֹא עָנְתָה |
| or [lit., and did **not**] pay attention | וְלֹא־שָׁתָה לִבָּהּ |

As I live, says the Lord, **even** (כִּי) if King Coniah **son** (בֶּן) of Jehoiakim of Judah **were** (יִהְיֶה) the signet ring on my right hand, **even** (כִּי) from there I would tear you off. (NRSV)

| | | | |
|---|---|---|---|
| הָיָה | to be, become, come to pass | | 3576x |
| *hāyâ* | | | S1961 |

בֶּן ➤ DAY 14          כִּי ➤ DAY 15

חַי־אָנִי נְאֻם־יְהוָה כִּי אִם־יִהְיֶה כָּנְיָהוּ בֶן־יְהוֹיָקִים מֶלֶךְ יְהוּדָה חוֹתָם עַל־יַד יְמִינִי כִּי מִשָּׁם אֶתְּקֶנְךָּ׃

| | |
|---|---|
| As I live | חַי־אָנִי |
| says the Lord | נְאֻם־יְהוָה |
| **even** if | כִּי אִם־ |
| King Coniah **son** of Jehoiakim of Judah | כָּנְיָהוּ בֶן־יְהוֹיָקִים מֶלֶךְ יְהוּדָה |
| **were** the signet ring | יִהְיֶה . . . חוֹתָם |
| on my right hand | עַל־יַד יְמִינִי |
| **even** from there | כִּי מִשָּׁם |
| I would tear you off | אֶתְּקֶנְךָּ |

So he died **according to (כְּ)** the word of the LORD that Elijah
had spoken. Jehoram became king in his place . . . **because (כִּי)**
Ahaziah had no son [lit., there **was (הָיָה)** no son to him]. (ESV)

| כְּ | | |
|---|---|---|
| *kĕ* | like, as, according to, approximately, about | 2902x |

כִּי ➤ DAY 15          היה ➤ DAY 16

וַיָּמָת כִּדְבַר יְהוָה אֲשֶׁר־דִּבֶּר אֵלִיָּהוּ וַיִּמְלֹךְ יְהוֹרָם תַּחְתָּיו . . . כִּי
לֹא־הָיָה לוֹ בֵּן:

| So he died | וַיָּמָת |
|---|---|
| **according to** the word of the LORD | כִּדְבַר יְהוָה |
| that Elijah had spoken | אֲשֶׁר־דִּבֶּר אֵלִיָּהוּ |
| Jehoram became king | וַיִּמְלֹךְ יְהוֹרָם |
| in his place . . . | תַּחְתָּיו . . . |
| **because** Ahaziah had no son [lit., there **was** no son to him] | כִּי לֹא־הָיָה לוֹ בֵּן |

And **it will be** (תִּהְיֶה) righteousness for us, if we are careful **to do** (עֲשׂוֹת) all this commandment before the Lord our God, **as** (כַּ) he has commanded us. (ESV)

| עָשָׂה | to do, make | | 2629x |
|---|---|---|---|
| ʿāśâ | | | S6213 |

| היה | ➤ | DAY 16 | | כְּ | ➤ | DAY 17 |
|---|---|---|---|---|---|---|

וּצְדָקָה תִּהְיֶה־לָּנוּ כִּי־נִשְׁמֹר לַעֲשׂוֹת אֶת־כָּל־הַמִּצְוָה הַזֹּאת לִפְנֵי
יְהוָה אֱלֹהֵינוּ כַּאֲשֶׁר צִוָּנוּ׃

| And **it will be** righteousness for us | וּצְדָקָה תִּהְיֶה־לָּנוּ |
|---|---|
| if we are careful | כִּי־נִשְׁמֹר |
| **to do** | לַעֲשׂוֹת |
| all this commandment | אֶת־כָּל־הַמִּצְוָה הַזֹּאת |
| before the Lord our God | לִפְנֵי יְהוָה אֱלֹהֵינוּ |
| **as** he has commanded us | כַּאֲשֶׁר צִוָּנוּ |

But he has slandered your servant to my master the king. Still, my master the king is **like (כְּ)** an angel of **God (אֱלֹהִים)**, so **do (עָשָׂה)** what seems good in your eyes. (MLB)

| אֱלֹהִים | God, gods | 2602x |
| --- | --- | --- |
| ʾĕlōhîm | | S430 |

כְּ  ➤  DAY 17          עשׂה  ➤  DAY 18

וַיְרַגֵּל בְּעַבְדְּךָ אֶל־אֲדֹנִי הַמֶּלֶךְ וַאדֹנִי הַמֶּלֶךְ כְּמַלְאַךְ הָאֱלֹהִים וַעֲשֵׂה הַטּוֹב בְּעֵינֶיךָ:

| But he has slandered your servant | וַיְרַגֵּל בְּעַבְדְּךָ |
| --- | --- |
| to my master the king | אֶל־אֲדֹנִי הַמֶּלֶךְ |
| Still, my master the king | וַאדֹנִי הַמֶּלֶךְ |
| is **like** an angel of **God** | כְּמַלְאַךְ הָאֱלֹהִים |
| so **do** | וַעֲשֵׂה |
| what seems good | הַטּוֹב |
| in your eyes | בְּעֵינֶיךָ |

The LORD also stirred up the spirit of Zerubbabel . . . and the spirit of Joshua . . . and the spirit of all the remnant of the people. **They came (וַיָּבֹאוּ)** and worked [lit., **performed (וַיַּעֲשׂוּ)** work] on the house of the LORD of hosts, their **God (אֱלֹהֵיהֶם)**. (MLB)

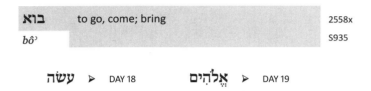

| בּוֹא | to go, come; bring | 2558x |
|---|---|---|
| bôʾ | | S935 |

עָשָׂה   ➢   DAY 18          אֱלֹהִים   ➢   DAY 19

וַיָּעַר יְהוָה אֶת־רוּחַ זְרֻבָּבֶל . . . וְאֶת־רוּחַ יְהוֹשֻׁעַ . . . וְאֶת־רוּחַ כֹּל
שְׁאֵרִית הָעָם וַיָּבֹאוּ וַיַּעֲשׂוּ מְלָאכָה בְּבֵית־יְהוָה צְבָאוֹת אֱלֹהֵיהֶם:

| | |
|---|---|
| The LORD also stirred up | וַיָּעַר יְהוָה |
| the spirit of Zerubbabel . . . | אֶת־רוּחַ זְרֻבָּבֶל . . . |
| and the spirit of Joshua . . . | וְאֶת־רוּחַ יְהוֹשֻׁעַ . . . |
| and the spirit of all the remnant of the people | וְאֶת־רוּחַ כֹּל שְׁאֵרִית הָעָם |
| **They came** | וַיָּבֹאוּ |
| and worked [lit., **performed** work] | וַיַּעֲשׂוּ מְלָאכָה |
| on the house of the LORD of hosts | בְּבֵית־יְהוָה צְבָאוֹת |
| their **God** | אֱלֹהֵיהֶם |

You will flee by the valley of My mountains . . . ; yes, you will flee just as you fled before the earthquake in the days of Uzziah **king** (מֶלֶךְ) of Judah. Then the LORD, my **God** (אֱלֹהַי), **will come** (וּבָא), and all the holy ones with Him! (NASB)

| מֶלֶךְ | king | 2528x |
|---|---|---|
| *melek* | | S4428 |

אֱלֹהִים    ➤    DAY 19        בוֹא    ➤    DAY 20

וְנַסְתֶּם גֵּיא־הָרַי . . . וְנַסְתֶּם כַּאֲשֶׁר נַסְתֶּם מִפְּנֵי הָרַעַשׁ בִּימֵי עֻזִּיָּה מֶלֶךְ־יְהוּדָה וּבָא יְהוָה אֱלֹהַי כָּל־קְדֹשִׁים עִמָּךְ׃

| | |
|---|---|
| You will flee by the valley of My mountains . . . | וְנַסְתֶּם גֵּיא־הָרַי . . . |
| yes, you will flee just as you fled | וְנַסְתֶּם כַּאֲשֶׁר נַסְתֶּם |
| before the earthquake | מִפְּנֵי הָרַעַשׁ |
| in the days of Uzziah **king** of Judah | בִּימֵי עֻזִּיָּה מֶלֶךְ־יְהוּדָה |
| Then the LORD, my **God**, **will come** | וּבָא יְהוָה אֱלֹהַי |
| and all the holy ones with Him! | כָּל־קְדֹשִׁים עִמָּךְ |

So they searched for a beautiful girl throughout all the territory of
**Israel** (יִשְׂרָאֵל), and found Abishag the Shunammite, and **brought**
(וַיָּבִאוּ) her to the **king** (מֶלֶךְ). (NRSV)

| יִשְׂרָאֵל | Israel | 2507x |
|---|---|---|
| *yiśrā'ēl* | | S3478 |

בוֹא   ▷   DAY 20          מֶלֶךְ   ▷   DAY 21

וַיְבַקְשׁוּ נַעֲרָה יָפָה בְּכֹל גְּבוּל יִשְׂרָאֵל וַיִּמְצְאוּ אֶת־אֲבִישַׁג הַשּׁוּנַמִּית
וַיָּבִאוּ אֹתָהּ לַמֶּלֶךְ׃

| English | Hebrew |
|---|---|
| So they searched for | וַיְבַקְשׁוּ |
| a beautiful girl | נַעֲרָה יָפָה |
| throughout all the territory of **Israel** | בְּכֹל גְּבוּל יִשְׂרָאֵל |
| and found | וַיִּמְצְאוּ |
| Abishag the Shunammite | אֶת־אֲבִישַׁג הַשּׁוּנַמִּית |
| and **brought** her | וַיָּבִאוּ אֹתָהּ |
| to the **king** | לַמֶּלֶךְ |

Now these are the **kings** (מַלְכֵי) of the **land** (אֶרֶץ) whom the sons
of **Israel** (יִשְׂרָאֵל) defeated, and whose **land** (אַרְצָם) they possessed
beyond the Jordan toward the sunrise, from the valley of the Arnon
as far as Mount Hermon, and all the Arabah to the east: . . . (NASB)

| | | |
|---|---|---|
| אֶרֶץ | land, earth, country | 2505x |
| ʾereṣ | | S776 |

מֶלֶךְ ▸ DAY 21          יִשְׂרָאֵל ▸ DAY 22

וְאֵלֶּה מַלְכֵי הָאָרֶץ אֲשֶׁר הִכּוּ בְנֵי־יִשְׂרָאֵל וַיִּרְשׁוּ אֶת־אַרְצָם בְּעֵבֶר
הַיַּרְדֵּן מִזְרְחָה הַשָּׁמֶשׁ מִנַּחַל אַרְנוֹן עַד־הַר חֶרְמוֹן וְכָל־הָעֲרָבָה
מִזְרָחָה:

| | |
|---|---|
| Now these are the **kings** of the **land** | וְאֵלֶּה מַלְכֵי הָאָרֶץ |
| whom the sons of **Israel** defeated | אֲשֶׁר הִכּוּ בְנֵי־יִשְׂרָאֵל |
| and whose **land** they possessed | וַיִּרְשׁוּ אֶת־אַרְצָם |
| beyond the Jordan | בְּעֵבֶר הַיַּרְדֵּן |
| toward the sunrise | מִזְרְחָה הַשָּׁמֶשׁ |
| from the valley of the Arnon | מִנַּחַל אַרְנוֹן |
| as far as Mount Hermon | עַד־הַר חֶרְמוֹן |
| and all the Arabah to the east | וְכָל־הָעֲרָבָה מִזְרָחָה |

There will be a highway for the remnant of his people who will survive from Assyria, as there was for **Israel** (יִשְׂרָאֵל) when [lit., on the **day** (יוֹם)] they came up from the **land** (אֶרֶץ) of Egypt. (CSB)

| יוֹם | day | 2298x |
|---|---|---|
| yôm | | S3117 |

יִשְׂרָאֵל  ➤ DAY 22        אֶרֶץ  ➤ DAY 23

וְהָיְתָה מְסִלָּה לִשְׁאָר עַמּוֹ אֲשֶׁר יִשָּׁאֵר מֵאַשּׁוּר כַּאֲשֶׁר הָיְתָה לְיִשְׂרָאֵל בְּיוֹם עֲלֹתוֹ מֵאֶרֶץ מִצְרָיִם:

| There will be a highway | וְהָיְתָה מְסִלָּה |
|---|---|
| for the remnant of his people | לִשְׁאָר עַמּוֹ |
| who will survive | אֲשֶׁר יִשָּׁאֵר |
| from Assyria | מֵאַשּׁוּר |
| as there was | כַּאֲשֶׁר הָיְתָה |
| for **Israel** | לְיִשְׂרָאֵל |
| when [lit., on the **day**] they came up | בְּיוֹם עֲלֹתוֹ |
| from the **land** of Egypt | מֵאֶרֶץ מִצְרָיִם |

In the **days** (בִּימֵי) when the judges ruled there was a famine in the **land** (אֶרֶץ), and a **man** (אִישׁ) of Bethlehem in Judah went to sojourn in the country of Moab, he and his wife and his two sons. (ESV)

| אִישׁ | man, husband | 2187x |
| אׁs | | S376 |

אֶרֶץ  ➤  DAY 23          יוֹם  ➤  DAY 24

וַיְהִי בִּימֵי שְׁפֹט הַשֹּׁפְטִים וַיְהִי רָעָב בָּאָרֶץ וַיֵּלֶךְ אִישׁ מִבֵּית לֶחֶם יְהוּדָה לָגוּר בִּשְׂדֵי מוֹאָב הוּא וְאִשְׁתּוֹ וּשְׁנֵי בָנָיו:

| In the **days** when | וַיְהִי בִּימֵי |
| the judges ruled | שְׁפֹט הַשֹּׁפְטִים |
| there was a famine | וַיְהִי רָעָב |
| in the **land** | בָּאָרֶץ |
| and a **man** . . . went | וַיֵּלֶךְ אִישׁ |
| of Bethlehem in Judah | מִבֵּית לֶחֶם יְהוּדָה |
| to sojourn | לָגוּר |
| in the country of Moab | בִּשְׂדֵי מוֹאָב |
| he and his wife | הוּא וְאִשְׁתּוֹ |
| and his two sons | וּשְׁנֵי בָנָיו |

And the battle was very fierce that **day** (יוֹם). And Abner and the **men** (אַנְשֵׁי) of Israel were beaten before [lit., to the **face** (פְּנֵי) of] the servants of David. (ESV)

| פָּנֶה<br>*pānê* | face | 2127x<br>S6440 |

יוֹם ➤ DAY 24        אִישׁ ➤ DAY 25

וַתְּהִי הַמִּלְחָמָה קָשָׁה עַד־מְאֹד בַּיּוֹם הַהוּא וַיִּנָּגֶף אַבְנֵר וְאַנְשֵׁי יִשְׂרָאֵל לִפְנֵי עַבְדֵי דָוִד:

| And the battle was | וַתְּהִי הַמִּלְחָמָה |
| very fierce | קָשָׁה עַד־מְאֹד |
| that **day** | בַּיּוֹם הַהוּא |
| And . . . were beaten | וַיִּנָּגֶף |
| Abner | אַבְנֵר |
| and the **men** of Israel | וְאַנְשֵׁי יִשְׂרָאֵל |
| before [lit., to the **face** of] | לִפְנֵי |
| the servants of David | עַבְדֵי דָוִד |

as if a **man** (אִישׁ) fled from [the **presence** (פְּנֵי) of] a lion, and a bear met him, or went into the **house** (בַּיִת) and leaned his hand against the wall, and a serpent bit him. (ESV)

| בַּיִת | house, palace, temple | 2047x |
| bayit | | S1004 |

| אִישׁ | ➤ | DAY 25 | פָּנֶה | ➤ | DAY 26 |

כַּאֲשֶׁר יָנוּס **אִישׁ** מִ**פְּנֵי** הָאֲרִי וּפְגָעוֹ הַדֹּב וּבָא הַ**בַּיִת** וְסָמַךְ יָדוֹ עַל־הַקִּיר וּנְשָׁכוֹ הַנָּחָשׁ:

| as if a **man** fled | כַּאֲשֶׁר יָנוּס **אִישׁ** |
| from [the **presence** of] a lion | מִ**פְּנֵי** הָאֲרִי |
| and a bear met him | וּפְגָעוֹ הַדֹּב |
| or went into the **house** | וּבָא הַ**בַּיִת** |
| and leaned his hand | וְסָמַךְ יָדוֹ |
| against the wall | עַל־הַקִּיר |
| and a serpent bit him | וּנְשָׁכוֹ הַנָּחָשׁ |

Then I set [lit., **I gave (וָאֶתֵּן)**] before [lit., in the **presence (פְּנֵי) of**] the sons of the **house (בֵית)** of the Rechabites pitchers full of wine and cups, and I said to them, "Drink wine." (MLB)

| נתן | to give | 2014x |
|---|---|---|
| nātan | | S5414 |

| פָּנֶה | ▷ | DAY 26 | | בַּיִת | ▷ | DAY 27 |
|---|---|---|---|---|---|---|

וָאֶתֵּן לִפְנֵי בְּנֵי בֵית־הָרֵכָבִים גְּבִעִים מְלֵאִים יַיִן וְכֹסוֹת וָאֹמַר אֲלֵיהֶם שְׁתוּ־יָיִן:

| Then I set [lit., **I gave**] | וָאֶתֵּן |
|---|---|
| before [lit., in the **presence of**] | לִפְנֵי |
| the sons of the **house** of the Rechabites | בְּנֵי בֵית־הָרֵכָבִים |
| pitchers | גְּבִעִים |
| full of wine | מְלֵאִים יַיִן |
| and cups | וְכֹסוֹת |
| and I said to them | וָאֹמַר אֲלֵיהֶם |
| Drink wine | שְׁתוּ־יָיִן |

Jeremiah also said to King Zedekiah, "What wrong have I
done against you or your servants or this **people** (עָם), that
**you have put** (נְתַתֶּם) me in prison [lit., the **house** (בֵּית) of
imprisonment]?" (MLB)

| עָם | people, nation | 1866x |
|---|---|---|
| ʿam | | S5971 |

בֵּית ➤ DAY 27        נתן ➤ DAY 28

וַיֹּאמֶר יִרְמְיָהוּ אֶל־הַמֶּלֶךְ צִדְקִיָּהוּ מֶה חָטָאתִי לְךָ וְלַעֲבָדֶיךָ וְלָעָם
הַזֶּה כִּי־נְתַתֶּם אוֹתִי אֶל־בֵּית הַכֶּלֶא:

| Jeremiah also said | וַיֹּאמֶר יִרְמְיָהוּ |
|---|---|
| to King Zedekiah | אֶל־הַמֶּלֶךְ צִדְקִיָּהוּ |
| What wrong have I done | מֶה חָטָאתִי |
| against you or your servants | לְךָ וְלַעֲבָדֶיךָ |
| or this **people** | וְלָעָם הַזֶּה |
| that **you have put** me | כִּי־נְתַתֶּם אוֹתִי |
| in prison [lit., the **house** of imprisonment]? | אֶל־בֵּית הַכֶּלֶא |

**I will lay** (וְנָתַתִּי) my vengeance upon Edom by the **hand** (יַד) of my **people** (עַמִּי) Israel; and they shall act in Edom according to my anger and according to my wrath; and they shall know my vengeance, says the Lord GOD. (NRSV)

| יָד | hand, strength, power | 1627x |
|---|---|---|
| yād | | S3027 |

נתן ➤ DAY 28　　　　　עַם ➤ DAY 29

וְנָתַתִּי אֶת־נִקְמָתִי בֶּאֱדוֹם בְּיַד עַמִּי יִשְׂרָאֵל וְעָשׂוּ בֶאֱדוֹם כְּאַפִּי
וְכַחֲמָתִי וְיָדְעוּ אֶת־נִקְמָתִי נְאֻם אֲדֹנָי יְהוִה:

| | |
|---|---|
| **I will lay** my vengeance | וְנָתַתִּי אֶת־נִקְמָתִי |
| upon Edom | בֶּאֱדוֹם |
| by the **hand** of my **people** Israel | בְּיַד עַמִּי יִשְׂרָאֵל |
| and they shall act in Edom | וְעָשׂוּ בֶאֱדוֹם |
| according to my anger | כְּאַפִּי |
| and according to my wrath | וְכַחֲמָתִי |
| and they shall know my vengeance | וְיָדְעוּ אֶת־נִקְמָתִי |
| says the Lord GOD | נְאֻם אֲדֹנָי יְהוִה |

I spread forth My **hands** (יָדַי) all day long to a rebellious **people** (עַם), who **walk** (הֹלְכִים) in a way which is not good, after their own devices. (MLB)

| הלך | to walk, go | 1554x |
|---|---|---|
| hālak | | S1980 |

עַם    ➤    DAY 29        יָד    ➤    DAY 30

פֵּרַשְׂתִּי יָדַי כָּל־הַיּוֹם אֶל־עַם סוֹרֵר הַהֹלְכִים הַדֶּרֶךְ לֹא־טוֹב אַחַר מַחְשְׁבֹתֵיהֶם:

| I spread forth My **hands** | פֵּרַשְׂתִּי יָדַי |
|---|---|
| all day long | כָּל־הַיּוֹם |
| to a rebellious **people** | אֶל־עַם סוֹרֵר |
| who **walk** in a way | הַהֹלְכִים הַדֶּרֶךְ |
| which is not good | לֹא־טוֹב |
| after their own devices | אַחַר מַחְשְׁבֹתֵיהֶם |

So the elders of Moab and the elders of Midian **departed** (וַיֵּלְכוּ)
with the fees for divination in their **hand** (יָדָם); and they came to
Balaam and repeated Balak's **words** (דִּבְרֵי) to him. (NASB)

| | | |
|---|---|---|
| דָּבָר | word, matter, thing | 1454x |
| *dāvār* | | S1697 |

יָד ➤ DAY 30            הלך ➤ DAY 31

וַיֵּלְכוּ זִקְנֵי מוֹאָב וְזִקְנֵי מִדְיָן וּקְסָמִים בְּיָדָם וַיָּבֹאוּ אֶל־בִּלְעָם וַיְדַבְּרוּ
אֵלָיו דִּבְרֵי בָלָק:

| | |
|---|---|
| So . . . **departed** | וַיֵּלְכוּ |
| the elders of Moab | זִקְנֵי מוֹאָב |
| and the elders of Midian | וְזִקְנֵי מִדְיָן |
| with the fees for divination | וּקְסָמִים |
| in their **hand** | בְּיָדָם |
| and they came | וַיָּבֹאוּ |
| to Balaam | אֶל־בִּלְעָם |
| and repeated . . . to him | וַיְדַבְּרוּ אֵלָיו |
| Balak's **words** | דִּבְרֵי בָלָק |

And she said, "According to your **words** (דִּבְרֵיכֶם), so be **it** (הוּא)." Then she sent them away, and **they departed** (וַיֵּלֵכוּ). And she tied the scarlet cord in the window. (ESV)

| הוּא | he, it, that | 1398x |
|------|--------------|-------|
| *hûʾ* | | S1931 |

הלך    ➤    DAY 31        דָּבַר    ➤    DAY 32

וַתֹּאמֶר כְּדִבְרֵיכֶם כֶּן־**הוּא** וַתְּשַׁלְּחֵם **וַיֵּלֵכוּ** וַתִּקְשֹׁר אֶת־תִּקְוַת הַשָּׁנִי בַּחַלּוֹן:

| | |
|---|---|
| And she said | וַתֹּאמֶר |
| According to your **words** | כְּדִבְרֵיכֶם |
| so be **it** | כֶּן־**הוּא** |
| Then she sent them away | וַתְּשַׁלְּחֵם |
| and **they departed** | **וַיֵּלֵכוּ** |
| And she tied | וַתִּקְשֹׁר |
| the scarlet cord | אֶת־תִּקְוַת הַשָּׁנִי |
| in the window | בַּחַלּוֹן |

Is there **anything (דָּבָר)** of which one might say, "**See (רָאָה)** this,
**it (הוּא)** is new"? Already it has existed for ages which were before
us. (NASB)

| רָאָה | to see; appear | 1301x |
|-------|----------------|-------|
| rāʾâ  |                | S7200 |

דָּבָר    ➤    DAY 32        הוּא    ➤    DAY 33

יֵשׁ דָּבָר שֶׁיֹּאמַר רְאֵה־זֶה חָדָשׁ הוּא כְּבָר הָיָה לְעֹלָמִים אֲשֶׁר הָיָה
מִלְּפָנֵנוּ:

| Is there **anything** | יֵשׁ דָּבָר |
|-----------------------|------------|
| of which one might say | שֶׁיֹּאמַר |
| **See** this | רְאֵה־זֶה |
| **it** is new | חָדָשׁ הוּא |
| Already | כְּבָר |
| it has existed | הָיָה |
| for ages | לְעֹלָמִים |
| which were | אֲשֶׁר הָיָה |
| before us | מִלְּפָנֵנוּ |

Then we set out from Horeb and went through all **that** (הוּא)
great and terrifying wilderness that **you saw** (רְאִיתֶם), . . . And we
came **to** (עַד) Kadesh-barnea. (ESV)

| עַד | | until, as far as | | 1263x |
|---|---|---|---|---|
| ʿad | | | | S5704 |

הוּא   ➤   DAY 33      רָאָה   ➤   DAY 34

וַנִּסַּע מֵחֹרֵב וַנֵּלֶךְ אֵת כָּל־הַמִּדְבָּר הַגָּדוֹל וְהַנּוֹרָא הַהוּא אֲשֶׁר
רְאִיתֶם . . . וַנָּבֹא עַד קָדֵשׁ בַּרְנֵעַ:

| Then we set out from Horeb | וַנִּסַּע מֵחֹרֵב |
|---|---|
| and went through | וַנֵּלֶךְ |
| all **that** . . . wilderness | אֵת כָּל־הַמִּדְבָּר . . . הַהוּא |
| great and terrifying | הַגָּדוֹל וְהַנּוֹרָא |
| that **you saw**, . . . | אֲשֶׁר רְאִיתֶם . . . |
| And we came | וַנָּבֹא |
| **to** Kadesh-barnea | עַד קָדֵשׁ בַּרְנֵעַ |

They will fill your houses, all your officials' houses, and the houses of all the Egyptians—something your **fathers** (אֲבֹתֶיךָ) and grandfathers [lit., the **fathers** (אֲבוֹת) of your **fathers** (אֲבֹתֶיךָ)] never **saw** (רָאוּ) since the time they occupied the land **until** (עַד) today. (CSB)

| אָב | father, ancestor | 1210x |
|---|---|---|
| ʾāv | | S1 |

רָאה ▷ DAY 34      עַד ▷ DAY 35

וּמָלְאוּ בָתֶּיךָ וּבָתֵּי כָל־עֲבָדֶיךָ וּבָתֵּי כָל־מִצְרַיִם אֲשֶׁר לֹא־רָאוּ
אֲבֹתֶיךָ וַאֲבוֹת אֲבֹתֶיךָ מִיּוֹם הֱיוֹתָם עַל־הָאֲדָמָה עַד הַיּוֹם
הַזֶּה

| They will fill your houses | וּמָלְאוּ בָתֶּיךָ |
|---|---|
| all your officials' houses | וּבָתֵּי כָל־עֲבָדֶיךָ |
| and the houses of all the Egyptians | וּבָתֵּי כָל־מִצְרַיִם |
| something your **fathers** | אֲשֶׁר . . . אֲבֹתֶיךָ |
| and grandfathers [lit., the **fathers** of your **fathers**] | וַאֲבוֹת אֲבֹתֶיךָ |
| never **saw** | לֹא־רָאוּ |
| since the time | מִיּוֹם |
| they occupied the land | הֱיוֹתָם עַל־הָאֲדָמָה |
| **until** today | עַד הַיּוֹם הַזֶּה |

So while these nations feared the Lᴏʀᴅ, they also served their idols; their children likewise and their grandchildren, as their **fathers** (אֲבֹתָם) did, so they do **to** (עַד) **this** (זֶה) day. (NASB)

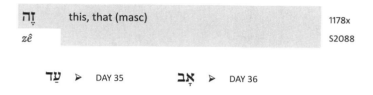

| זֶה | this, that (masc) | 1178x |
| zê | | S2088 |

עַד  ▷  DAY 35      אָב  ▷  DAY 36

וַיִּהְיוּ הַגּוֹיִם הָאֵלֶּה יְרֵאִים אֶת־יְהוָה וְאֶת־פְּסִילֵיהֶם הָיוּ עֹבְדִים גַּם־בְּנֵיהֶם וּבְנֵי בְנֵיהֶם כַּאֲשֶׁר עָשׂוּ אֲבֹתָם הֵם עֹשִׂים עַד הַיּוֹם הַזֶּה:

| So while these nations | וַיִּהְיוּ הַגּוֹיִם הָאֵלֶּה |
| feared the Lᴏʀᴅ | יְרֵאִים אֶת־יְהוָה |
| they also served their idols | וְאֶת־פְּסִילֵיהֶם הָיוּ עֹבְדִים |
| their children likewise | גַּם־בְּנֵיהֶם |
| and their grandchildren | וּבְנֵי בְנֵיהֶם |
| as their **fathers** did | כַּאֲשֶׁר עָשׂוּ אֲבֹתָם |
| so they do | הֵם עֹשִׂים |
| **to this** day | עַד הַיּוֹם הַזֶּה |

For I earnestly admonished your **fathers** (אֲבוֹתֵיכֶם) in the day that I brought them up out of the land of Egypt, even to **this** (זֶה) day, rising up early and admonishing, saying, **Obey** (שִׁמְעוּ) My voice. (MLB)

| שָׁמַע | to hear, obey | 1165x |
|---|---|---|
| *šāmaʻ* | | S8085 |

אָב  ▷  DAY 36          זֶה  ▷  DAY 37

כִּי הָעֵד הַעִדֹתִי בַּאֲבוֹתֵיכֶם בְּיוֹם הַעֲלוֹתִי אוֹתָם מֵאֶרֶץ מִצְרַיִם
וְעַד־הַיּוֹם הַזֶּה הַשְׁכֵּם וְהָעֵד לֵאמֹר שִׁמְעוּ בְּקוֹלִי:

| | |
|---|---|
| For I earnestly admonished | כִּי הָעֵד הַעִדֹתִי |
| your **fathers** | בַּאֲבוֹתֵיכֶם |
| in the day that I brought them up | בְּיוֹם הַעֲלוֹתִי אוֹתָם |
| out of the land of Egypt | מֵאֶרֶץ מִצְרַיִם |
| even to **this** day | וְעַד־הַיּוֹם הַזֶּה |
| rising up early and admonishing | הַשְׁכֵּם וְהָעֵד |
| saying | לֵאמֹר |
| **Obey** My voice | שִׁמְעוּ בְּקוֹלִי |

**Hear** (שִׁמְעוּ) **this** (זֶה) word that the LORD **has spoken** (דִּבֶּר) against you, O people of Israel, against the whole family that I brought up out of the land of Egypt. (ESV)

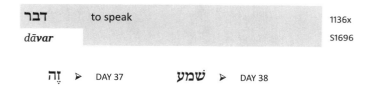

| דבר | to speak | 1136x |
| --- | --- | --- |
| *dāvar* | | S1696 |

זֶה　➤　DAY 37　　　　שׁמע　➤　DAY 38

שִׁמְעוּ אֶת־הַדָּבָר הַזֶּה אֲשֶׁר דִּבֶּר יְהוָה עֲלֵיכֶם בְּנֵי יִשְׂרָאֵל עַל כָּל־הַמִּשְׁפָּחָה אֲשֶׁר הֶעֱלֵיתִי מֵאֶרֶץ מִצְרָיִם

| | |
| --- | --- |
| **Hear** | שִׁמְעוּ |
| **this** word | אֶת־הַדָּבָר הַזֶּה |
| that the LORD **has spoken** | אֲשֶׁר דִּבֶּר יְהוָה |
| against you | עֲלֵיכֶם |
| O people of Israel | בְּנֵי יִשְׂרָאֵל |
| against the whole family | עַל כָּל־הַמִּשְׁפָּחָה |
| that I brought up | אֲשֶׁר הֶעֱלֵיתִי |
| out of the land of Egypt | מֵאֶרֶץ מִצְרָיִם |

But then a wise woman shouted from the **city** (עִיר), "Listen (שִׁמְעוּ)! **Listen** (שִׁמְעוּ)! Tell Joab now, 'Come here, so **I can speak** (אֲדַבְּרָה) with you!'" (MLB)

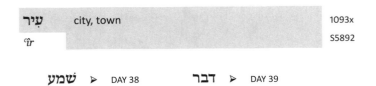

| עִיר | city, town | 1093x |
|---|---|---|
| ʿîr | | S5892 |

שָׁמַע   ➤   DAY 38        דבר   ➤   DAY 39

וַתִּקְרָא אִשָּׁה חֲכָמָה מִן־הָעִיר שִׁמְעוּ שִׁמְעוּ אִמְרוּ־נָא אֶל־יוֹאָב
קְרַב עַד־הֵנָּה וַאֲדַבְּרָה אֵלֶיךָ:

| But then a wise woman shouted | וַתִּקְרָא אִשָּׁה חֲכָמָה |
|---|---|
| from the **city** | מִן־הָעִיר |
| **Listen! Listen!** | שִׁמְעוּ שִׁמְעוּ |
| Tell Joab now | אִמְרוּ־נָא אֶל־יוֹאָב |
| Come here | קְרַב עַד־הֵנָּה |
| so **I can speak** with you! | וַאֲדַבְּרָה אֵלֶיךָ |

There were men passing by who saw the corpse thrown on the road and the lion standing beside it [lit., the corpse], and they went and **spoke** (וַיְדַבְּרוּ) about it in the **city** (עִיר) where the old prophet **lived** (יֹשֵׁב). (CSB)

| יָשַׁב | to sit, dwell | 1087x |
|--------|---------------|-------|
| *yāšav* | | S3427 |

דבר  ➤  DAY 39          עִיר  ➤  DAY 40

וְהִנֵּה אֲנָשִׁים עֹבְרִים וַיִּרְאוּ אֶת־הַנְּבֵלָה מֻשְׁלֶכֶת בַּדֶּרֶךְ וְאֶת־הָאַרְיֵה עֹמֵד אֵצֶל הַנְּבֵלָה וַיָּבֹאוּ וַיְדַבְּרוּ בָעִיר אֲשֶׁר הַנָּבִיא הַזָּקֵן יֹשֵׁב בָּהּ:

| There were men passing by | וְהִנֵּה אֲנָשִׁים עֹבְרִים |
|---|---|
| who saw the corpse | וַיִּרְאוּ אֶת־הַנְּבֵלָה |
| thrown on the road | מֻשְׁלֶכֶת בַּדֶּרֶךְ |
| and the lion | וְאֶת־הָאַרְיֵה |
| standing beside it [lit., the corpse] | עֹמֵד אֵצֶל הַנְּבֵלָה |
| and they went and **spoke** about it | וַיָּבֹאוּ וַיְדַבְּרוּ |
| in the **city** where | בָעִיר אֲשֶׁר . . . בָּהּ |
| the old prophet **lived** | הַנָּבִיא הַזָּקֵן יֹשֵׁב |

**David** (דָּוִד) then **took up residence** (וַיֵּשֶׁב) in the fortress, and so it was called the **City** (עִיר) of **David** (דָּוִד). (NIV)

| דָּוִד | David | 1075x |
|---|---|---|
| *dāvīd* | | S1732 |

עִיר ▷ DAY 40          יָשַׁב ▷ DAY 41

וַיֵּשֶׁב דָּוִיד בַּמְצָד עַל־כֵּן קָרְאוּ־לֹו עִיר דָּוִיד:

| David then **took up residence** | וַיֵּשֶׁב דָּוִיד |
|---|---|
| in the fortress | בַּמְצָד |
| and so | עַל־כֵּן |
| it was called | קָרְאוּ־לֹו |
| the **City** of **David** | עִיר דָּוִיד |

Thus says the LORD concerning the king who **sits** (יוֹשֵׁב) on the throne of **David** (דָוִד), and concerning all the people who **live** (יוֹשֵׁב) in this city, your kinsfolk who **did** not **go out** (יָצְאוּ) with you into exile: . . . (NRSV)

| יָצָא | to go out | 1075x |
|------|-----------|-------|
| yāṣāʾ | | S3318 |

יָשַׁב ➤ DAY 41          דָוִד ➤ DAY 42

כִּי־כֹה אָמַר יְהוָה אֶל־הַמֶּלֶךְ הַיּוֹשֵׁב אֶל־כִּסֵּא דָוִד וְאֶל־כָּל־הָעָם הַיּוֹשֵׁב בָּעִיר הַזֹּאת אֲחֵיכֶם אֲשֶׁר לֹא־יָצְאוּ אִתְּכֶם בַּגּוֹלָה:

| | |
|---|---|
| Thus says the LORD | כִּי־כֹה אָמַר יְהוָה |
| concerning the king | אֶל־הַמֶּלֶךְ |
| who **sits** on the throne of **David** | הַיּוֹשֵׁב אֶל־כִּסֵּא דָוִד |
| and concerning all the people | וְאֶל־כָּל־הָעָם |
| who **live** in this city | הַיּוֹשֵׁב בָּעִיר הַזֹּאת |
| your kinsfolk who | אֲחֵיכֶם אֲשֶׁר |
| **did** not **go out** with you | לֹא־יָצְאוּ אִתְּכֶם |
| into exile | בַּגּוֹלָה |

When Joab **came out** (וַיֵּצֵא) from **David**'s (דָּוִד) presence, he sent messengers after Abner, and **they brought** him **back** (וַיָּשִׁבוּ) from the cistern of Sirah. But **David** (דָּוִד) did not know about it. (ESV)

| | | |
|---|---|---|
| **שׁוּב** *šûv* | to return, turn | 1075x S7725 |

דָּוִד ➤ DAY 42 יצא ➤ DAY 43

וַיֵּצֵא יוֹאָב מֵעִם דָּוִד וַיִּשְׁלַח מַלְאָכִים אַחֲרֵי אַבְנֵר וַיָּשִׁבוּ אֹתוֹ מִבּוֹר הַסִּרָה וְדָוִד לֹא יָדָע׃

| | |
|---|---|
| When Joab **came out** | וַיֵּצֵא יוֹאָב |
| from **David**'s presence | מֵעִם דָּוִד |
| he sent messengers | וַיִּשְׁלַח מַלְאָכִים |
| after Abner | אַחֲרֵי אַבְנֵר |
| and **they brought** him **back** | וַיָּשִׁבוּ אֹתוֹ |
| from the cistern of Sirah | מִבּוֹר הַסִּרָה |
| But **David** did not know about it | וְדָוִד לֹא יָדָע |

So is my word that **goes out (יֵצֵא)** from my mouth: **It will** not
**return (יָשׁוּב)** to me empty, but [lit., for **if (אִם)**] will accomplish
what I desire and achieve the purpose for which I sent it. (NIV)

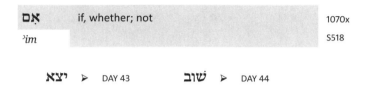

| אִם | if, whether; not | 1070x |
| --- | --- | --- |
| ʾim | | S518 |

יָצָא  ➤  DAY 43        שׁוּב  ➤  DAY 44

כֵּן יִהְיֶה דְבָרִי אֲשֶׁר יֵצֵא מִפִּי לֹא־יָשׁוּב אֵלַי רֵיקָם כִּי אִם־עָשָׂה אֶת־
אֲשֶׁר חָפַצְתִּי וְהִצְלִיחַ אֲשֶׁר שְׁלַחְתִּיו:

| | |
| --- | --- |
| So is my word | כֵּן יִהְיֶה דְבָרִי |
| that **goes out** from my mouth | אֲשֶׁר יֵצֵא מִפִּי |
| **It will** not **return** to me | לֹא־יָשׁוּב אֵלַי |
| empty | רֵיקָם |
| but [lit., for **if**] will accomplish | כִּי אִם־עָשָׂה |
| what I desire | אֶת־אֲשֶׁר חָפַצְתִּי |
| and achieve the purpose | וְהִצְלִיחַ |
| for which I sent it | אֲשֶׁר שְׁלַחְתִּיו |

When **he returned** (וַיָּשָׁב) to the man of God . . . he said, "**Behold** (הִנֵּה)** now, I know that there is no God in all the earth, but [lit., for **if** (אִם)] in Israel; so please take a present from your servant now." (NASB)

| הִנֵּה | behold! | 1061x |
|--------|---------|-------|
| *hinnê* |  | S2009 |

שׁוּב ➤ DAY 44          אִם ➤ DAY 45

וַיָּשָׁב אֶל־אִישׁ הָאֱלֹהִים . . . וַיֹּאמֶר הִנֵּה־נָא יָדַעְתִּי כִּי אֵין אֱלֹהִים
בְּכָל־הָאָרֶץ כִּי אִם־בְּיִשְׂרָאֵל וְעַתָּה קַח־נָא בְרָכָה מֵאֵת עַבְדֶּךָ:

| When **he returned** to the man of God . . . | וַיָּשָׁב אֶל־אִישׁ הָאֱלֹהִים . . . |
|---|---|
| he said | וַיֹּאמֶר |
| **Behold** now | הִנֵּה־נָא |
| I know that | יָדַעְתִּי כִּי |
| there is no God | אֵין אֱלֹהִים |
| in all the earth | בְּכָל־הָאָרֶץ |
| but [lit., for **if**] in Israel | כִּי אִם־בְּיִשְׂרָאֵל |
| so . . . now | וְעַתָּה |
| please take a present | קַח־נָא בְרָכָה |
| from your servant | מֵאֵת עַבְדֶּךָ |

**Look** (הִנֵּה), I am **with** (עִמָּךְ) you and will watch over you wherever you go. I will bring you back to this land, for I will not leave you until [lit., until which **if** (אִם)] I have done what I have promised you. (CSB)

| עִם | with | | 1048x |
| --- | --- | --- | --- |
| ʿim | | | S5973 |

| אִם | ➤ | DAY 45 | | הִנֵּה | ➤ | DAY 46 |
| --- | --- | --- | --- | --- | --- | --- |

וְהִנֵּה אָנֹכִי **עִמָּךְ** וּשְׁמַרְתִּיךָ בְּכֹל אֲשֶׁר־תֵּלֵךְ וַהֲשִׁבֹתִיךָ אֶל־הָאֲדָמָה הַזֹּאת כִּי לֹא אֶעֱזָבְךָ עַד אֲשֶׁר **אִם־**עָשִׂיתִי אֵת אֲשֶׁר־דִּבַּרְתִּי לָךְ׃

| **Look**, I am **with** you | וְהִנֵּה אָנֹכִי **עִמָּךְ** |
| --- | --- |
| and will watch over you | וּשְׁמַרְתִּיךָ |
| wherever you go | בְּכֹל אֲשֶׁר־תֵּלֵךְ |
| I will bring you back | וַהֲשִׁבֹתִיךָ |
| to this land | אֶל־הָאֲדָמָה הַזֹּאת |
| for I will not leave you | כִּי לֹא אֶעֱזָבְךָ |
| until [lit., until which **if**] I have done | עַד אֲשֶׁר **אִם־**עָשִׂיתִי |
| what I have promised you | אֵת אֲשֶׁר־דִּבַּרְתִּי לָךְ |

**One** (אֶחָד) of the young men answered, "**Behold** (הִנֵּה), I have seen a son of Jesse the Bethlehemite, who is skillful in playing, a man of valor, a man of war, prudent in speech, and a man of good presence, and the LORD is **with** (עִמּוֹ) him." (ESV)

| | | |
|---|---|---|
| אֶחָד | one, first | 976x |
| ʾeḥād | | S259 |

הִנֵּה ➤ DAY 46          עִם ➤ DAY 47

וַיַּעַן אֶחָד מֵהַנְּעָרִים וַיֹּאמֶר הִנֵּה רָאִיתִי בֵּן לְיִשַׁי בֵּית הַלַּחְמִי יֹדֵעַ נַגֵּן וְגִבּוֹר חַיִל וְאִישׁ מִלְחָמָה וּנְבוֹן דָּבָר וְאִישׁ תֹּאַר וַיהוָה עִמּוֹ:

| | |
|---|---|
| **One** of the young men answered | וַיַּעַן אֶחָד מֵהַנְּעָרִים וַיֹּאמֶר |
| **Behold**, I have seen | הִנֵּה רָאִיתִי |
| a son of Jesse the Bethlehemite | בֵּן לְיִשַׁי בֵּית הַלַּחְמִי |
| who is skillful in playing | יֹדֵעַ נַגֵּן |
| a man of valor | וְגִבּוֹר חַיִל |
| a man of war | וְאִישׁ מִלְחָמָה |
| prudent in speech | וּנְבוֹן דָּבָר |
| and a man of good presence | וְאִישׁ תֹּאַר |
| and the LORD is **with** him | וַיהוָה עִמּוֹ |

David responded, "**Here is** (הִנֵּה) the spear, O king; let **one** (אֶחָד) of the young men come over and **get** (וְיִקָּחֶהָ) it." (MLB)

| לקח | to take | 966x |
|---|---|---|
| lāqaḥ | | S3947 |

הִנֵּה　➤　DAY 46　　　　אֶחָד　➤　DAY 48

וַיַּעַן דָּוִד וַיֹּאמֶר הִנֵּה חֲנִית הַמֶּלֶךְ וְיַעֲבֹר אֶחָד מֵהַנְּעָרִים וְיִקָּחֶהָ:

| David responded | וַיַּעַן דָּוִד וַיֹּאמֶר |
|---|---|
| **Here is** the spear | הִנֵּה חֲנִית |
| O king | הַמֶּלֶךְ |
| let **one** of the young men come over | וְיַעֲבֹר אֶחָד מֵהַנְּעָרִים |
| and **get** it | וְיִקָּחֶהָ |

Then the LORD God said, "See, the man has become like **one** (אֶחָד) of us, **knowing** (דַעַת) good and evil; and now, he might reach out his hand and **take** (וְלָקַח) also from the tree of life, and eat, and live forever." (NRSV)

| ידע | to know | 952x |
|---|---|---|
| *yāda'* | | S3045 |

אֶחָד  ➤  DAY 48          לקח  ➤  DAY 49

וַיֹּאמֶר יְהוָה אֱלֹהִים הֵן הָאָדָם הָיָה כְּאַחַד מִמֶּנּוּ לָדַעַת טוֹב וָרָע
וְעַתָּה פֶּן־יִשְׁלַח יָדוֹ וְלָקַח גַּם מֵעֵץ הַחַיִּים וְאָכַל וָחַי לְעֹלָם:

| Then the LORD God said | וַיֹּאמֶר יְהוָה אֱלֹהִים |
|---|---|
| See, the man | הֵן הָאָדָם |
| has become like **one** of us | הָיָה כְּאַחַד מִמֶּנּוּ |
| **knowing** good and evil | לָדַעַת טוֹב וָרָע |
| and now | וְעַתָּה |
| he might reach out his hand | פֶּן־יִשְׁלַח יָדוֹ |
| and **take** also | וְלָקַח גַּם |
| from the tree of life | מֵעֵץ הַחַיִּים |
| and eat | וְאָכַל |
| and live forever | וָחַי לְעֹלָם |

The LORD said to Joshua: Today I shall begin to exalt you in the
**eyes** (עֵינֵי) of all Israel, so that **they may know** (יֵדְעוּן) that, as I
was **with** (עִם) Moses, I shall be **with** (עִמָּךְ) you. (MLB)

| עַיִן | eye, appearance, fountain | 901x |
|---|---|---|
| ʿ**ayin** | | S5869 |

עִם    ➤    DAY 47        יָדַע    ➤    DAY 50

וַיֹּאמֶר יְהוָה אֶל־יְהוֹשֻׁעַ הַיּוֹם הַזֶּה אָחֵל גַּדֶּלְךָ בְּעֵינֵי כָּל־יִשְׂרָאֵל
אֲשֶׁר יֵדְעוּן כִּי כַּאֲשֶׁר הָיִיתִי עִם־מֹשֶׁה אֶהְיֶה עִמָּךְ:

| | |
|---|---|
| The LORD said | וַיֹּאמֶר יְהוָה |
| to Joshua | אֶל־יְהוֹשֻׁעַ |
| Today | הַיּוֹם הַזֶּה |
| I shall begin | אָחֵל |
| to exalt you | גַּדֶּלְךָ |
| in the **eyes** of | בְּעֵינֵי |
| all Israel | כָּל־יִשְׂרָאֵל |
| so that **they may know** that | אֲשֶׁר יֵדְעוּן כִּי |
| as I was | כַּאֲשֶׁר הָיִיתִי |
| **with** Moses | עִם־מֹשֶׁה |
| I shall be **with** you | אֶהְיֶה עִמָּךְ |

And Achish answered David and said, "**I know** (יָדַעְתִּי) that you are as blameless in my **sight** (עֵינַי) as an angel of God. Nevertheless, the commanders of the Philistines have said, '**He shall** not **go up** (יַעֲלֶה) with us to the battle.'" (ESV)

| | | |
|---|---|---|
| עלה | to go up; offer | 894x |
| ʿālâ | | S5927 |

ידע  ➤  DAY 50          עַיִן  ➤  DAY 51

וַיַּעַן אָכִישׁ וַיֹּאמֶר אֶל־דָּוִד **יָדַעְתִּי** כִּי טוֹב אַתָּה בְּעֵינַי כְּמַלְאַךְ
אֱלֹהִים אַךְ שָׂרֵי פְלִשְׁתִּים אָמְרוּ לֹא־**יַעֲלֶה** עִמָּנוּ בַּמִּלְחָמָה:

| | |
|---|---|
| And Achish answered David and said | וַיַּעַן אָכִישׁ וַיֹּאמֶר אֶל־דָּוִד |
| **I know** that | **יָדַעְתִּי** כִּי |
| you are as blameless | טוֹב אַתָּה |
| in my **sight** | בְּעֵינַי |
| as an angel of God | כְּמַלְאַךְ אֱלֹהִים |
| Nevertheless | אַךְ |
| the commanders of the Philistines have said | שָׂרֵי פְלִשְׁתִּים אָמְרוּ |
| **He shall** not **go up** with us | לֹא־**יַעֲלֶה** עִמָּנוּ |
| to the battle | בַּמִּלְחָמָה |

For (כִּי) our transgressions before you are many, and our sins testify against us. Our transgressions **indeed** (כִּי) are **with** (אִתָּנוּ) us, and **we know** (יְדַעֲנוּם) our iniquities. (NRSV)

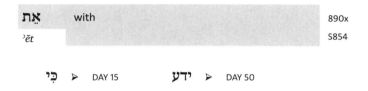

| אֵת | with | 890x |
|---|---|---|
| ʾēt | | S854 |

כִּי ▷ DAY 15          יָדַע ▷ DAY 50

כִּי־רַבּוּ פְשָׁעֵינוּ נֶגְדֶּךָ וְחַטֹּאותֵינוּ עָנְתָה בָּנוּ כִּי־פְשָׁעֵינוּ אִתָּנוּ
וַעֲוֹנֹתֵינוּ יְדַעֲנוּם:

| | |
|---|---|
| **For** our transgressions | כִּי־ . . . פְשָׁעֵינוּ |
| before you | נֶגְדֶּךָ |
| are many | רַבּוּ |
| and our sins | וְחַטֹּאותֵינוּ |
| testify against us | עָנְתָה בָּנוּ |
| Our transgressions **indeed** | כִּי־פְשָׁעֵינוּ |
| are **with** us | אִתָּנוּ |
| and . . . our iniquities | וַעֲוֹנֹתֵינוּ |
| **we know** | יְדַעֲנוּם |

And he remained **with** (אִתָּהּ) her six **years** (שָׁנִים), hidden in the house of the LORD, while Athaliah reigned over the **land** (אֶרֶץ).
(ESV)

| שָׁנָה | year | 878x |
|---|---|---|
| *šānâ* | | S8141 |

אֶרֶץ  ➤  DAY 23          אֵת  ➤  DAY 53

וַיְהִי אִתָּהּ בֵּית יְהוָה מִתְחַבֵּא שֵׁשׁ שָׁנִים וַעֲתַלְיָה מֹלֶכֶת עַל־הָאָרֶץ:

| | |
|---|---|
| And he remained | וַיְהִי |
| **with** her | אִתָּהּ |
| six **years** | שֵׁשׁ שָׁנִים |
| hidden | מִתְחַבֵּא |
| in the house of the LORD | בֵּית יְהוָה |
| while Athaliah reigned | וַעֲתַלְיָה מֹלֶכֶת |
| over the **land** | עַל־הָאָרֶץ |

In the first **year** (שְׁנַת) of his reign, **I** (אֲנִי), Daniel, observed in the books the number of the **years** (שָׁנִים) which was revealed as the **word** (דְּבַר) of the LORD to Jeremiah the prophet for the completion of the desolations of Jerusalem, namely, seventy **years** (שָׁנָה). (NASB)

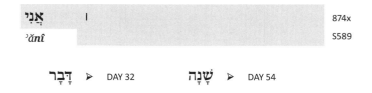

| אֲנִי | I | 874x |
|---|---|---|
| ʾănî | | S589 |

דְּבַר ➤ DAY 32     שָׁנָה ➤ DAY 54

בִּשְׁנַת אַחַת לְמָלְכוֹ אֲנִי דָנִיֵּאל בִּינֹתִי בַּסְּפָרִים מִסְפַּר הַשָּׁנִים
אֲשֶׁר הָיָה דְבַר־יְהוָה אֶל־יִרְמִיָה הַנָּבִיא לְמַלֹּאות לְחָרְבוֹת יְרוּשָׁלַ֫ם
שִׁבְעִים שָׁנָה:

| In the first **year** of his reign | בִּשְׁנַת אַחַת לְמָלְכוֹ |
|---|---|
| **I**, Daniel, observed in the books | אֲנִי דָנִיֵּאל בִּינֹתִי בַּסְּפָרִים |
| the number of the **years** | מִסְפַּר הַשָּׁנִים |
| which was revealed as the **word** of the LORD | אֲשֶׁר הָיָה דְבַר־יְהוָה |
| to Jeremiah the prophet | אֶל־יִרְמִיָה הַנָּבִיא |
| for the completion of the desolations of Jerusalem | לְמַלֹּאות לְחָרְבוֹת יְרוּשָׁלַ֫ם |
| namely, seventy **years** | שִׁבְעִים שָׁנָה |

Cursed be the cheat who has a male in his flock, and vows it, and yet sacrifices to the Lord what is blemished. For **I** (אֲנִי) am a great **King** (מֶלֶךְ), says the LORD of hosts, and my **name** (שְׁמִי) will be feared among the nations. (ESV)

| | | |
|---|---|---|
| שֵׁם | name | 864x |
| *šēm* | | S8034 |

מֶלֶךְ ▷ DAY 21      אֲנִי ▷ DAY 55

וְאָרוּר נוֹכֵל וְיֵשׁ בְּעֶדְרוֹ זָכָר וְנֹדֵר וְזֹבֵחַ מָשְׁחָת לַאדֹנָי כִּי מֶלֶךְ גָּדוֹל אָנִי אָמַר יְהוָה צְבָאוֹת וּשְׁמִי נוֹרָא בַּגּוֹיִם:

| | |
|---|---|
| Cursed be the cheat | וְאָרוּר נוֹכֵל |
| who has a male | וְיֵשׁ . . . זָכָר |
| in his flock | בְּעֶדְרוֹ |
| and vows it | וְנֹדֵר |
| and yet sacrifices to the Lord | וְזֹבֵחַ . . . לַאדֹנָי |
| what is blemished | מָשְׁחָת |
| For **I** am a great **King** | כִּי מֶלֶךְ גָּדוֹל אָנִי |
| says the LORD of hosts | אָמַר יְהוָה צְבָאוֹת |
| and my **name** will be feared | וּשְׁמִי נוֹרָא |
| among the nations | בַּגּוֹיִם |

Please do not let my lord pay attention to this worthless man,
Nabal, for as his **name** (שְׁמוֹ) is, so is he. Nabal is his **name** (שְׁמוֹ)
and folly is with him; but **I** (אֲנִי) your maidservant did not see the
young men of my lord whom **you sent** (שָׁלָחְתָּ). (NASB)

| שׁלח | to send | 847x |
|---|---|---|
| šālaḥ | | S7971 |

אֲנִי   ➤   DAY 55          שֵׁם   ➤   DAY 56

אַל־נָא יָשִׂים אֲדֹנִי אֶת־לִבּוֹ אֶל־אִישׁ הַבְּלִיַּעַל הַזֶּה עַל־נָבָל כִּי
כִשְׁמוֹ כֶּן־הוּא נָבָל שְׁמוֹ וּנְבָלָה עִמּוֹ וַאֲנִי אֲמָתְךָ לֹא רָאִיתִי אֶת־
נַעֲרֵי אֲדֹנִי אֲשֶׁר שָׁלָחְתָּ:

| Please do not let my lord pay attention | אַל־נָא יָשִׂים אֲדֹנִי אֶת־לִבּוֹ |
|---|---|
| to this worthless man, Nabal | אֶל־אִישׁ הַבְּלִיַּעַל הַזֶּה עַל־נָבָל |
| for as his **name** is | כִּי כִשְׁמוֹ |
| so is he | כֶּן־הוּא |
| Nabal is his **name** | נָבָל שְׁמוֹ |
| and folly is with him | וּנְבָלָה עִמּוֹ |
| but **I** your maidservant | וַאֲנִי אֲמָתְךָ |
| did not see | לֹא רָאִיתִי |
| the young men of my lord | אֶת־נַעֲרֵי אֲדֹנִי |
| whom **you sent** | אֲשֶׁר שָׁלָחְתָּ |

And when the king of Israel read the letter, he tore his clothes and said, "Am **I** (אֲנִי) God, **to kill** (הָמִית) and to make alive, that this man **sends** (שֹׁלֵחַ) word to me to cure a man of his leprosy? Only consider, and see how he is seeking a quarrel with me." (ESV)

| מוּת | to die | 845x |
|------|--------|------|
| *mût* | | S4191 |

אֲנִי  ➤  DAY 55          שֹׁלֵחַ  ➤  DAY 57

וַיְהִי כִּקְרֹא מֶלֶךְ־יִשְׂרָאֵל אֶת־הַסֵּפֶר וַיִּקְרַע בְּגָדָיו וַיֹּאמֶר הַאֱלֹהִים
אָנִי לְהָמִית וּלְהַחֲיוֹת כִּי־זֶה שֹׁלֵחַ אֵלַי לֶאֱסֹף אִישׁ מִצָּרַעְתּוֹ כִּי אַךְ־
דְּעוּ־נָא וּרְאוּ כִּי־מִתְאַנֶּה הוּא לִי:

| And when the king of Israel read | וַיְהִי כִּקְרֹא מֶלֶךְ־יִשְׂרָאֵל |
|---|---|
| the letter | אֶת־הַסֵּפֶר |
| he tore his clothes and said | וַיִּקְרַע בְּגָדָיו וַיֹּאמֶר |
| Am **I** God | הַאֱלֹהִים אָנִי |
| **to kill** and to make alive | לְהָמִית וּלְהַחֲיוֹת |
| that this man **sends** word to me | כִּי־זֶה שֹׁלֵחַ אֵלַי |
| to cure a man of his leprosy? | לֶאֱסֹף אִישׁ מִצָּרַעְתּוֹ |
| Only | כִּי אַךְ־ |
| consider and see | דְּעוּ־נָא וּרְאוּ |
| how he | כִּי־ . . . הוּא |
| is seeking a quarrel with me | מִתְאַנֶּה . . . לִי |

Then the elders of his city **shall send** (וְשָׁלְחוּ) and take him from **there** (שָׁם) and deliver him into the hand of the avenger of blood, that **he may die** (וָמֵת). (NASB)

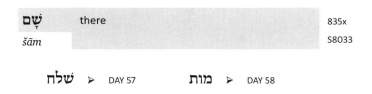

| שָׁם | there | | 835x |
|------|-------|-|------|
| *šām* | | | S8033 |

שָׁלַח  ➤  DAY 57          מוּת  ➤  DAY 58

וְשָׁלְחוּ זִקְנֵי עִירוֹ וְלָקְחוּ אֹתוֹ מִשָּׁם וְנָתְנוּ אֹתוֹ בְּיַד גֹּאֵל הַדָּם וָמֵת:

| Then the elders of his city **shall send** | וְשָׁלְחוּ זִקְנֵי עִירוֹ |
|---|---|
| and take him | וְלָקְחוּ אֹתוֹ |
| from **there** | מִשָּׁם |
| and deliver him | וְנָתְנוּ אֹתוֹ |
| into the hand of | בְּיַד |
| the avenger of blood | גֹּאֵל הַדָּם |
| that **he may die** | וָמֵת |

I will take the remnant of **Judah** (יְהוּדָה) who have set their faces to come to the land of Egypt to live [**there** (שָׁם)], and they shall all be consumed. . . . From the least to the greatest, **they shall die** (יָמֻתוּ) by the sword and by famine. (ESV)

| יְהוּדָה | Judah | 819x |
| --- | --- | --- |
| *yĕhûdâ* | | S3063 |

**מוּת**  ▷  DAY 58       **שָׁם**  ▷  DAY 59

וְלָקַחְתִּי אֶת־שְׁאֵרִית **יְהוּדָה** אֲשֶׁר־שָׂמוּ פְנֵיהֶם לָבוֹא אֶרֶץ־מִצְרַיִם לָגוּר **שָׁם** וְתַמּוּ כֹל . . . מִקָּטֹן וְעַד־גָּדוֹל בַּחֶרֶב וּבָרָעָב **יָמֻתוּ**

| I will take | וְלָקַחְתִּי |
| --- | --- |
| the remnant of **Judah** | אֶת־שְׁאֵרִית **יְהוּדָה** |
| who have set their faces | אֲשֶׁר־שָׂמוּ פְנֵיהֶם |
| to come to the land of Egypt | לָבוֹא אֶרֶץ־מִצְרַיִם |
| to live [**there**] | לָגוּר שָׁם |
| and they shall all be consumed. . . . | וְתַמּוּ כֹל . . . |
| From the least to the greatest | מִקָּטֹן וְעַד־גָּדוֹל |
| **they shall die** | **יָמֻתוּ** |
| by the sword and by famine | בַּחֶרֶב וּבָרָעָב |

And Amaziah said to Amos, "O seer, go, flee away to the land of **Judah** (יְהוּדָה), and **eat** (אֱכָל) bread **there** (שָׁם), and prophesy **there** (שָׁם)." (ESV)

| אכל | to eat, consume | 814x |
|---|---|---|
| ʾāḵal | | S398 |

שָׁם　➤　DAY 59　　　　　יְהוּדָה　➤　DAY 60

וַיֹּאמֶר אֲמַצְיָה אֶל־עָמוֹס חֹזֶה לֵךְ בְּרַח־לְךָ אֶל־אֶרֶץ יְהוּדָה וֶאֱכָל־
שָׁם לֶחֶם וְשָׁם תִּנָּבֵא:

| And Amaziah said | וַיֹּאמֶר אֲמַצְיָה |
|---|---|
| to Amos | אֶל־עָמוֹס |
| O seer | חֹזֶה |
| go | לֵךְ |
| flee away | בְּרַח־לְךָ |
| to the land of **Judah** | אֶל־אֶרֶץ יְהוּדָה |
| and **eat** bread **there** | וֶאֱכָל־שָׁם לֶחֶם |
| and prophesy **there** | וְשָׁם תִּנָּבֵא |

Uriah said to David, "The ark and Israel and **Judah** (יְהוּדָה) are staying in temporary shelters, and my lord Joab and the **servants** (עַבְדֵי) of my lord are camping in the open field. Shall I then go to my house **to eat** (אֱכֹל) and to drink and to lie with my wife?" (NASB)

| עֶבֶד | servant | 806x |
|---|---|---|
| ʿeved | | S5650 |

יְהוּדָה   ▷   DAY 60          אכל   ▷   DAY 61

וַיֹּאמֶר אוּרִיָּה אֶל־דָּוִד הָאָרוֹן וְיִשְׂרָאֵל וִיהוּדָה יֹשְׁבִים בַּסֻּכּוֹת וַאדֹנִי יוֹאָב וְעַבְדֵי אֲדֹנִי עַל־פְּנֵי הַשָּׂדֶה חֹנִים וַאֲנִי אָבוֹא אֶל־בֵּיתִי לֶאֱכֹל וְלִשְׁתּוֹת וְלִשְׁכַּב עִם־אִשְׁתִּי

| | |
|---|---|
| Uriah said to David | וַיֹּאמֶר אוּרִיָּה אֶל־דָּוִד |
| The ark and Israel and **Judah** | הָאָרוֹן וְיִשְׂרָאֵל וִיהוּדָה |
| are staying in temporary shelters | יֹשְׁבִים בַּסֻּכּוֹת |
| and my lord Joab | וַאדֹנִי יוֹאָב |
| and the **servants** of my lord | וְעַבְדֵי אֲדֹנִי |
| are camping | חֹנִים |
| in the open field | עַל־פְּנֵי הַשָּׂדֶה |
| Shall I then go to my house | וַאֲנִי אָבוֹא אֶל־בֵּיתִי |
| **to eat** and to drink | לֶאֱכֹל וְלִשְׁתּוֹת |
| and to lie with my wife? | וְלִשְׁכַּב עִם־אִשְׁתִּי |

And Pharaoh rose up in the night, he and all his **servants** (עֲבָדָיו) and all the Egyptians. And there was a great cry in Egypt, for **there was not** (אֵין) a house where [lit., which . . . **there** (שָׁם)] someone **was not** (אֵין) dead. (ESV)

| אֵין | not, nothing, no | 790x |
|---|---|---|
| ʾên | | S369 |

שָׁם ➤ DAY 59　　　עֶבֶד ➤ DAY 62

וַיָּקָם פַּרְעֹה לַיְלָה הוּא וְכָל־עֲבָדָיו וְכָל־מִצְרַיִם וַתְּהִי צְעָקָה גְדֹלָה בְּמִצְרָיִם כִּי־אֵין בַּיִת אֲשֶׁר אֵין־שָׁם מֵת:

| And Pharaoh rose up | וַיָּקָם פַּרְעֹה |
|---|---|
| in the night | לַיְלָה |
| he and all his **servants** | הוּא וְכָל־עֲבָדָיו |
| and all the Egyptians | וְכָל־מִצְרַיִם |
| And there was a great cry | וַתְּהִי צְעָקָה גְדֹלָה |
| in Egypt | בְּמִצְרָיִם |
| for **there was not** a house | כִּי־אֵין בַּיִת |
| where [lit., which . . . **there**] | אֲשֶׁר . . . שָׁם |
| someone **was not** dead | אֵין־ . . . מֵת |

But Jezebel his **wife** (אִשְׁתּוֹ) came to him and said to him, "How is it that your spirit is so sullen that you **are not** (אֵינְךָ) **eating** (אֹכֵל) food?" (NASB)

| אִשָּׁה | woman, wife | 781x |
|---|---|---|
| *'iššâ* | | S802 |

אֹכֵל ▷ DAY 61      אֵין ▷ DAY 63

וַתָּבֹא אֵלָיו אִיזֶבֶל **אִשְׁתּוֹ** וַתְּדַבֵּר אֵלָיו מַה־זֶּה רוּחֲךָ סָרָה וְאֵינְךָ אֹכֵל לָחֶם:

| But Jezebel his **wife** came to him | וַתָּבֹא אֵלָיו אִיזֶבֶל **אִשְׁתּוֹ** |
|---|---|
| and said to him | וַתְּדַבֵּר אֵלָיו |
| How is it that | מַה־זֶּה |
| your spirit | רוּחֲךָ |
| is so sullen | סָרָה |
| that you **are not** | וְאֵינְךָ |
| **eating** | אֹכֵל |
| food? | לָחֶם |

When his **master** (אֲדֹנָיו) heard the words that his **wife** (אִשְׁתּוֹ) spoke to him, saying, "This is the way your **servant** (עַבְדֶּךָ) treated me," he became enraged. (NRSV)

| אָדוֹן | sovereign, lord, master, owner | 774x |
|---|---|---|
| ʾādôn | | S113 |

עֶבֶד ➤ DAY 62　　　　　　　אִשָּׁה ➤ DAY 64

וַיְהִי כִשְׁמֹעַ אֲדֹנָיו אֶת־דִּבְרֵי אִשְׁתּוֹ אֲשֶׁר דִּבְּרָה אֵלָיו לֵאמֹר
כַּדְּבָרִים הָאֵלֶּה עָשָׂה לִי עַבְדֶּךָ וַיִּחַר אַפּוֹ:

| When his **master** heard | וַיְהִי כִשְׁמֹעַ אֲדֹנָיו |
|---|---|
| the words that his **wife** spoke to him, saying | אֶת־דִּבְרֵי אִשְׁתּוֹ אֲשֶׁר דִּבְּרָה אֵלָיו לֵאמֹר |
| This is the way | כַּדְּבָרִים הָאֵלֶּה |
| your **servant** treated me | עָשָׂה לִי עַבְדֶּךָ |
| he became enraged | וַיִּחַר אַפּוֹ |

and who says to me, "You [lit., **Both** (גַּם) you] drink, and I will draw for your camels, **too** (גַם)," let her be the **woman** (אִשָּׁה) whom the LORD has designated for my **master's** (אֲדֹנִי) son. (MLB)

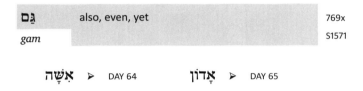

| גַּם | also, even, yet | 769x |
| gam | | S1571 |

אִשָּׁה ➤ DAY 64          אָדוֹן ➤ DAY 65

וְאָמְרָה אֵלַי גַּם־אַתָּה שְׁתֵה וְגַם לִגְמַלֶּיךָ אֶשְׁאָב הִוא הָאִשָּׁה אֲשֶׁר־הֹכִיחַ יְהוָה לְבֶן־אֲדֹנִי:

| and who says to me | וְאָמְרָה אֵלַי |
| You [lit., **Both** you] drink | גַּם־אַתָּה שְׁתֵה |
| and . . . for your camels, **too** | וְגַם לִגְמַלֶּיךָ |
| I will draw | אֶשְׁאָב |
| let her be the **woman** | הִוא הָאִשָּׁה |
| whom the LORD has designated | אֲשֶׁר־הֹכִיחַ יְהוָה |
| for my **master's** son | לְבֶן־אֲדֹנִי |

So David went up there, along with [lit., and **also (גַם)**] his **two** (שְׁתֵּי) **wives** (נָשָׁיו), Ahinoam of Jezreel, and Abigail the widow [lit., **wife (אֵשֶׁת)**)] of Nabal of Carmel. (NRSV)

שְׁנַיִם      two      769x

šěnayim      S8147

אִשָּׁה ◄    DAY 64      גַּם ◄    DAY 66

וַיַּעַל שָׁם דָּוִד וְגַם שְׁתֵּי נָשָׁיו אֲחִינֹעַם הַיִּזְרְעֵלִית וַאֲבִיגַיִל אֵשֶׁת נָבָל הַכַּרְמְלִי:

| So David went up there | וַיַּעַל שָׁם דָּוִד |
| --- | --- |
| along with [lit., and **also**] | וְגַם |
| his **two wives** | שְׁתֵּי נָשָׁיו |
| Ahinoam of Jezreel | אֲחִינֹעַם הַיִּזְרְעֵלִית |
| and Abigail | וַאֲבִיגַיִל |
| the widow [lit., **wife**] of Nabal of Carmel | אֵשֶׁת נָבָל הַכַּרְמְלִי |

**Nothing** (אֵין) was in the ark except the **two** (שְׁנֵי) tablets of stone which **Moses** (מֹשֶׁה) put there at Horeb, where the LORD made a covenant [lit., cut] with the children of Israel when they came out of the land of Egypt. (MLB)

| מֹשֶׁה | Moses | 766x |
|--------|-------|------|
| *mōšê* | | S4872 |

אֵין ▷ DAY 63        שְׁנַיִם ▷ DAY 67

אֵין בָּאָרוֹן רַק שְׁנֵי לֻחוֹת הָאֲבָנִים אֲשֶׁר הִנִּחַ שָׁם מֹשֶׁה בְּחֹרֵב
אֲשֶׁר כָּרַת יְהוָה עִם־בְּנֵי יִשְׂרָאֵל בְּצֵאתָם מֵאֶרֶץ מִצְרָיִם:

| | |
|---|---|
| **Nothing** was in the ark | אֵין בָּאָרוֹן |
| except | רַק |
| the **two** tablets of stone | שְׁנֵי לֻחוֹת הָאֲבָנִים |
| which **Moses** | אֲשֶׁר . . . מֹשֶׁה |
| put there at Horeb | הִנִּחַ שָׁם . . . בְּחֹרֵב |
| where the LORD made a covenant [lit., cut] | אֲשֶׁר כָּרַת יְהוָה |
| with the children of Israel | עִם־בְּנֵי יִשְׂרָאֵל |
| when they came out | בְּצֵאתָם |
| of the land of Egypt | מֵאֶרֶץ מִצְרָיִם |

And the LORD said to **Moses (מֹשֶׁה)** in Midian, "Go back [lit., go, **return (שֵׁב)**] to Egypt, for all the men who were seeking your **life (נַפְשֶׁךָ)** are dead." (ESV)

| נֶפֶשׁ | soul, life, breath, throat | 757x |
|---|---|---|
| *nefeš* | | S5315 |

שׁוּב ▷ DAY 44          מֹשֶׁה ▷ DAY 68

וַיֹּאמֶר יְהוָה אֶל־מֹשֶׁה בְּמִדְיָן לֵךְ שֵׁב מִצְרָיִם כִּי־מֵתוּ כָּל־הָאֲנָשִׁים הַמְבַקְשִׁים אֶת־נַפְשֶׁךָ׃

| And the LORD said | וַיֹּאמֶר יְהוָה |
|---|---|
| to **Moses** | אֶל־מֹשֶׁה |
| in Midian | בְּמִדְיָן |
| Go back [lit., go, **return**] | לֵךְ שֵׁב |
| to Egypt | מִצְרָיִם |
| for all the men | כִּי־ . . . כָּל־הָאֲנָשִׁים |
| who were seeking | הַמְבַקְשִׁים |
| your **life** | אֶת־נַפְשֶׁךָ |
| are dead | מֵתוּ |

They said to **Moses** (מֹשֶׁה): "Is it because **there are no** (אֵין) graves in Egypt that you have taken us away to die in the wilderness? **What** (מַה) have you done to us by bringing us out of Egypt?" (CSB)

| | | |
|---|---|---|
| מָה | what? how! | 754x |
| *mâ* | | S4100 |

אֵין    ▷    DAY 63        מֹשֶׁה    ▷    DAY 68

וַיֹּאמְרוּ אֶל־מֹשֶׁה הַמִבְּלִי אֵין־קְבָרִים בְּמִצְרַיִם לְקַחְתָּנוּ לָמוּת
בַּמִּדְבָּר מַה־זֹּאת עָשִׂיתָ לָּנוּ לְהוֹצִיאָנוּ מִמִּצְרָיִם:

| | |
|---|---|
| They said to **Moses** | וַיֹּאמְרוּ אֶל־מֹשֶׁה |
| Is it because | הַמִבְּלִי |
| **there are no** graves in Egypt | אֵין־קְבָרִים בְּמִצְרַיִם |
| that you have taken us away | לְקַחְתָּנוּ |
| to die in the wilderness? | לָמוּת בַּמִּדְבָּר |
| **What** have you done to us | מַה־זֹּאת עָשִׂיתָ לָּנוּ |
| by bringing us out of Egypt? | לְהוֹצִיאָנוּ מִמִּצְרָיִם |

And when these went into Micah's house and took the carved image, the ephod, the household gods, and the metal image, the **priest** (כֹּהֵן) said to them, "**What** (מָה) **are** you **doing** (עֹשִׂים)?" (ESV)

| | | |
|---|---|---|
| כֹּהֵן | priest | 750x |
| kōhēn | | S3548 |

עָשָׂה ➤ DAY 18        מָה ➤ DAY 70

וְאֵלֶּה בָּאוּ בֵּית מִיכָה וַיִּקְחוּ אֶת־פֶּסֶל הָאֵפוֹד וְאֶת־הַתְּרָפִים וְאֶת־הַמַּסֵּכָה וַיֹּאמְרוּ אֲלֵיהֶם הַכֹּהֵן מָה אַתֶּם עֹשִׂים:

| And when these went | וְאֵלֶּה בָּאוּ |
|---|---|
| into Micah's house | בֵּית מִיכָה |
| and took | וַיִּקְחוּ |
| the carved image, the ephod | אֶת־פֶּסֶל הָאֵפוֹד |
| the household gods | וְאֶת־הַתְּרָפִים |
| and the metal image | וְאֶת־הַמַּסֵּכָה |
| the **priest** said to them | וַיֹּאמְרוּ אֲלֵיהֶם הַכֹּהֵן |
| **What are** you **doing**? | מָה אַתֶּם עֹשִׂים |

Now **listen** (שְׁמַע), Joshua the high **priest** (כֹּהֵן), **you** (אַתָּה) and your friends who are sitting in front of you—indeed they are men who are a symbol, for behold, I am going to bring in My servant the Branch. (NASB)

| אַתָּה | you (masc sg) | 749x |
|---|---|---|
| ʾattâ | | S859 |

שְׁמַע ➤ DAY 38          כֹּהֵן ➤ DAY 71

שְׁמַֽע־נָא יְהוֹשֻׁעַ הַכֹּהֵן הַגָּדוֹל אַתָּה וְרֵעֶיךָ הַיֹּשְׁבִים לְפָנֶיךָ כִּי־אַנְשֵׁי מוֹפֵת הֵמָּה כִּי־הִנְנִי מֵבִיא אֶת־עַבְדִּי צֶמַח׃

| Now **listen** | שְׁמַֽע־נָא |
|---|---|
| Joshua the high **priest** | יְהוֹשֻׁעַ הַכֹּהֵן הַגָּדוֹל |
| **you** and your friends | אַתָּה וְרֵעֶיךָ |
| who are sitting in front of you | הַיֹּשְׁבִים לְפָנֶיךָ |
| indeed they are | כִּי־ . . . הֵמָּה |
| men who are a symbol | אַנְשֵׁי מוֹפֵת |
| for behold, I am going to bring in | כִּי־הִנְנִי מֵבִיא |
| My servant the Branch | אֶת־עַבְדִּי צֶמַח |

Has any people ever heard (הֲשָׁמַע עָם) the voice of a god
**speaking** (מְדַבֵּר) out of a fire, as **you** (אַתָּה) have heard, and
lived? (NRSV)

| הֲ | (interrogative particle) | 748x |
|---|---|---|
| hă | | |

הֲ            דבר  ➤  DAY 39                  אַתָּה  ➤  DAY 72

הֲשָׁמַע עָם קוֹל אֱלֹהִים מְדַבֵּר מִתּוֹךְ־הָאֵשׁ כַּאֲשֶׁר־שָׁמַעְתָּ אַתָּה
וַיֶּחִי:

| Has any people ever heard | הֲשָׁמַע עָם |
|---|---|
| the voice of a god | קוֹל אֱלֹהִים |
| **speaking** | מְדַבֵּר |
| out of a fire | מִתּוֹךְ־הָאֵשׁ |
| as **you** have heard | כַּאֲשֶׁר־שָׁמַעְתָּ אַתָּה |
| and lived? | וַיֶּחִי |

Who has heard of such a thing? Who **has seen** (רָאָה) such things
[lit., such as **these** (אֵלֶּה)]? Can a land be born (הֲיוּחַל אֶרֶץ) in one
day or a nation be delivered in an instant? Yet as soon as Zion was
in labor, she gave birth to her sons. (CSB)

| | | |
|---|---|---|
| **אֵלֶּה** | these, those | 745x |
| ʾēllê | | S428 |

| רָאָה | ▷ | DAY 34 | הֲ | ▷ | DAY 73 |
|---|---|---|---|---|---|

מִי־שָׁמַע כָּזֹאת מִי רָאָה כָּאֵלֶּה הֲיוּחַל אֶרֶץ בְּיוֹם אֶחָד אִם־יִוָּלֵד גּוֹי
פַּעַם אֶחָת כִּי־חָלָה גַּם־יָלְדָה צִיּוֹן אֶת־בָּנֶיהָ׃

| | |
|---|---|
| Who has heard of such a thing? | מִי־שָׁמַע כָּזֹאת |
| Who **has seen** such things [lit., such as **these**]? | מִי רָאָה כָּאֵלֶּה |
| Can a land be born | הֲיוּחַל אֶרֶץ |
| in one day | בְּיוֹם אֶחָד |
| or a nation be delivered | אִם־יִוָּלֵד גּוֹי |
| in an instant? | פַּעַם אֶחָת |
| Yet as soon as Zion was in labor | כִּי־חָלָה . . . צִיּוֹן |
| she gave birth to her sons | גַּם־יָלְדָה . . . אֶת־בָּנֶיהָ |

Take care that you be not ensnared to follow them, after they have been destroyed before you, and that you do not inquire about their gods, saying, "How did **these (אֵלֶּה)** nations serve their gods?—that **I (אֲנִי)** also may do the same [lit., **thus (כֵּן)**]." (ESV)

| כֵּן | thus, therefore | 741x |
| kēn | | S3651 |

אֲנִי   ➤   DAY 55          אֵלֶּה   ➤   DAY 74

הִשָּׁמֶר לְךָ פֶּן־תִּנָּקֵשׁ אַחֲרֵיהֶם אַחֲרֵי הִשָּׁמְדָם מִפָּנֶיךָ וּפֶן־תִּדְרֹשׁ לֵאלֹהֵיהֶם לֵאמֹר אֵיכָה יַעַבְדוּ הַגּוֹיִם הָאֵלֶּה אֶת־אֱלֹהֵיהֶם וְאֶעֱשֶׂה־כֵּן גַּם־אָנִי:

| Take care | הִשָּׁמֶר לְךָ |
| that you be not ensnared to follow them | פֶּן־תִּנָּקֵשׁ אַחֲרֵיהֶם |
| after they have been destroyed before you | אַחֲרֵי הִשָּׁמְדָם מִפָּנֶיךָ |
| and that you do not inquire | וּפֶן־תִּדְרֹשׁ |
| about their gods, saying | לֵאלֹהֵיהֶם לֵאמֹר |
| How did **these** nations | אֵיכָה . . . הַגּוֹיִם הָאֵלֶּה |
| serve their gods? | יַעַבְדוּ . . . אֶת־אֱלֹהֵיהֶם |
| that **I** also | גַּם־אָנִי |
| may do the same [lit., **thus**] | וְאֶעֱשֶׂה־כֵּן |

Therefore [lit., upon **thus** (כֵּן)] **they called** (קָרְאוּ) **these** (אֵלֶּה)
days Purim, after the term Pur. Therefore [lit., upon **thus** (כֵּן)],
because of all that was written in this letter, and of what they had
faced in this matter, and of what had happened to them, . . . (ESV)

| קרא | to call, proclaim | 739x |
|---|---|---|
| qārā' | | S7121 |

אֵלֶּה ◄  ➤  DAY 74          כֵּן  ➤  DAY 75

עַל־כֵּן קָרְאוּ לַיָּמִים הָאֵלֶּה פוּרִים עַל־שֵׁם הַפּוּר עַל־כֵּן עַל־כָּל־
דִּבְרֵי הָאִגֶּרֶת הַזֹּאת וּמָה־רָאוּ עַל־כָּכָה וּמָה הִגִּיעַ אֲלֵיהֶם:

| Therefore [lit., upon **thus**] | עַל־כֵּן |
|---|---|
| **they called these** days | קָרְאוּ לַיָּמִים הָאֵלֶּה |
| Purim | פוּרִים |
| after the term Pur | עַל־שֵׁם הַפּוּר |
| Therefore [lit., upon **thus**] | עַל־כֵּן |
| because of all that was written in this letter | עַל־כָּל־דִּבְרֵי הָאִגֶּרֶת הַזֹּאת |
| and of what they had faced in this matter | וּמָה־רָאוּ עַל־כָּכָה |
| and of what had happened to them | וּמָה הִגִּיעַ אֲלֵיהֶם |

Then **they cried out** (וַיִּקְרְאוּ) to the LORD, "Please, O LORD, we pray, do **not** (אַל) let us perish on account of this man's **life** (נֶפֶשׁ). Do **not** (אַל) make us guilty of innocent blood; for you, O LORD, have done as it pleased you." (NRSV)

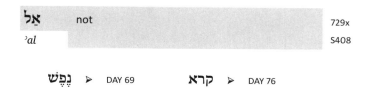

| אַל | not | | 729x |
|---|---|---|---|
| ʾal | | | S408 |

נֶפֶשׁ ➤ DAY 69　　　　קרא ➤ DAY 76

וַיִּקְרְאוּ אֶל־יְהוָה וַיֹּאמְרוּ אָנָּה יְהוָה אַל־נָא נֹאבְדָה בְּנֶפֶשׁ הָאִישׁ הַזֶּה וְאַל־תִּתֵּן עָלֵינוּ דָּם נָקִיא כִּי־אַתָּה יְהוָה כַּאֲשֶׁר חָפַצְתָּ עָשִׂיתָ׃

| Then **they cried out** to the LORD | וַיִּקְרְאוּ אֶל־יְהוָה וַיֹּאמְרוּ |
|---|---|
| O LORD, we pray | אָנָּה יְהוָה |
| Please . . . do **not** let us perish | אַל־נָא נֹאבְדָה |
| on account of this man's **life** | בְּנֶפֶשׁ הָאִישׁ הַזֶּה |
| Do **not** make us guilty of | וְאַל־תִּתֵּן עָלֵינוּ |
| innocent blood | דָּם נָקִיא |
| for you, O LORD | כִּי־אַתָּה יְהוָה |
| have done | עָשִׂיתָ |
| as it pleased you | כַּאֲשֶׁר חָפַצְתָּ |

Do **not** (אַל) be like your fathers, to whom the former prophets **cried out** (קָרְאוּ), "Thus says the LORD of hosts, Return from your evil **ways** (דַּרְכֵיכֶם) and from your evil deeds." But they did not hear or pay attention to me, declares the LORD. (ESV)

| | | |
|---|---|---|
| דֶּרֶךְ | road, way | 712x |
| *derek* | | S1870 |

קָרָא    ➤    DAY 76        אַל    ➤    DAY 77

אַל־תִּהְיוּ כַאֲבֹתֵיכֶם אֲשֶׁר קָרְאוּ־אֲלֵיהֶם הַנְּבִיאִים הָרִאשֹׁנִים לֵאמֹר
כֹּה אָמַר יְהוָה צְבָאוֹת שׁוּבוּ נָא מִדַּרְכֵיכֶם הָרָעִים וּמַעֲלְלֵיכֶם
הָרָעִים וְלֹא שָׁמְעוּ וְלֹא־הִקְשִׁיבוּ אֵלַי נְאֻם־יְהוָה׃

| | |
|---|---|
| Do **not** be like your fathers | אַל־תִּהְיוּ כַאֲבֹתֵיכֶם |
| to whom | אֲשֶׁר . . . אֲלֵיהֶם |
| the former prophets **cried out** | קָרְאוּ־ . . . הַנְּבִיאִים הָרִאשֹׁנִים לֵאמֹר |
| Thus says the LORD of hosts | כֹּה אָמַר יְהוָה צְבָאוֹת |
| Return from your evil **ways** | שׁוּבוּ נָא מִדַּרְכֵיכֶם הָרָעִים |
| and from your evil deeds | וּמַעֲלְלֵיכֶם הָרָעִים |
| But they did not hear | וְלֹא שָׁמְעוּ |
| or pay attention to me | וְלֹא־הִקְשִׁיבוּ אֵלַי |
| declares the LORD | נְאֻם־יְהוָה |

I have sent to you all my servants the prophets, sending them persistently, saying, "Turn now every one of you from his evil **way** (דַּרְכּוֹ), and amend your deeds, and do **not** (אַל) go **after** (אַחֲרֵי) other gods to serve them." (ESV)

| אַחַר | after, behind | 711x |
|---|---|---|
| ʾaḥar | | S310 |

אַל ➤ DAY 77          דֶּרֶךְ ➤ DAY 78

וָאֶשְׁלַח אֲלֵיכֶם אֶת־כָּל־עֲבָדַי הַנְּבִאִים הַשְׁכֵּים וְשָׁלֹחַ לֵאמֹר שֻׁבוּ־נָא אִישׁ מִדַּרְכּוֹ הָרָעָה וְהֵיטִיבוּ מַעַלְלֵיכֶם וְאַל־תֵּלְכוּ אַחֲרֵי אֱלֹהִים אֲחֵרִים לְעָבְדָם

| I have sent to you | וָאֶשְׁלַח אֲלֵיכֶם |
|---|---|
| all my servants the prophets | אֶת־כָּל־עֲבָדַי הַנְּבִאִים |
| sending them persistently, saying | הַשְׁכֵּים וְשָׁלֹחַ לֵאמֹר |
| Turn now | שֻׁבוּ־נָא |
| every one of you | אִישׁ |
| from his evil **way** | מִדַּרְכּוֹ הָרָעָה |
| and amend your deeds | וְהֵיטִיבוּ מַעַלְלֵיכֶם |
| and do **not** go **after** | וְאַל־תֵּלְכוּ אַחֲרֵי |
| other gods | אֱלֹהִים אֲחֵרִים |
| to serve them | לְעָבְדָם |

Then it came about **after** (אַחַר) these things, the cupbearer and the baker for the king of **Egypt** (מִצְרַיִם) offended their **lord** (אֲדֹנֵיהֶם), the king of **Egypt** (מִצְרַיִם). (NASB)

| מִצְרַיִם | Egypt | 681x |
|---|---|---|
| *miṣrayim* | | S4714 |

| אָדוֹן | ➤ | DAY 65 | | אַחַר | ➤ | DAY 79 |
|---|---|---|---|---|---|---|

וַיְהִי אַחַר הַדְּבָרִים הָאֵלֶּה חָטְאוּ מַשְׁקֵה מֶלֶךְ־מִצְרַיִם וְהָאֹפֶה לַאֲדֹנֵיהֶם לְמֶלֶךְ מִצְרָיִם:

| | |
|---|---|
| Then it came about | וַיְהִי |
| **after** these things | אַחַר הַדְּבָרִים הָאֵלֶּה |
| the cupbearer . . . for the king of **Egypt** | מַשְׁקֵה מֶלֶךְ־מִצְרַיִם |
| and the baker | וְהָאֹפֶה |
| offended | חָטְאוּ |
| their **lord** | לַאֲדֹנֵיהֶם |
| the king of **Egypt** | לְמֶלֶךְ מִצְרַיִם |

When Pharaoh drew near, the people of Israel **lifted up** (וַיִּשְׂאוּ)
their eyes, and behold, the Egyptians were [lit., **Egypt** (מִצְרַיִם)
was] marching **after** (אַחֲרֵיהֶם) them, and they feared greatly. And
the people of Israel cried out to the Lord. (ESV)

| נשׂא | to lift, bear, pardon | 658x |
|---|---|---|
| nāśā' | | S5375 |

אַחַר ➤ DAY 79     מִצְרַיִם ➤ DAY 80

וּפַרְעֹה הִקְרִיב וַיִּשְׂאוּ בְנֵי־יִשְׂרָאֵל אֶת־עֵינֵיהֶם וְהִנֵּה מִצְרַיִם נֹסֵעַ
אַחֲרֵיהֶם וַיִּירְאוּ מְאֹד וַיִּצְעֲקוּ בְנֵי־יִשְׂרָאֵל אֶל־יְהוָה:

| When Pharaoh drew near | וּפַרְעֹה הִקְרִיב |
|---|---|
| the people of Israel **lifted up** | וַיִּשְׂאוּ בְנֵי־יִשְׂרָאֵל |
| their eyes | אֶת־עֵינֵיהֶם |
| and behold | וְהִנֵּה |
| the Egyptians were [lit., **Egypt** was] marching **after** them | מִצְרַיִם נֹסֵעַ אַחֲרֵיהֶם |
| and they feared greatly | וַיִּירְאוּ מְאֹד |
| And the people of Israel cried out | וַיִּצְעֲקוּ בְנֵי־יִשְׂרָאֵל |
| to the Lord | אֶל־יְהוָה |

So the king took counsel, and made two calves of gold. He said to the people [lit., them], "You **have gone up** (עָלוֹת) to **Jerusalem** (יְרוּשָׁלַ͏ִם) long enough. Here are your gods, O Israel, who **brought you up** (הֶעֱלוּךָ) out of the land of **Egypt** (מִצְרָיִם)." (NRSV)

| יְרוּשָׁלַ͏ִם | Jerusalem | 643x |
|---|---|---|
| *yĕrûšālayim* | | S3389 |

עָלָה ▹ DAY 52　　　　מִצְרַיִם ▹ DAY 80

וַיִּוָּעַץ הַמֶּלֶךְ וַיַּעַשׂ שְׁנֵי עֶגְלֵי זָהָב וַיֹּאמֶר אֲלֵהֶם רַב־לָכֶם מֵעֲלוֹת
יְרוּשָׁלַ͏ִם הִנֵּה אֱלֹהֶיךָ יִשְׂרָאֵל אֲשֶׁר הֶעֱלוּךָ מֵאֶרֶץ מִצְרָיִם:

| So the king took counsel | וַיִּוָּעַץ הַמֶּלֶךְ |
|---|---|
| and made two calves of gold | וַיַּעַשׂ שְׁנֵי עֶגְלֵי זָהָב |
| He said to the people [lit., them] | וַיֹּאמֶר אֲלֵהֶם |
| You **have gone up** to **Jerusalem** long enough | רַב־לָכֶם מֵעֲלוֹת יְרוּשָׁלַ͏ִם |
| Here are your gods | הִנֵּה אֱלֹהֶיךָ |
| O Israel | יִשְׂרָאֵל |
| who **brought** you **up** | אֲשֶׁר הֶעֱלוּךָ |
| out of the land of **Egypt** | מֵאֶרֶץ מִצְרָיִם |

Then I put Hanani my **brother** (אָחִי), and Hananiah the commander of the fortress, in charge of **Jerusalem** (יְרוּשָׁלָם), for he was a faithful man and feared **God** (אֱלֹהִים) more than many. (NASB)

| אָח | brother | 632x |
|---|---|---|
| ʾāḥ | | S251 |

אֱלֹהִים ▷ DAY 19       יְרוּשָׁלַם ▷ DAY 82

וָאֲצַוֶּה אֶת־חֲנָנִי אָחִי וְאֶת־חֲנַנְיָה שַׂר הַבִּירָה עַל־יְרוּשָׁלָם כִּי־הוּא כְאִישׁ אֱמֶת וְיָרֵא אֶת־הָאֱלֹהִים מֵרַבִּים:

| Then I put . . . in charge | וָאֲצַוֶּה |
|---|---|
| Hanani my **brother** | אֶת־חֲנָנִי אָחִי |
| and Hananiah | וְאֶת־חֲנַנְיָה |
| the commander of the fortress | שַׂר הַבִּירָה |
| of **Jerusalem** | עַל־יְרוּשָׁלָם |
| for he was a faithful man | כִּי־הוּא כְאִישׁ אֱמֶת |
| and feared **God** | וְיָרֵא אֶת־הָאֱלֹהִים |
| more than many | מֵרַבִּים |

Now therefore, my son, **obey** (שְׁמַע) my voice. **Arise** (קוּם), flee to Laban my **brother** (אָחִי) in Haran. (ESV)

| | | |
|---|---|---|
| **קוּם** | to arise; raise up | 627x |
| *qûm* | | S6965 |

שְׁמַע  ▷  DAY 38        אָח  ▷  DAY 83

וְעַתָּה בְנִי שְׁמַע בְּקֹלִי וְקוּם בְּרַח־לְךָ אֶל־לָבָן אָחִי חָרָנָה:

| | |
|---|---|
| Now therefore | וְעַתָּה |
| my son | בְנִי |
| **obey** my voice | שְׁמַע בְּקֹלִי |
| **Arise** | וְקוּם |
| flee | בְּרַח־לְךָ |
| to Laban | אֶל־לָבָן |
| my **brother** | אָחִי |
| in Haran | חָרָנָה |

One person could not see another [lit., his **brother** (אָחִיו)], and for **three** (שְׁלֹשֶׁת) days they did not move [lit., **they did** not **rise** (קָמוּ)] from where they were. Yet all the Israelites had light where they lived. (CSB)

| שָׁלֹשׁ | three | 606x |
|---|---|---|
| šālōš | | S7991 |

אָח ▷ DAY 83　　　　קוּם ▷ DAY 84

לֹא־רָאוּ אִישׁ אֶת־אָחִיו וְלֹא־קָמוּ אִישׁ מִתַּחְתָּיו שְׁלֹשֶׁת יָמִים וּלְכָל־
בְּנֵי יִשְׂרָאֵל הָיָה אוֹר בְּמוֹשְׁבֹתָם׃

| One person could not see | לֹא־רָאוּ אִישׁ |
|---|---|
| another [lit., his **brother**] | אֶת־אָחִיו |
| and for **three** days | שְׁלֹשֶׁת יָמִים |
| they did not move [lit., **they did** not **rise**] | וְלֹא־קָמוּ |
| from where they were | אִישׁ מִתַּחְתָּיו |
| Yet all the Israelites had light | וּלְכָל־בְּנֵי יִשְׂרָאֵל הָיָה אוֹר |
| where they lived | בְּמוֹשְׁבֹתָם |

And [he] said, "Far be it from me, O LORD, that I should do **this** (זֹאת). Shall I drink the blood of the men who went at the risk of their lives?" Therefore he would not drink it [lit., them]. **These things** (אֵלֶּה) the **three** (שְׁלֹשֶׁת) mighty men did. (ESV)

| | | |
|---|---|---|
| **זֹאת** | this, that (fem) | 605x |
| zō't | | S2063 |

אֵלֶּה  ➤  DAY 74          שָׁלֹשׁ  ➤  DAY 85

וַיֹּאמֶר חָלִילָה לִּי יְהוָה מֵעֲשֹׂתִי **זֹאת** הֲדַם הָאֲנָשִׁים הַהֹלְכִים בְּנַפְשׁוֹתָם וְלֹא אָבָה לִשְׁתּוֹתָם **אֵלֶּה** עָשׂוּ **שְׁלֹשֶׁת** הַגִּבֹּרִים:

| | |
|---|---|
| And [he] said | וַיֹּאמֶר |
| Far be it from me, O LORD | חָלִילָה לִּי יְהוָה |
| that I should do **this** | מֵעֲשֹׂתִי **זֹאת** |
| Shall I drink the blood of | הֲדַם |
| the men who went | הָאֲנָשִׁים הַהֹלְכִים |
| at the risk of their lives? | בְּנַפְשׁוֹתָם |
| Therefore he would not | וְלֹא אָבָה |
| drink it [lit., them] | לִשְׁתּוֹתָם |
| **These things** | אֵלֶּה |
| the **three** mighty men did | עָשׂוּ **שְׁלֹשֶׁת** הַגִּבֹּרִים |

Then Moses said, "This is how [lit., by **this (זֹאת)**] you will know that the Lᴏʀᴅ **sent (שְׁלָחַנִי)** me to do all these things and that it was not of my own will [lit., **heart (לִבִּי)**]." (CSB)

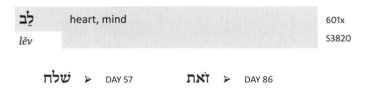

| לֵב | heart, mind | 601x |
| --- | --- | --- |
| *lēv* | | S3820 |

שׁלח   ➤   DAY 57        זֹאת   ➤   DAY 86

וַיֹּאמֶר מֹשֶׁה בְּזֹאת תֵּדְעוּן כִּי־יְהוָה שְׁלָחַנִי לַעֲשׂוֹת אֵת כָּל־הַמַּעֲשִׂים הָאֵלֶּה כִּי־לֹא מִלִּבִּי׃

| Then Moses said | וַיֹּאמֶר מֹשֶׁה |
| --- | --- |
| This is how [lit., by **this**] | בְּזֹאת |
| you will know | תֵּדְעוּן |
| that the Lᴏʀᴅ **sent** me | כִּי־יְהוָה שְׁלָחַנִי |
| to do | לַעֲשׂוֹת |
| all these things | אֵת כָּל־הַמַּעֲשִׂים הָאֵלֶּה |
| and that it was not | כִּי־לֹא |
| of my own will [lit., **heart**] | מִלִּבִּי |

And he told her all his **heart** (לִבּוֹ), and said to her, "A razor has never come upon my **head** (רֹאשִׁי), for **I** (אֲנִי) have been a Nazirite to God from my mother's womb. If my head is shaved, then my strength will leave me." (ESV)

| רֹאשׁ | head, chief | 600x |
|---|---|---|
| rōʾš | | S7218 |

אֲנִי   ➤   DAY 55      לֵב   ➤   DAY 87

וַיַּגֶּד־לָהּ אֶת־כָּל־לִבּוֹ וַיֹּאמֶר לָהּ מוֹרָה לֹא־עָלָה עַל־רֹאשִׁי כִּי־נְזִיר אֱלֹהִים אֲנִי מִבֶּטֶן אִמִּי אִם־גֻּלַּחְתִּי וְסָר מִמֶּנִּי כֹחִי

| | |
|---|---|
| And he told her | וַיַּגֶּד־לָהּ |
| all his **heart** | אֶת־כָּל־לִבּוֹ |
| and said to her | וַיֹּאמֶר לָהּ |
| A razor | מוֹרָה |
| has never come upon my **head** | לֹא־עָלָה עַל־רֹאשִׁי |
| for **I** have been | כִּי־ . . . אֲנִי |
| a Nazirite to God | נְזִיר אֱלֹהִים |
| from my mother's womb | מִבֶּטֶן אִמִּי |
| If my head is shaved | אִם־גֻּלַּחְתִּי |
| then my strength will leave me | וְסָר מִמֶּנִּי כֹחִי |

The man said to me, "Son of man, **look** (רְאֵה) with your eyes, hear with your ears, and **take** (שִׂים) to **heart** (לִבְּךָ) all that I **shall show** (מַרְאֶה) you; for you were brought here so that I **might show** (הַרְאוֹתְכָה) it to you." (MLB)

| שִׂים | to put, place | | 588x |
|---|---|---|---|
| *śîm* | | | S7760 |

רָאָה   ➤   DAY 34      לֵב   ➤   DAY 87

וַיְדַבֵּר אֵלַי הָאִישׁ בֶּן־אָדָם רְאֵה בְעֵינֶיךָ וּבְאָזְנֶיךָ שְׁמָע וְשִׂים לִבְּךָ לְכֹל אֲשֶׁר־אֲנִי מַרְאֶה אוֹתָךְ כִּי לְמַעַן הַרְאוֹתְכָה הֻבָאתָה הֵנָּה

| The **man** said to me | וַיְדַבֵּר אֵלַי הָאִישׁ |
|---|---|
| Son of man | בֶּן־אָדָם |
| **look** with your eyes | רְאֵה בְעֵינֶיךָ |
| hear with your ears | וּבְאָזְנֶיךָ שְׁמָע |
| and **take** to **heart** all that | וְשִׂים לִבְּךָ לְכֹל אֲשֶׁר־ |
| I **shall show** you | אֲנִי מַרְאֶה אוֹתָךְ |
| for you were brought here | כִּי . . . הֻבָאתָה הֵנָּה |
| so that I **might show** it to you | לְמַעַן הַרְאוֹתְכָה |

And you, son of man, **set** (שִׂים) your face against the **daughters** (בְּנוֹת) of your people, who prophesy from their own **minds** (לִבְּהֶן). Prophesy against them . . . (MLB)

| בַּת | daughter | 587x |
|------|----------|------|
| *bat* | | S1323 |

לֵב ➤ DAY 87      שִׂים ➤ DAY 89

וְאַתָּה בֶן־אָדָם **שִׂים** פָּנֶיךָ אֶל־**בְּנוֹת** עַמְּךָ הַמִּתְנַבְּאוֹת מִ**לִּבְּהֶן** וְהִנָּבֵא עֲלֵיהֶן:

| | |
|---|---|
| And you | וְאַתָּה |
| son of man | בֶן־אָדָם |
| **set** your face | **שִׂים** פָּנֶיךָ |
| against the **daughters** of your people | אֶל־**בְּנוֹת** עַמְּךָ |
| who prophesy | הַמִּתְנַבְּאוֹת |
| from their own **minds** | מִ**לִּבְּהֶן** |
| Prophesy against them | וְהִנָּבֵא עֲלֵיהֶן |

Then Abraham fell on his face and laughed, and said to himself [lit., in his **heart** (לִבּוֹ)], "Can a child be born to a man who is a hundred years old [lit., to a son of a **hundred** (מֵאָה) years]? Can Sarah, who is ninety years old [lit., a **daughter** (בַּת) of ninety years], bear a child?" (NRSV)

| מֵאָה | hundred | 584x |
|---|---|---|
| mēʾâ | | S3967 |

לֵב ➤ DAY 87   בַּת ➤ DAY 90

וַיִּפֹּל אַבְרָהָם עַל־פָּנָיו וַיִּצְחָק וַיֹּאמֶר בְּלִבּוֹ הַלְבֶן מֵאָה־שָׁנָה יִוָּלֵד וְאִם־שָׂרָה הֲבַת־תִּשְׁעִים שָׁנָה תֵּלֵד:

| Then Abraham fell | וַיִּפֹּל אַבְרָהָם |
|---|---|
| on his face | עַל־פָּנָיו |
| and laughed | וַיִּצְחָק |
| and said to himself [lit., in his **heart**] | וַיֹּאמֶר בְּלִבּוֹ |
| Can a child be born to a man who is a hundred years old [lit., to a son of a **hundred** years]? | הַלְבֶן מֵאָה־שָׁנָה יִוָּלֵד |
| Can Sarah | וְאִם־שָׂרָה |
| who is ninety years old [lit., a **daughter** of ninety years] | הֲבַת־תִּשְׁעִים שָׁנָה |
| bear a child? | תֵּלֵד |

Now the number of those who lapped, putting their hand to their mouth, was 300 (שְׁלֹשׁ מֵאוֹת) men; but all the rest of the **people** (עָם) kneeled [on their knees] to drink **water** (מַיִם). (NASB)

| מַיִם | water | 584x |
|---|---|---|
| *mayim* | | S4325 |

עָם  ▷  DAY 29      מֵאָה  ▷  DAY 91

וַיְהִי מִסְפַּר הַמֲלַקְקִים בְּיָדָם אֶל־פִּיהֶם שְׁלֹשׁ **מֵאוֹת** אִישׁ וְכֹל יֶתֶר הָעָם כָּרְעוּ עַל־בִּרְכֵיהֶם לִשְׁתּוֹת מָיִם:

| Now the number of | וַיְהִי מִסְפַּר |
|---|---|
| those who lapped | הַמֲלַקְקִים |
| putting their hand | בְּיָדָם |
| to their mouth | אֶל־פִּיהֶם |
| was 300 men | שְׁלֹשׁ מֵאוֹת אִישׁ |
| but all the rest of the **people** | וְכֹל יֶתֶר הָעָם |
| kneeled [on their knees] | כָּרְעוּ עַל־בִּרְכֵיהֶם |
| to drink **water** | לִשְׁתּוֹת מָיִם |

**Thus** (כֹּה) the LORD spoke to me: Go and buy a linen waistcloth, **put** (וְשַׂמְתּוֹ) it on your loins, and do not dip it in **water** (מַיִם).
(MLB)

| כֹּה | thus, here, now | 577x |
|------|-----------------|------|
| *kô* | | S3541 |

שִׂים ➤ DAY 89        מַיִם ➤ DAY 92

כֹּה־אָמַר יְהוָה אֵלַי הָלוֹךְ וְקָנִיתָ לְּךָ אֵזוֹר פִּשְׁתִּים וְשַׂמְתּוֹ עַל־מָתְנֶיךָ
וּבַמַּיִם לֹא תְבִאֵהוּ:

| | |
|---|---|
| **Thus** the LORD spoke to me | כֹּה־אָמַר יְהוָה אֵלַי |
| Go | הָלוֹךְ |
| and buy | וְקָנִיתָ לְּךָ |
| a linen waistcloth | אֵזוֹר פִּשְׁתִּים |
| **put** it | וְשַׂמְתּוֹ |
| on your loins | עַל־מָתְנֶיךָ |
| and . . . in **water** | וּבַמַּיִם |
| do not dip it | לֹא תְבִאֵהוּ |

Therefore **thus (כֹּה)** says the Lord GOD: Your slain whom **you
have laid (שַׂמְתֶּם)** in the midst of it, **they (הֵמָּה)** are the meat, and
this city [lit., it] is the cauldron, but you shall be brought out of
the midst of it. (ESV)

| הֵם | they (masc) | 564x |
|---|---|---|
| hēm | | S1992 |

שִׂים ➤ DAY 89     כֹּה ➤ DAY 93

לָכֵן כֹּה־אָמַר אֲדֹנָי יְהוִה חַלְלֵיכֶם אֲשֶׁר שַׂמְתֶּם בְּתוֹכָהּ הֵמָּה
הַבָּשָׂר וְהִיא הַסִּיר וְאֶתְכֶם הוֹצִיא מִתּוֹכָהּ:

| Therefore | לָכֵן |
|---|---|
| **thus** says | כֹּה־אָמַר |
| the Lord GOD | אֲדֹנָי יְהוִה |
| Your slain | חַלְלֵיכֶם |
| whom **you have laid** | אֲשֶׁר שַׂמְתֶּם |
| in the midst of it | בְּתוֹכָהּ |
| **they** are the meat | הֵמָּה הַבָּשָׂר |
| and this city [lit., it] is the cauldron | וְהִיא הַסִּיר |
| but you shall be brought out | וְאֶתְכֶם הוֹצִיא |
| of the midst of it | מִתּוֹכָהּ |

Thus (כֹּה) says the Lᴏʀᴅ: "Learn not the way of the **nations** (גּוֹיִם), nor be dismayed at the signs of the heavens because the **nations** (גּוֹיִם) are dismayed at **them** (הֵמָּה)." (ESV)

| גּוֹי | nation, people | 560x |
|------|----------------|------|
| gôy  |                | S1471 |

כֹּה ➤ DAY 93         הֵם ➤ DAY 94

כֹּה אָמַר יְהוָה אֶל־דֶּרֶךְ הַגּוֹיִם אַל־תִּלְמָדוּ וּמֵאֹתוֹת הַשָּׁמַיִם אַל־
תֵּחָתּוּ כִּי־יֵחַתּוּ הַגּוֹיִם מֵהֵמָּה:

| | |
|---|---|
| **Thus** says the Lᴏʀᴅ | כֹּה אָמַר יְהוָה |
| Learn not | אַל־תִּלְמָדוּ |
| the way of the **nations** | אֶל־דֶּרֶךְ הַגּוֹיִם |
| nor be dismayed | אַל־תֵּחָתּוּ |
| at the signs of the heavens | וּמֵאֹתוֹת הַשָּׁמַיִם |
| because the **nations** | כִּי־ . . . הַגּוֹיִם |
| are dismayed at **them** | יֵחַתּוּ . . . מֵהֵמָּה |

**For** (כִּי) as you have drunk on my holy **mountain** (הַר), so all the **nations** (גּוֹיִם) shall drink continually; they shall drink and swallow, and shall be as though they had never been. (ESV)

| הַר | mountain | 559x |
|---|---|---|
| *har* | | S2022 |

כִּי ➤ DAY 15          גּוֹי ➤ DAY 95

כִּי כַּאֲשֶׁר שְׁתִיתֶם עַל־הַר קָדְשִׁי יִשְׁתּוּ כָל־הַגּוֹיִם תָּמִיד וְשָׁתוּ וְלָעוּ וְהָיוּ כְּלוֹא הָיוּ׃

| **For** as you have drunk | כִּי כַּאֲשֶׁר שְׁתִיתֶם |
|---|---|
| on my holy **mountain** | עַל־הַר קָדְשִׁי |
| so all the **nations** shall drink | יִשְׁתּוּ כָל־הַגּוֹיִם |
| continually | תָּמִיד |
| they shall drink | וְשָׁתוּ |
| and swallow | וְלָעוּ |
| and shall be | וְהָיוּ |
| as though they had never been | כְּלוֹא הָיוּ |

The **mountains** (הָרִים) saw you, and writhed; a torrent of water **swept by** (עָבָר); the deep gave forth its voice. The sun raised high its **hands** (יָדֵיהוּ). (NRSV)

| עבר | to cross, pass over | 556x |
|---|---|---|
| *ʿāvar* | | S5674 |

יָד ➤ DAY 30           הַר ➤ DAY 96

רָאוּךָ יָחִילוּ הָרִים זֶרֶם מַיִם עָבָר נָתַן תְּהוֹם קוֹלוֹ רוֹם יָדֵיהוּ נָשָׂא:

| The **mountains** saw you | רָאוּךָ . . . הָרִים |
|---|---|
| and writhed | יָחִילוּ |
| a torrent of water | זֶרֶם מַיִם |
| **swept by** | עָבָר |
| the deep gave forth | נָתַן תְּהוֹם |
| its voice | קוֹלוֹ |
| The sun raised high | רוֹם . . . נָשָׂא |
| its **hands** | יָדֵיהוּ |

For **I will go through** (וְעָבַרְתִּי) the land of **Egypt** (מִצְרַיִם) on that night, and will strike down all the firstborn in the land of **Egypt** (מִצְרַיִם), both **man** (אָדָם) and beast; and against all the gods of **Egypt** (מִצְרַיִם) I will execute judgments—I am the LORD. (NASB)

| אָדָם | man, human being, humankind | 546x |
|---|---|---|
| ʾādām | | S120 |

מִצְרַיִם   ➤   DAY 80      עבר   ➤   DAY 97

וְעָבַרְתִּי בְאֶרֶץ־מִצְרַיִם בַּלַּיְלָה הַזֶּה וְהִכֵּיתִי כָל־בְּכוֹר בְּאֶרֶץ מִצְרַיִם
מֵאָדָם וְעַד־בְּהֵמָה וּבְכָל־אֱלֹהֵי מִצְרַיִם אֶעֱשֶׂה שְׁפָטִים אֲנִי יְהוָה:

| | |
|---|---|
| For **I will go through** the land of **Egypt** | וְעָבַרְתִּי בְאֶרֶץ־מִצְרַיִם |
| on that night | בַּלַּיְלָה הַזֶּה |
| and will strike down all the firstborn | וְהִכֵּיתִי כָל־בְּכוֹר |
| in the land of **Egypt** | בְּאֶרֶץ מִצְרַיִם |
| both **man** and beast | מֵאָדָם וְעַד־בְּהֵמָה |
| and against all the gods of **Egypt** | וּבְכָל־אֱלֹהֵי מִצְרַיִם |
| I will execute judgments | אֶעֱשֶׂה שְׁפָטִים |
| I am the LORD | אֲנִי יְהוָה |

A **man's** (אָדָם) gift makes room for him and brings him before [lit., in the **presence** (פְּנֵי) of] **great men** (גְדֹלִים). (MLB)

| גָּדוֹל | great, large | 527x |
| gādôl | | S1419 |

פָּנֶה  ➤  DAY 26        אָדָם  ➤  DAY 98

מַתָּן אָדָם יַרְחִיב לוֹ וְלִפְנֵי גְדֹלִים יַנְחֶנּוּ:

| A **man's** gift | מַתָּן אָדָם |
| makes room for him | יַרְחִיב לוֹ |
| and . . . before [lit., in the **presence** of] **great men** | וְלִפְנֵי גְדֹלִים |
| brings him | יַנְחֶנּוּ |

And, **standing** (וַיַּעֲמֹד), he blessed the **whole** (כָּל) congregation of Israel with a loud [lit., **large** (גָּדוֹל)] voice. (MLB)

| עמד | to stand | 524x |
|---|---|---|
| *ʿāmad* | | S5975 |

כֹּל   ➤   DAY 11        גָּדוֹל   ➤   DAY 99

וַיַּעֲמֹד וַיְבָרֶךְ אֵת כָּל־קְהַל יִשְׂרָאֵל קוֹל גָּדוֹל

| And, **standing** | וַיַּעֲמֹד |
|---|---|
| he blessed | וַיְבָרֶךְ |
| the **whole** congregation | אֵת כָּל־קְהַל |
| of Israel | יִשְׂרָאֵל |
| with a loud [lit., **large**] voice | קוֹל גָּדוֹל |

**I saw** (רָאִיתִי) all the living, who move about **under** (תַּחַת) the sun, follow [lit., with] a second youth who succeeds him [lit., **stands** (יַעֲמֹד) **in** his **stead** (תַּחְתָּיו)]. (CSB)

| תַּחַת | below, under, in place of | 511x |
|---|---|---|
| *taḥat* | | S8478 |

רָאָה ➤ DAY 34　　　עמד ➤ DAY 100

רָאִיתִי אֶת־כָּל־הַחַיִּים הַמְהַלְּכִים תַּחַת הַשֶּׁמֶשׁ עִם הַיֶּלֶד הַשֵּׁנִי אֲשֶׁר יַעֲמֹד תַּחְתָּיו:

| I saw | רָאִיתִי |
|---|---|
| all the living | אֶת־כָּל־הַחַיִּים |
| who move about | הַמְהַלְּכִים |
| **under** the sun | תַּחַת הַשֶּׁמֶשׁ |
| follow [lit., with] a second youth | עִם הַיֶּלֶד הַשֵּׁנִי |
| who succeeds him [lit., **stands in** his **stead**] | אֲשֶׁר יַעֲמֹד תַּחְתָּיו |

Now therefore, what do you have on hand [lit., **what** (מַה) is there **under** (תַּחַת) your hand]? Give me [lit., in my hand] **five** (חֲמִשָּׁה) loaves of bread, or whatever can be found. (NASB)

| חָמֵשׁ | five | | 508x |
|---|---|---|---|
| ḥāmēš | | | S2568 |

מָה ➤ DAY 70          תַּחַת ➤ DAY 101

וְעַתָּה מַה־יֵּשׁ תַּחַת־יָדְךָ חֲמִשָּׁה־לֶחֶם תְּנָה בְיָדִי אוֹ הַנִּמְצָא:

| Now therefore | וְעַתָּה |
|---|---|
| what do you have on hand [lit., **what** is there **under** your hand]? | מַה־יֵּשׁ תַּחַת־יָדְךָ |
| Give me [lit., in my hand] | תְּנָה בְיָדִי |
| **five** loaves of bread | חֲמִשָּׁה־לֶחֶם |
| or | אוֹ |
| whatever can be found | הַנִּמְצָא |

The LORD utters [lit., **gives (נָתַן)**] his **voice (קוֹלוֹ)** before his
army, for his camp is exceedingly great; he who executes his word
is powerful. For the day of the LORD is **great (גָּדוֹל)** and very
awesome; who can endure it? (ESV)

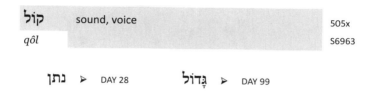

| | קוֹל |
| sound, voice | 505x |
| *qôl* | S6963 |

נתן  ➤  DAY 28          גָּדוֹל  ➤  DAY 99

וַיהוָה **נָתַן קוֹלוֹ** לִפְנֵי חֵילוֹ כִּי רַב מְאֹד מַחֲנֵהוּ כִּי עָצוּם עֹשֵׂה דְבָרוֹ
כִּי־**גָדוֹל** יוֹם־יְהוָה וְנוֹרָא מְאֹד וּמִי יְכִילֶנּוּ:

| The LORD utters [lit., **gives**] his **voice** | וַיהוָה **נָתַן קוֹלוֹ** |
| before his army | לִפְנֵי חֵילוֹ |
| for his camp is exceedingly great | כִּי רַב מְאֹד מַחֲנֵהוּ |
| he who executes his word is powerful | כִּי עָצוּם עֹשֵׂה דְבָרוֹ |
| For the day of the LORD is **great** | כִּי־**גָדוֹל** יוֹם־יְהוָה |
| and very awesome | וְנוֹרָא מְאֹד |
| who can endure it? | וּמִי יְכִילֶנּוּ |

Then he said to him, "Because you have not obeyed the **voice** (קוֹל) of the LORD, as soon as you have left [lit., **have gone** (הוֹלֵךְ) from] me, a lion **will kill** (וְהִכְּךָ) you." And when he had left [lit., **he had gone** (וַיֵּלֶךְ) from] him, a lion met him and **killed** (וַיַּכֵּהוּ) him. (NRSV)

| נכה | to strike, smite | 501x |
|---|---|---|
| nāḵâ | | S5221 |

**הָלַךְ** ▷ DAY 31        **קוֹל** ▷ DAY 103

וַיֹּאמֶר לוֹ יַעַן אֲשֶׁר לֹא־שָׁמַעְתָּ בְּקוֹל יְהוָה הִנְּךָ הוֹלֵךְ מֵאִתִּי וְהִכְּךָ הָאַרְיֵה וַיֵּלֶךְ מֵאֶצְלוֹ וַיִּמְצָאֵהוּ הָאַרְיֵה וַיַּכֵּהוּ׃

| Then he said to him | וַיֹּאמֶר לוֹ |
|---|---|
| Because | יַעַן אֲשֶׁר |
| you have not obeyed the **voice** of the LORD | לֹא־שָׁמַעְתָּ בְּקוֹל יְהוָה |
| as soon as you have left [lit., **have gone** from] me | הִנְּךָ הוֹלֵךְ מֵאִתִּי |
| a lion **will kill** you | וְהִכְּךָ הָאַרְיֵה |
| And when he had left [lit., **he had gone** from] him | וַיֵּלֶךְ מֵאֶצְלוֹ |
| a lion met him | וַיִּמְצָאֵהוּ הָאַרְיֵה |
| and **killed** him | וַיַּכֵּהוּ |

It is **certainly** (גַּם) not **good** (טוֹב) to fine an innocent person or **to beat** (הַכּוֹת) a noble for his [lit., nobles for] honesty. (CSB)

| טוֹב | good | 499x |
| *ṭôv* | | S2896 |

גַּם ➤ DAY 66          נכה ➤ DAY 104

גַּם עֲנוֹשׁ לַצַּדִּיק לֹא־טוֹב לְהַכּוֹת נְדִיבִים עַל־יֹשֶׁר:

| It is **certainly** not **good** | גַּם . . . לֹא־טוֹב |
| to fine | עֲנוֹשׁ |
| an innocent person | לַצַּדִּיק |
| or **to beat** | לְהַכּוֹת |
| a noble for his [lit., nobles for] | נְדִיבִים עַל־ |
| honesty | יֹשֶׁר |

And the L‍ord opened the **mouth** (פִּי) of the donkey, and she said to Balaam, "What have I done to you, that **you have struck** (הִכִּיתַנִי) me these **three** (שָׁלֹשׁ) times?" (NASB)

| פֶּה | mouth | | 498x |
|---|---|---|---|
| pê | | | S6310 |

| שָׁלֹשׁ | ▷ | DAY 85 | נכה | ▷ | DAY 104 |
|---|---|---|---|---|---|

וַיִּפְתַּח יְהוָה אֶת־פִּי הָאָתוֹן וַתֹּאמֶר לְבִלְעָם מֶה־עָשִׂיתִי לְךָ כִּי הִכִּיתַנִי זֶה שָׁלֹשׁ רְגָלִים:

| And the L‍ord opened | וַיִּפְתַּח יְהוָה |
|---|---|
| the **mouth** of the donkey | אֶת־פִּי הָאָתוֹן |
| and she said to Balaam | וַתֹּאמֶר לְבִלְעָם |
| What have I done to you | מֶה־עָשִׂיתִי לְךָ |
| that **you have struck** me | כִּי הִכִּיתַנִי |
| these | זֶה |
| **three** times? | שָׁלֹשׁ רְגָלִים |

The law of your **mouth** (פִּיךָ) is **better** (טוֹב) to me than **thousands** (אַלְפֵי) of gold and silver pieces. (NRSV)

| אֶלֶף | thousand | 496x |
|---|---|---|
| ʾelef | | S505 |

טוֹב    ➤    DAY 105        פֶּה    ➤    DAY 106

טוֹב־לִי תוֹרַת־פִּיךָ מֵאַלְפֵי זָהָב וָכָסֶף:

| The law of your **mouth** | תוֹרַת־פִּיךָ |
|---|---|
| is **better** | טוֹב־ |
| to me | לִי |
| than **thousands** of | מֵאַלְפֵי |
| gold and silver pieces | זָהָב וָכָסֶף |

He remembers his covenant forever, the **word** (דָּבָר) that **he commanded** (צִוָּה), for a **thousand** (אֶלֶף) generations. (ESV)

| | | |
|---|---|---|
| **צוה** | to command | 496x |
| ṣāvâ | | S6680 |

דָּבָר　▷　DAY 32　　　　אֶלֶף　▷　DAY 107

זָכַר לְעוֹלָם בְּרִיתוֹ דָּבָר צִוָּה לְאֶלֶף דּוֹר:

| | |
|---|---|
| He remembers | זָכַר |
| his covenant | בְּרִיתוֹ |
| forever | לְעוֹלָם |
| the **word** | דָּבָר |
| that **he commanded** | צִוָּה |
| for a **thousand** | לְאֶלֶף |
| generations | דּוֹר |

The woman became pregnant and **gave birth to** (וַתֵּלֶד) a son;
when **she saw** (וַתֵּרֶא) that he was **beautiful** (טוֹב), she hid him for
three months. (CSB)

| | | |
|---|---|---|
| **יָלַד** | to bear, beget | 495x |
| *yālad* | | S3205 |

| | | | | |
|---|---|---|---|---|
| **רָאָה** | ▷ | DAY 34 | **טוֹב** ▷ | DAY 105 |

וַתַּהַר הָאִשָּׁה וַתֵּלֶד בֵּן וַתֵּרֶא אֹתוֹ כִּי־טוֹב הוּא וַתִּצְפְּנֵהוּ שְׁלֹשָׁה
יְרָחִים׃

| The woman became pregnant | וַתַּהַר הָאִשָּׁה |
|---|---|
| and **gave birth to** a son | וַתֵּלֶד בֵּן |
| when **she saw** that he was **beautiful** | וַתֵּרֶא אֹתוֹ כִּי־טוֹב הוּא |
| she hid him | וַתִּצְפְּנֵהוּ |
| for three months | שְׁלֹשָׁה יְרָחִים |

But Abijah grew strong. **He took (וַיִּשָּׂא)** fourteen wives, and
**became the father of (וַיּוֹלֶד) twenty**-two (עֶשְׂרִים וּשְׁנַיִם) sons and
sixteen daughters. (NRSV)

| עֶשֶׂר | ten | 492x |
|---|---|---|
| ʿeśer | | S6235 |

נשׂא  ▷  DAY 81          ילד  ▷  DAY 109

וַיִּתְחַזֵּק אֲבִיָּהוּ וַיִּשָּׂא־לוֹ נָשִׁים אַרְבַּע עֶשְׂרֵה וַיּוֹלֶד עֶשְׂרִים וּשְׁנַיִם
בָּנִים וְשֵׁשׁ עֶשְׂרֵה בָּנוֹת:

| | |
|---|---|
| But Abijah grew strong | וַיִּתְחַזֵּק אֲבִיָּהוּ |
| **He took** . . . wives | וַיִּשָּׂא־לוֹ נָשִׁים |
| fourteen | אַרְבַּע עֶשְׂרֵה |
| and **became the father of** | וַיּוֹלֶד |
| **twenty**-two | עֶשְׂרִים וּשְׁנַיִם |
| sons | בָּנִים |
| and sixteen | וְשֵׁשׁ עֶשְׂרֵה |
| daughters | בָּנוֹת |

They struck down (וַיַּכּוּ) at that (הִיא) time about ten (עֲשֶׂרֶת)
thousand Moabites, all robust and valiant men; and no one
escaped. (NASB)

| הִיא | she, it, that | 491x |
| hî | | S1931 |

נכה  ➤  DAY 104          עָשַׂר  ➤  DAY 110

וַיַּכּוּ אֶת־מוֹאָב בָּעֵת הַהִיא כַּעֲשֶׂרֶת אֲלָפִים אִישׁ כָּל־שָׁמֵן וְכָל־אִישׁ
חָיִל וְלֹא נִמְלַט אִישׁ:

| They struck down | וַיַּכּוּ |
| at **that** time | בָּעֵת הַהִיא |
| about **ten** thousand Moabites | אֶת־מוֹאָב . . . כַּעֲשֶׂרֶת אֲלָפִים אִישׁ |
| all robust | כָּל־שָׁמֵן |
| and valiant men | וְכָל־אִישׁ חָיִל |
| and no one escaped | וְלֹא נִמְלַט אִישׁ |

The manna ceased on the day after they **had eaten** (אָכְלָם) some of the produce of the land, so that the sons of Israel no **longer** (עוֹד) had manna, but **they ate** (וַיֹּאכְלוּ) some of the yield of the land of Canaan during **that** (הִיא) year. (NASB)

| עוֹד | again, still, more | 491x |
|---|---|---|
| ʿôd | | S5750 |

אכל　▷　DAY 61　　　　הִיא　▷　DAY 111

וַיִּשְׁבֹּת הַמָּן מִמָּחֳרָת בְּאָכְלָם מֵעֲבוּר הָאָרֶץ וְלֹא־הָיָה עוֹד לִבְנֵי יִשְׂרָאֵל מָן וַיֹּאכְלוּ מִתְּבוּאַת אֶרֶץ כְּנַעַן בַּשָּׁנָה הַהִיא:

| The manna ceased | וַיִּשְׁבֹּת הַמָּן |
|---|---|
| on the day after they **had eaten** | מִמָּחֳרָת בְּאָכְלָם |
| some of the produce of the land | מֵעֲבוּר הָאָרֶץ |
| so that the sons of Israel no **longer** had manna | וְלֹא־הָיָה עוֹד לִבְנֵי יִשְׂרָאֵל מָן |
| but **they ate** | וַיֹּאכְלוּ |
| some of the yield of the land of Canaan | מִתְּבוּאַת אֶרֶץ כְּנַעַן |
| during **that** year | בַּשָּׁנָה הַהִיא |

So he waited **yet (עוֹד)** another **seven (שִׁבְעַת) days (יָמִים)**; and
again he sent out the dove from the ark. (NASB)

| שֶׁבַע | seven | 490x |
|---|---|---|
| *ševa‘* | | S7651 |

יוֹם ➤ DAY 24          עוֹד ➤ DAY 112

וַיָּחֶל עוֹד שִׁבְעַת יָמִים אֲחֵרִים וַיֹּסֶף שַׁלַּח אֶת־הַיּוֹנָה מִן־הַתֵּבָה:

| | |
|---|---|
| So he waited | וַיָּחֶל |
| **yet** another | עוֹד . . . אֲחֵרִים |
| **seven days** | שִׁבְעַת יָמִים |
| and again he sent out | וַיֹּסֶף שַׁלַּח |
| the dove | אֶת־הַיּוֹנָה |
| from the ark | מִן־הַתֵּבָה |

The Arameans fled before Israel; and David killed of the Arameans **seven** (שֶׁבַע) hundred chariot teams, and forty thousand horsemen, and **wounded** (הִכָּה) Shobach the commander of their **army** (צְבָאוֹ), so that he died there. (NRSV)

| צָבָא | army, host | 486x |
|-------|-----------|------|
| ṣāvā' | | S6635 |

| נכה | ▷ | DAY 104 |    שֶׁבַע | ▷ | DAY 113 |
|-----|---|---------|-------------|---|---------|

וַיָּנָס אֲרָם מִפְּנֵי יִשְׂרָאֵל וַיַּהֲרֹג דָּוִד מֵאֲרָם שְׁבַע מֵאוֹת רֶכֶב
וְאַרְבָּעִים אֶלֶף פָּרָשִׁים וְאֵת שׁוֹבַךְ שַׂר־צְבָאוֹ הִכָּה וַיָּמָת שָׁם:

| | |
|---|---|
| The Arameans fled | וַיָּנָס אֲרָם |
| before Israel | מִפְּנֵי יִשְׂרָאֵל |
| and David killed of the Arameans | וַיַּהֲרֹג דָּוִד מֵאֲרָם |
| **seven** hundred chariot teams | שְׁבַע מֵאוֹת רֶכֶב |
| and forty thousand horsemen | וְאַרְבָּעִים אֶלֶף פָּרָשִׁים |
| and **wounded** Shobach | וְאֵת שׁוֹבַךְ . . . הִכָּה |
| the commander of their **army** | שַׂר־צְבָאוֹ |
| so that he died there | וַיָּמָת שָׁם |

The Captain of the Lord's **host** (צְבָא) said to Joshua: Remove your shoes from your feet, because the place upon which **you** (אַתָּה) are standing is **holy** (קֹדֶשׁ). And Joshua did so. (MLB)

| קֹדֶשׁ | holiness, holy place | | 470x |
|---|---|---|---|
| qōdeš | | | S6944 |

| אַתָּה | ➤ DAY 72 | צְבָא | ➤ DAY 114 |
|---|---|---|---|

וַיֹּאמֶר שַׂר־צְבָא יְהוָה אֶל־יְהוֹשֻׁעַ שַׁל־נַעַלְךָ מֵעַל רַגְלֶךָ כִּי הַמָּקוֹם אֲשֶׁר אַתָּה עֹמֵד עָלָיו קֹדֶשׁ הוּא וַיַּעַשׂ יְהוֹשֻׁעַ כֵּן:

| The Captain of the Lord's **host** said | וַיֹּאמֶר שַׂר־צְבָא יְהוָה |
|---|---|
| to Joshua | אֶל־יְהוֹשֻׁעַ |
| Remove your shoes | שַׁל־נַעַלְךָ |
| from your feet | מֵעַל רַגְלֶךָ |
| because the place | כִּי הַמָּקוֹם |
| upon which | אֲשֶׁר . . . עָלָיו |
| **you** are standing | אַתָּה עֹמֵד |
| is **holy** | קֹדֶשׁ הוּא |
| And Joshua did so | וַיַּעַשׂ יְהוֹשֻׁעַ כֵּן |

**Observe** (וּשְׁמַרְתֶּם) the Sabbath, for it is **holy** (קֹדֶשׁ) to you. Whoever profanes it **must be put to death** (מוֹת יוּמָת). If anyone does work on it, that person must be cut off from his people. (CSB)

| שָׁמַר | to guard, protect | 469x |
|---|---|---|
| *šāmar* | | S8104 |

מוֹת ▷ DAY 58       קֹדֶשׁ ▷ DAY 115

וּשְׁמַרְתֶּם אֶת־הַשַּׁבָּת כִּי קֹדֶשׁ הִוא לָכֶם מְחַלְלֶיהָ מוֹת יוּמָת כִּי כָּל־הָעֹשֶׂה בָהּ מְלָאכָה וְנִכְרְתָה הַנֶּפֶשׁ הַהִוא מִקֶּרֶב עַמֶּיהָ:

| | |
|---|---|
| **Observe** the Sabbath | וּשְׁמַרְתֶּם אֶת־הַשַּׁבָּת |
| for it is **holy** to you | כִּי קֹדֶשׁ הִוא לָכֶם |
| Whoever profanes it | מְחַלְלֶיהָ |
| **must be put to death** | מוֹת יוּמָת |
| If anyone does work on it | כִּי כָּל־הָעֹשֶׂה בָהּ מְלָאכָה |
| that person | הַנֶּפֶשׁ הַהִוא |
| must be cut off | וְנִכְרְתָה |
| from his people | מִקֶּרֶב עַמֶּיהָ |

The **watchmen** (שֹׁמְרִים) **found** (מְצָאוּנִי) me as they went about in the city. "Have you seen him whom my **soul** (נַפְשִׁי) loves?"
(ESV)

| מצא | to find | 457x |
|---|---|---|
| *māṣā'* | | S4672 |

נֶפֶשׁ ➤ DAY 69        שָׁמַר ➤ DAY 116

מְצָאוּנִי הַשֹּׁמְרִים הַסֹּבְבִים בָּעִיר אֵת שֶׁאָהֲבָה נַפְשִׁי רְאִיתֶם:

| The **watchmen** | הַשֹּׁמְרִים |
|---|---|
| **found** me | מְצָאוּנִי |
| as they went about | הַסֹּבְבִים |
| in the city | בָּעִיר |
| Have you seen | רְאִיתֶם |
| him whom my **soul** loves? | אֵת שֶׁאָהֲבָה נַפְשִׁי |

Once **again** (עוֹד) he spoke to him, "What if only **forty** (אַרְבָּעִים) **are found** (יִמָּצְאוּן) there?" He said, "For the sake of **forty** (אַרְבָּעִים), I will not do it." (NIV)

| אַרְבַּע | four | | 456x |
|---|---|---|---|
| ʾarbaʿ | | | S702 |

עוֹד ➤ DAY 112      מצא ➤ DAY 117

וַיֹּסֶף עוֹד לְדַבֵּר אֵלָיו וַיֹּאמַר אוּלַי יִמָּצְאוּן שָׁם אַרְבָּעִים וַיֹּאמֶר לֹא
אֶעֱשֶׂה בַּעֲבוּר הָאַרְבָּעִים:

| Once **again** he spoke to him | וַיֹּסֶף עוֹד לְדַבֵּר אֵלָיו וַיֹּאמַר |
|---|---|
| What if only | אוּלַי |
| **forty** | אַרְבָּעִים |
| **are found** there? | יִמָּצְאוּן שָׁם |
| He said | וַיֹּאמֶר |
| For the sake of | בַּעֲבוּר |
| **forty** | הָאַרְבָּעִים |
| I will not do it | לֹא אֶעֱשֶׂה |

the Maker of heaven and **earth (אֶרֶץ)**, the sea and all that is in them; who **keeps (שָׁמַר)** faith forever [lit., to **eternity (עוֹלָם)**].
(MLB)

| עוֹלָם | eternity, always, forever | 439x |
|---|---|---|
| *ʿôlām* | | S5769 |

אֶרֶץ ➤ DAY 23          שָׁמַר ➤ DAY 116

עֹשֶׂה שָׁמַיִם וָאָרֶץ אֶת־הַיָּם וְאֶת־כָּל־אֲשֶׁר־בָּם הַשֹּׁמֵר אֱמֶת לְעוֹלָם:

| | |
|---|---|
| the Maker | עֹשֶׂה |
| of heaven and **earth** | שָׁמַיִם וָאָרֶץ |
| the sea | אֶת־הַיָּם |
| and all that is in them | וְאֶת־כָּל־אֲשֶׁר־בָּם |
| who **keeps** faith | הַשֹּׁמֵר אֱמֶת |
| forever [lit., to **eternity**] | לְעוֹלָם |

In that day **I will raise up** (אָקִים) the **fallen** (נֹפֶלֶת) tabernacle of David; I will repair its breaks; **I will raise up** (אָקִים) its ruins and build it as in the days of **old** (עוֹלָם). (MLB)

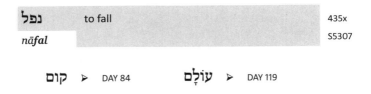

| נָפַל | to fall | 435x |
|---|---|---|
| *nāfal* | | S5307 |

קוּם ▷ DAY 84        עוֹלָם ▷ DAY 119

בַּיּוֹם הַהוּא אָקִים אֶת־סֻכַּת דָּוִיד הַנֹּפֶלֶת וְגָדַרְתִּי אֶת־פִּרְצֵיהֶן
וַהֲרִסֹתָיו אָקִים וּבְנִיתִיהָ כִּימֵי עוֹלָם:

| In that day | בַּיּוֹם הַהוּא |
|---|---|
| **I will raise up** | אָקִים |
| the **fallen** tabernacle of David | אֶת־סֻכַּת דָּוִיד הַנֹּפֶלֶת |
| I will repair | וְגָדַרְתִּי |
| its breaks | אֶת־פִּרְצֵיהֶן |
| **I will raise up** | אָקִים |
| its ruins | וַהֲרִסֹתָיו |
| and build it | וּבְנִיתִיהָ |
| as in the days of **old** | כִּימֵי עוֹלָם |

**Now** (עַתָּה) therefore, do not **let** my blood **fall** (יִפֹּל) to the ground, away from the **presence** (פְּנֵי) of the LORD; for the king of Israel has come out to seek a single flea, like one who hunts a partridge in the mountains. (NRSV)

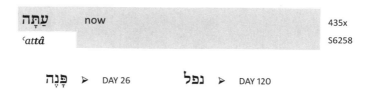

| עַתָּה | now | 435x |
| 'attâ | | S6258 |

| פָּנָה | ➤ | DAY 26 | | נפל | ➤ | DAY 120 |

וְעַתָּה אַל־יִפֹּל דָּמִי אַרְצָה מִנֶּגֶד פְּנֵי יְהוָה כִּי־יָצָא מֶלֶךְ יִשְׂרָאֵל
לְבַקֵּשׁ אֶת־פַּרְעֹשׁ אֶחָד כַּאֲשֶׁר יִרְדֹּף הַקֹּרֵא בֶּהָרִים:

| | |
|---|---|
| **Now** therefore | וְעַתָּה |
| do not **let** my blood **fall** | אַל־יִפֹּל דָּמִי |
| to the ground | אַרְצָה |
| away from the **presence** of the LORD | מִנֶּגֶד פְּנֵי יְהוָה |
| for the king of Israel has come out | כִּי־יָצָא מֶלֶךְ יִשְׂרָאֵל |
| to seek a single flea | לְבַקֵּשׁ אֶת־פַּרְעֹשׁ אֶחָד |
| like one who hunts a partridge | כַּאֲשֶׁר יִרְדֹּף הַקֹּרֵא |
| in the mountains | בֶּהָרִים |

**Who** (מִי) is there left among you who saw this **house** (בַּיִת) in its former glory? And how do you see it **now** (עַתָּה)? Is it not in your eyes nothing when compared with it? (MLB)

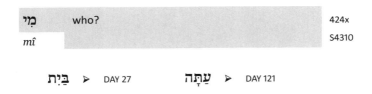

| | | |
|---|---|---|
| **מִי** | who? | 424x |
| mî | | S4310 |

בַּיִת ▷ DAY 27          עַתָּה ▷ DAY 121

מִי בָכֶם הַנִּשְׁאָר אֲשֶׁר רָאָה אֶת־הַבַּיִת הַזֶּה בִּכְבוֹדוֹ הָרִאשׁוֹן וּמָה
אַתֶּם רֹאִים אֹתוֹ עַתָּה הֲלוֹא כָמֹהוּ כְּאַיִן בְּעֵינֵיכֶם:

| | |
|---|---|
| **Who** is there left | מִי . . . הַנִּשְׁאָר |
| among you | בָכֶם |
| who saw | אֲשֶׁר רָאָה |
| this **house** | אֶת־הַבַּיִת הַזֶּה |
| in its former glory? | בִּכְבוֹדוֹ הָרִאשׁוֹן |
| And how do you see it **now**? | וּמָה אַתֶּם רֹאִים אֹתוֹ עַתָּה |
| Is it not . . . nothing | הֲלוֹא . . . כְּאַיִן |
| in your eyes | בְּעֵינֵיכֶם |
| when compared with it? | כָמֹהוּ |

And **what (מִי) great (גָּדוֹל)** nation is there, that has statutes and
**rules (מִשְׁפָּטִים)** so righteous as all this law that I set before you
today? (ESV)

| מִשְׁפָּט | law, judgment, justice | 424x |
|---|---|---|
| mišpāṭ | | S4941 |

**גָּדוֹל** ➤ DAY 99      **מִי** ➤ DAY 122

וּמִי גּוֹי גָּדוֹל אֲשֶׁר־לוֹ חֻקִּים וּמִשְׁפָּטִים צַדִּיקִם כְּכֹל הַתּוֹרָה הַזֹּאת
אֲשֶׁר אָנֹכִי נֹתֵן לִפְנֵיכֶם הַיּוֹם:

| | |
|---|---|
| And **what great** nation is there | וּמִי גּוֹי גָּדוֹל |
| that has | אֲשֶׁר־לוֹ |
| statutes and **rules** | חֻקִּים וּמִשְׁפָּטִים |
| so righteous | צַדִּיקִם |
| as all this law | כְּכֹל הַתּוֹרָה הַזֹּאת |
| that I set | אֲשֶׁר אָנֹכִי נֹתֵן |
| before you | לִפְנֵיכֶם |
| today? | הַיּוֹם |

You came down also upon **Mount** (הַר) Sinai, and spoke with them from **heaven** (שָׁמַיִם), and gave them right **ordinances** (מִשְׁפָּטִים) and true laws, good statutes and commandments. (NRSV)

| שָׁמַיִם | sky, heavens | 421x |
|---|---|---|
| *šāmayim* | | S8064 |

הַר  ➤  DAY 96          מִשְׁפָּט  ➤  DAY 123

וְעַל הַר־סִינַי יָרַדְתָּ וְדַבֵּר עִמָּהֶם מִשָּׁמָיִם וַתִּתֵּן לָהֶם מִשְׁפָּטִים יְשָׁרִים וְתוֹרוֹת אֱמֶת חֻקִּים וּמִצְוֺת טוֹבִים:

| You came down | יָרַדְתָּ |
|---|---|
| also upon **Mount** Sinai | וְעַל הַר־סִינַי |
| and spoke with them | וְדַבֵּר עִמָּהֶם |
| from **heaven** | מִשָּׁמָיִם |
| and gave them | וַתִּתֵּן לָהֶם |
| right **ordinances** | מִשְׁפָּטִים יְשָׁרִים |
| and true laws | וְתוֹרוֹת אֱמֶת |
| good statutes and commandments | חֻקִּים וּמִצְוֺת טוֹבִים |

Elijah replied to the **captain** (שַׂר) of **fifty** (חֲמִשִּׁים), "If I am a man of God, let fire come down from **heaven** (שָׁמַיִם) and consume you and your **fifty** (חֲמִשֶּׁיךָ)." Then fire came down from **heaven** (שָׁמַיִם) and consumed him and his **fifty** (חֲמִשָּׁיו). (NASB)

| שַׂר | prince, captain, governor | 421x |
|---|---|---|
| śar | | S8269 |

חָמֵשׁ  ▸  DAY 102     שָׁמַיִם  ▸  DAY 124

וַיַּעֲנֶה אֵלִיָּהוּ וַיְדַבֵּר אֶל־שַׂר הַחֲמִשִּׁים וְאִם־אִישׁ אֱלֹהִים אָנִי תֵּרֶד
אֵשׁ מִן־הַשָּׁמַיִם וְתֹאכַל אֹתְךָ וְאֶת־חֲמִשֶּׁיךָ וַתֵּרֶד אֵשׁ מִן־הַשָּׁמַיִם
וַתֹּאכַל אֹתוֹ וְאֶת־חֲמִשָּׁיו:

| Elijah replied | וַיַּעֲנֶה אֵלִיָּהוּ וַיְדַבֵּר |
|---|---|
| to the **captain** of **fifty** | אֶל־שַׂר הַחֲמִשִּׁים |
| If I am a man of God | וְאִם־אִישׁ אֱלֹהִים אָנִי |
| let fire come down from **heaven** | תֵּרֶד אֵשׁ מִן־הַשָּׁמַיִם |
| and consume you and your **fifty** | וְתֹאכַל אֹתְךָ וְאֶת־חֲמִשֶּׁיךָ |
| Then fire came down from **heaven** | וַתֵּרֶד אֵשׁ מִן־הַשָּׁמַיִם |
| and consumed him and his **fifty** | וַתֹּאכַל אֹתוֹ וְאֶת־חֲמִשָּׁיו |

On the third day, which was Pharaoh's **birth**day (יוֹם הֻלֶּדֶת), he
made a feast for all his servants and lifted up the head of the **chief**
(שַׂר) cupbearer and the head of the **chief** (שַׂר) baker among [lit.,
in the **midst** (תוֹךְ) of] his servants. (ESV)

| תָּוֶךְ | midst, center | 420x |
|---|---|---|
| *tāvek* | | S8432 |

יֶלֶד   ➤   DAY 109          שַׂר   ➤   DAY 125

וַיְהִי בַּיּוֹם הַשְּׁלִישִׁי יוֹם הֻלֶּדֶת אֶת־פַּרְעֹה וַיַּעַשׂ מִשְׁתֶּה לְכָל־עֲבָדָיו
וַיִּשָּׂא אֶת־רֹאשׁ שַׂר הַמַּשְׁקִים וְאֶת־רֹאשׁ שַׂר הָאֹפִים בְּתוֹךְ עֲבָדָיו:

| On the third day | וַיְהִי בַּיּוֹם הַשְּׁלִישִׁי |
|---|---|
| which was Pharaoh's **birth**day | יוֹם הֻלֶּדֶת אֶת־פַּרְעֹה |
| he made a feast | וַיַּעַשׂ מִשְׁתֶּה |
| for all his servants | לְכָל־עֲבָדָיו |
| and lifted up the head of | וַיִּשָּׂא אֶת־רֹאשׁ |
| the **chief** cupbearer | שַׂר הַמַּשְׁקִים |
| and the head of | וְאֶת־רֹאשׁ |
| the **chief** baker | שַׂר הָאֹפִים |
| among [lit., in the **midst** of] his servants | בְּתוֹךְ עֲבָדָיו |

And **many** (רַבִּים) nations shall join themselves to the LORD in that day, and shall be my people. And I will dwell in your **midst** (תּוֹכֵךְ), and you shall know that the LORD of **hosts** (צְבָאוֹת) has sent me to you. (ESV)

| רַב | great, many | 419x |
| *rav* | | S7227 |

צָבָא  ▷  DAY 114          תָּוֶךְ  ▷  DAY 126

וְנִלְווּ גוֹיִם **רַבִּים** אֶל־יְהוָה בַּיּוֹם הַהוּא וְהָיוּ לִי לְעָם וְשָׁכַנְתִּי בְ**תוֹכֵךְ** וְיָדַעַתְּ כִּי־יְהוָה **צְבָאוֹת** שְׁלָחַנִי אֵלָיִךְ:

| And **many** nations shall join themselves | וְנִלְווּ גוֹיִם **רַבִּים** |
| to the LORD | אֶל־יְהוָה |
| in that day | בַּיּוֹם הַהוּא |
| and shall be my people | וְהָיוּ לִי לְעָם |
| And I will dwell in your **midst** | וְשָׁכַנְתִּי בְ**תוֹכֵךְ** |
| and you shall know that | וְיָדַעַתְּ כִּי־ |
| the LORD of **hosts** | יְהוָה **צְבָאוֹת** |
| has sent me to you | שְׁלָחַנִי אֵלָיִךְ |

As they fled before Israel . . . , the LORD threw down **huge** (גְּדֹלוֹת)
stones from heaven on them as far as Azekah, and they died;
there were **more** (רַבִּים) who died because of the hailstones than
the Israelites killed with the **sword** (חֶרֶב). (NRSV)

| חֶרֶב | sword | 413x |
|---|---|---|
| *ḥerev* | | S2719 |

גָּדוֹל ➤ DAY 99          רַב ➤ DAY 127

וַיְהִי בְּנֻסָם מִפְּנֵי יִשְׂרָאֵל . . . וַיהוָה הִשְׁלִיךְ עֲלֵיהֶם אֲבָנִים **גְּדֹלוֹת**
מִן־הַשָּׁמַיִם עַד־עֲזֵקָה וַיָּמֻתוּ **רַבִּים** אֲשֶׁר־מֵתוּ בְּאַבְנֵי הַבָּרָד מֵאֲשֶׁר
הָרְגוּ בְּנֵי יִשְׂרָאֵל בֶּחָרֶב:

| As they fled before Israel . . . | . . . וַיְהִי בְּנֻסָם מִפְּנֵי יִשְׂרָאֵל |
|---|---|
| the LORD threw down . . . on them | וַיהוָה הִשְׁלִיךְ עֲלֵיהֶם |
| **huge** stones from heaven | אֲבָנִים **גְּדֹלוֹת** מִן־הַשָּׁמַיִם |
| as far as Azekah | עַד־עֲזֵקָה |
| and they died | וַיָּמֻתוּ |
| there were **more** who died | **רַבִּים** אֲשֶׁר־מֵתוּ |
| because of the hailstones | בְּאַבְנֵי הַבָּרָד |
| than the Israelites | מֵאֲשֶׁר . . . בְּנֵי יִשְׂרָאֵל |
| killed with the **sword** | הָרְגוּ . . . בֶּחָרֶב |

He shall judge **between** (בֵּין) the nations, and shall arbitrate for **many** (רַבִּים) peoples; they shall beat their **swords** (חַרְבוֹתָם) into plowshares, and their spears into pruning hooks; nation shall not lift up **sword** (חֶרֶב) against nation, neither shall they learn war any more. (NRSV)

| בֵּין | between | 409x |
|---|---|---|
| bên | | S996 |

רַב ➤ DAY 127    חֶרֶב ➤ DAY 128

וְשָׁפַט בֵּין הַגּוֹיִם וְהוֹכִיחַ לְעַמִּים רַבִּים וְכִתְּתוּ חַרְבוֹתָם לְאִתִּים
וַחֲנִיתוֹתֵיהֶם לְמַזְמֵרוֹת לֹא־יִשָּׂא גוֹי אֶל־גּוֹי חֶרֶב וְלֹא־יִלְמְדוּ עוֹד
מִלְחָמָה:

| He shall judge **between** the nations | וְשָׁפַט בֵּין הַגּוֹיִם |
|---|---|
| and shall arbitrate for **many** peoples | וְהוֹכִיחַ לְעַמִּים רַבִּים |
| they shall beat their **swords** | וְכִתְּתוּ חַרְבוֹתָם |
| into plowshares | לְאִתִּים |
| and their spears | וַחֲנִיתוֹתֵיהֶם |
| into pruning hooks | לְמַזְמֵרוֹת |
| nation shall not lift up | לֹא־יִשָּׂא גוֹי |
| **sword** against nation | אֶל־גּוֹי חֶרֶב |
| neither shall they learn war any more | וְלֹא־יִלְמְדוּ עוֹד מִלְחָמָה |

And **now** (עַתָּה), residents of Jerusalem and men of Judah,
**please** (נָא) arbitrate **between** (בֵּינִי) Me and [**between** (בֵּין)] My
vineyard. (MLB)

| | | |
|---|---|---|
| נָא | (particle of entreaty), please | 406x |
| *nāʾ* | | S4994 |

עַתָּה　➤　DAY 121　　　　בֵּין　➤　DAY 129

וְעַתָּה יוֹשֵׁב יְרוּשָׁלַם וְאִישׁ יְהוּדָה שִׁפְטוּ־נָא בֵּינִי וּבֵין כַּרְמִי׃

| And **now** | וְעַתָּה |
|---|---|
| residents of Jerusalem | יוֹשֵׁב יְרוּשָׁלַם |
| and men of Judah | וְאִישׁ יְהוּדָה |
| **please** arbitrate | שִׁפְטוּ־נָא |
| **between** Me | בֵּינִי |
| and [**between**] My vineyard | וּבֵין כַּרְמִי |

Now the donkeys of Kish, **Saul**'s (שָׁאוּל) father, were lost. So Kish said to **Saul** (שָׁאוּל) his son, "Take [, **please** (נָא),] one of the young men **with** (אִתָּךְ) you, and arise, go and look for the donkeys." (ESV)

| שָׁאוּל | Saul | 406x |
|---|---|---|
| *šā'ûl* | | S7586 |

אֵת ➤ DAY 53　　　　נָא ➤ DAY 130

וַתֹּאבַדְנָה הָאֲתֹנוֹת לְקִישׁ אֲבִי שָׁאוּל וַיֹּאמֶר קִישׁ אֶל־שָׁאוּל בְּנוֹ קַח־נָא אִתְּךָ אֶת־אַחַד מֵהַנְּעָרִים וְקוּם לֵךְ בַּקֵּשׁ אֶת־הָאֲתֹנֹת:

| | |
|---|---|
| Now the donkeys of Kish . . . were lost | וַתֹּאבַדְנָה הָאֲתֹנוֹת לְקִישׁ |
| **Saul**'s father | אֲבִי שָׁאוּל |
| So Kish said | וַיֹּאמֶר קִישׁ |
| to **Saul** his son | אֶל־שָׁאוּל בְּנוֹ |
| Take [, **please**,] . . . **with** you | קַח־נָא אִתְּךָ |
| one of the young men | אֶת־אַחַד מֵהַנְּעָרִים |
| and arise, go | וְקוּם לֵךְ |
| and look for the donkeys | בַּקֵּשׁ אֶת־הָאֲתֹנֹת |

The servant answered **Saul** (שָׁאוּל) again and said, "Behold, I have [lit., **there is found** (נִמְצָא)] in my hand a fourth of a shekel of **silver** (כָּסֶף); I will give it to the man of God and he will tell us our way." (NASB)

| | | |
|---|---|---|
| כָּסֶף | silver, money | 403x |
| *kesef* | | S3701 |

מצא  ➢  DAY 117　　　　שָׁאוּל  ➢  DAY 131

וַיֹּסֶף הַנַּעַר לַעֲנוֹת אֶת־שָׁאוּל וַיֹּאמֶר הִנֵּה נִמְצָא בְיָדִי רֶבַע שֶׁקֶל כָּסֶף וְנָתַתִּי לְאִישׁ הָאֱלֹהִים וְהִגִּיד לָנוּ אֶת־דַּרְכֵּנוּ:

| | |
|---|---|
| The servant answered **Saul** again and said | וַיֹּסֶף הַנַּעַר לַעֲנוֹת אֶת־שָׁאוּל וַיֹּאמֶר |
| Behold | הִנֵּה |
| I have [lit., **there is found**] in my hand | נִמְצָא בְיָדִי |
| a fourth of a shekel of **silver** | רֶבַע שֶׁקֶל כָּסֶף |
| I will give it | וְנָתַתִּי |
| to the man of God | לְאִישׁ הָאֱלֹהִים |
| and he will tell us | וְהִגִּיד לָנוּ |
| our way | אֶת־דַּרְכֵּנוּ |

Then Jehoiada the priest took a chest, bored a hole through its lid, and placed it beside the **altar** (מִזְבֵּחַ), on the right side as one enters the house of the Lord. The priests who served as door**keepers** (שֹׁמְרֵי) put in it all the **money** (כֶּסֶף) brought to the house of the Lord. (MLB)

| מִזְבֵּחַ | altar | | 403x |
| --- | --- | --- | --- |
| mizbēaḥ | | | S4196 |

| שמר | ➤ | DAY 116 | כֶּסֶף | ➤ | DAY 132 |

וַיִּקַּח יְהוֹיָדָע הַכֹּהֵן אֲרוֹן אֶחָד וַיִּקֹּב חֹר בְּדַלְתּוֹ וַיִּתֵּן אֹתוֹ אֵצֶל הַמִּזְבֵּחַ מִיָּמִין בְּבוֹא־אִישׁ בֵּית יְהוָה וְנָתְנוּ־שָׁמָּה הַכֹּהֲנִים שֹׁמְרֵי הַסַּף אֶת־כָּל־הַכֶּסֶף הַמּוּבָא בֵית־יְהוָה:

| Then Jehoiada the priest took | וַיִּקַּח יְהוֹיָדָע הַכֹּהֵן |
| --- | --- |
| a chest | אֲרוֹן אֶחָד |
| bored a hole through its lid | וַיִּקֹּב חֹר בְּדַלְתּוֹ |
| and placed it beside the **altar** | וַיִּתֵּן אֹתוֹ אֵצֶל הַמִּזְבֵּחַ |
| on the right side as one enters the house of the Lord | מִיָּמִין בְּבוֹא־אִישׁ בֵּית יְהוָה |
| The priests who served as door**keepers** | הַכֹּהֲנִים שֹׁמְרֵי הַסַּף |
| put in it | וְנָתְנוּ־שָׁמָּה |
| all the **money** | אֶת־כָּל־הַכֶּסֶף |
| brought to the house of the Lord | הַמּוּבָא בֵית־יְהוָה |

David said to Ornan, "Give me the **site** (מָקוֹם) of the threshing floor that I may build on it an **altar** (מִזְבֵּחַ) to the LORD—give it to me at its full **price** (כֶּסֶף)—so that the plague may be averted from the people." (NRSV)

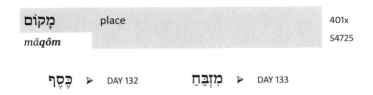

| מָקוֹם | place | 401x |
| māqôm | | S4725 |

כֶּסֶף ▷ DAY 132          מִזְבֵּחַ ▷ DAY 133

וַיֹּאמֶר דָּוִיד אֶל־אָרְנָן תְּנָה־לִּי מְקוֹם הַגֹּרֶן וְאֶבְנֶה־בּוֹ מִזְבֵּחַ לַיהוָה בְּכֶסֶף מָלֵא תְּנֵהוּ לִי וְתֵעָצַר הַמַּגֵּפָה מֵעַל הָעָם:

| David said to Ornan | וַיֹּאמֶר דָּוִיד אֶל־אָרְנָן |
| Give me | תְּנָה־לִּי |
| the **site** of the threshing floor | מְקוֹם הַגֹּרֶן |
| that I may build on it | וְאֶבְנֶה־בּוֹ |
| an **altar** to the LORD | מִזְבֵּחַ לַיהוָה |
| give it to me | תְּנֵהוּ לִי |
| at its full **price** | בְּכֶסֶף מָלֵא |
| so that the plague may be averted | וְתֵעָצַר הַמַּגֵּפָה |
| from the people | מֵעַל הָעָם |

Yet the number of the children of Israel shall be like the sand of the **sea** (יָם), which cannot be measured or numbered. And in the **place** (מְקוֹם) where it was said to **them** (הֶם), "You are not my people," it shall be said to **them** (הֶם), "Children of the living God." (ESV)

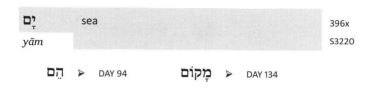

| יָם | sea | | 396x |
|---|---|---|---|
| *yām* | | | S3220 |

הֶם  ➤  DAY 94        מְקוֹם  ➤  DAY 134

וְהָיָה מִסְפַּר בְּנֵי־יִשְׂרָאֵל כְּחוֹל הַיָּם אֲשֶׁר לֹא־יִמַּד וְלֹא יִסָּפֵר וְהָיָה
בִּמְקוֹם אֲשֶׁר־יֵאָמֵר לָהֶם לֹא־עַמִּי אַתֶּם יֵאָמֵר לָהֶם בְּנֵי אֵל־חָי:

| Yet . . . shall be like the sand of the **sea** | וְהָיָה . . . כְּחוֹל הַיָּם |
|---|---|
| the number of the children of Israel | מִסְפַּר בְּנֵי־יִשְׂרָאֵל |
| which cannot be measured | אֲשֶׁר לֹא־יִמַּד |
| or numbered | וְלֹא יִסָּפֵר |
| And in the **place** | וְהָיָה בִּמְקוֹם |
| where it was said to **them** | אֲשֶׁר־יֵאָמֵר לָהֶם |
| You are not my people | לֹא־עַמִּי אַתֶּם |
| it shall be said to **them** | יֵאָמֵר לָהֶם |
| Children of the living God | בְּנֵי אֵל־חָי |

For the king had ships of Tarshish at **sea** (יָם) with Hiram's fleet, and once every **three** (שָׁלֹשׁ) years the ships of Tarshish would arrive bearing **gold** (זָהָב), silver, ivory, apes, and peacocks. (CSB)

| זָהָב | gold | 389x |
| --- | --- | --- |
| *zāhāv* | | S2091 |

שָׁלֹשׁ ➤ DAY 85          יָם ➤ DAY 135

כִּי אֳנִי תַרְשִׁישׁ לַמֶּלֶךְ בַּיָּם עִם אֳנִי חִירָם אַחַת לְשָׁלֹשׁ שָׁנִים תָּבוֹא
אֳנִי תַרְשִׁישׁ נֹשְׂאֵת זָהָב וָכֶסֶף שֶׁנְהַבִּים וְקֹפִים וְתֻכִּיִּים:

| For the king had | כִּי . . . לַמֶּלֶךְ |
| --- | --- |
| ships of Tarshish | אֳנִי תַרְשִׁישׁ |
| at **sea** | בַּיָּם |
| with Hiram's fleet | עִם אֳנִי חִירָם |
| and once every **three** years | אַחַת לְשָׁלֹשׁ שָׁנִים |
| the ships of Tarshish | אֳנִי תַרְשִׁישׁ |
| would arrive bearing | תָּבוֹא . . . נֹשְׂאֵת |
| **gold**, silver | זָהָב וָכֶסֶף |
| ivory | שֶׁנְהַבִּים |
| apes, and peacocks | וְקֹפִים וְתֻכִּיִּים |

The Levites **took down** (הוֹרִידוּ) the ark of the Lᴏʀᴅ and the box that was beside it, in which were the **gold** (זָהָב) objects, and **set** (וַיָּשִׂמוּ) them upon the large stone. (NRSV)

| | | |
|---|---|---|
| **יָרַד** | to descend, go down | 382x |
| *yārad* | | S3381 |

שִׂים   ➤   DAY 89          זָהָב   ➤   DAY 136

וְהַלְוִיִּם **הוֹרִידוּ** אֶת־אֲרוֹן יְהוָה וְאֶת־הָאַרְגַּז אֲשֶׁר־אִתּוֹ אֲשֶׁר־בּוֹ
כְּלֵי־**זָהָב וַיָּשִׂמוּ** אֶל־הָאֶבֶן הַגְּדוֹלָה

| | |
|---|---|
| The Levites **took down** | וְהַלְוִיִּם **הוֹרִידוּ** |
| the ark of the Lᴏʀᴅ | אֶת־אֲרוֹן יְהוָה |
| and the box | וְאֶת־הָאַרְגַּז |
| that was beside it | אֲשֶׁר־אִתּוֹ |
| in which | אֲשֶׁר־בּוֹ |
| were the **gold** objects | כְּלֵי־**זָהָב** |
| and **set** them | **וַיָּשִׂמוּ** |
| upon the large stone | אֶל־הָאֶבֶן הַגְּדוֹלָה |

All of **Mount** (הַר) Sinai was smoking, because the Lord **came down** (יָרַד) upon it in **fire** (אֵשׁ); its smoke went up like the smoke of a furnace and the whole **mountain** (הַר) quaked severely. (MLB)

| אֵשׁ | fire | | 378x |
| --- | --- | --- | --- |
| ʾēš | | | S784 |

הַר　▷　DAY 96　　　　　　יָרַד　▷　DAY 137

וְהַר סִינַי עָשַׁן כֻּלּוֹ מִפְּנֵי אֲשֶׁר יָרַד עָלָיו יְהוָה בָּאֵשׁ וַיַּעַל עֲשָׁנוֹ כְּעֶשֶׁן הַכִּבְשָׁן וַיֶּחֱרַד כָּל־הָהָר מְאֹד:

| All of **Mount** Sinai was smoking | וְהַר סִינַי עָשַׁן כֻּלּוֹ |
| --- | --- |
| because | מִפְּנֵי אֲשֶׁר |
| the Lord **came down** | יָרַד . . . יְהוָה |
| upon it in **fire** | עָלָיו . . . בָּאֵשׁ |
| its smoke went up | וַיַּעַל עֲשָׁנוֹ |
| like the smoke of a furnace | כְּעֶשֶׁן הַכִּבְשָׁן |
| and the whole **mountain** quaked | וַיֶּחֱרַד כָּל־הָהָר |
| severely | מְאֹד |

As I looked, behold, a storm **wind** (רוּחַ) was coming from the north, a great cloud with **fire** (אֵשׁ) flashing forth continually and a bright light around it, and in its midst something like [the **appearance** (עַיִן) of] glowing metal in the midst of the **fire** (אֵשׁ). (NASB)

| רוּחַ | wind, breath, spirit | 378x |
|---|---|---|
| *rûaḥ* | | S7307 |

עַיִן ➤ DAY 51　　　　　אֵשׁ ➤ DAY 138

וָאֵרֶא וְהִנֵּה רוּחַ סְעָרָה בָּאָה מִן־הַצָּפוֹן עָנָן גָּדוֹל וְאֵשׁ מִתְלַקַּחַת וְנֹגַהּ לוֹ סָבִיב וּמִתּוֹכָהּ כְּעֵין הַחַשְׁמַל מִתּוֹךְ הָאֵשׁ:

| As I looked, behold | וָאֵרֶא וְהִנֵּה |
|---|---|
| a storm **wind** | רוּחַ סְעָרָה |
| was coming from the north | בָּאָה מִן־הַצָּפוֹן |
| a great cloud | עָנָן גָּדוֹל |
| with **fire** flashing forth continually | וְאֵשׁ מִתְלַקַּחַת |
| and a bright light around it | וְנֹגַהּ לוֹ סָבִיב |
| and in its midst | וּמִתּוֹכָהּ |
| something like [the **appearance** of] glowing metal | כְּעֵין הַחַשְׁמַל |
| in the midst of the **fire** | מִתּוֹךְ הָאֵשׁ |

Then rose up the **heads** (רָאשֵׁי) of the fathers' houses of Judah and Benjamin, and the priests and the Levites, everyone whose **spirit** (רוּחוֹ) God had stirred to go up **to rebuild** (בְּנוֹת) the house of the LORD that is in Jerusalem. (ESV)

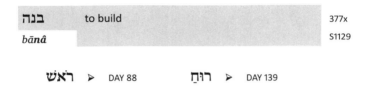

| בנה | to build | | 377x |
|-----|----------|--|------|
| *bānâ* | | | S1129 |

רֹאשׁ   ➤   DAY 88          רוּחַ   ➤   DAY 139

וַיָּקוּמוּ רָאשֵׁי הָאָבוֹת לִיהוּדָה וּבִנְיָמִן וְהַכֹּהֲנִים וְהַלְוִיִּם לְכֹל הֵעִיר הָאֱלֹהִים אֶת־רוּחוֹ לַעֲלוֹת לִבְנוֹת אֶת־בֵּית יְהוָה אֲשֶׁר בִּירוּשָׁלָם:

| Then rose up | וַיָּקוּמוּ |
|---|---|
| the **heads** of the fathers' houses | רָאשֵׁי הָאָבוֹת |
| of Judah and Benjamin | לִיהוּדָה וּבִנְיָמִן |
| and the priests and the Levites | וְהַכֹּהֲנִים וְהַלְוִיִּם |
| everyone whose **spirit** God had stirred | לְכֹל הֵעִיר הָאֱלֹהִים אֶת־רוּחוֹ |
| to go up **to rebuild** | לַעֲלוֹת לִבְנוֹת |
| the house of the LORD | אֶת־בֵּית יְהוָה |
| that is in Jerusalem | אֲשֶׁר בִּירוּשָׁלָם |

Therefore, thus says the Lord, **I have returned** (שַׁבְתִּי) to
Jerusalem with mercy; my house **shall be built** (יִבָּנֶה) in it,
declares [lit., **declaration** (נְאֻם) of] the Lord of hosts, and the
measuring line shall be stretched out over Jerusalem. (ESV)

| נְאֻם | oracle, declaration | 376x |
| *nĕ'ūm* | | S5002 |

שׁוּב　➤　DAY 44　　　בנה　➤　DAY 140

לָכֵן כֹּה־אָמַר יְהוָה שַׁבְתִּי לִירוּשָׁלַ͏ִם בְּרַחֲמִים בֵּיתִי יִבָּנֶה בָּהּ נְאֻם
יְהוָה צְבָאוֹת וְקָו יִנָּטֶה עַל־יְרוּשָׁלָ͏ִם:

| Therefore | לָכֵן |
| thus says the Lord | כֹּה־אָמַר יְהוָה |
| **I have returned** to Jerusalem | שַׁבְתִּי לִירוּשָׁלַ͏ִם |
| with mercy | בְּרַחֲמִים |
| my house **shall be built** in it | בֵּיתִי יִבָּנֶה בָּהּ |
| declares [lit., **declaration** of] the Lord of hosts | נְאֻם יְהוָה צְבָאוֹת |
| and the measuring line shall be stretched out | וְקָו יִנָּטֶה |
| over Jerusalem | עַל־יְרוּשָׁלָ͏ִם |

Behold, the days are coming, **declares** (נְאֻם) the Lᴏʀᴅ, when the city **shall be rebuilt** (וְנִבְנְתָה) for the Lᴏʀᴅ from the Tower of Hananel to the Corner **Gate** (שַׁעַר). (ESV)

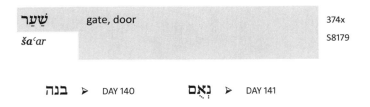

| שַׁעַר | gate, door | 374x |
| šaʿar | | S8179 |

בנה  ➤  DAY 140          נְאֻם  ➤  DAY 141

הִנֵּה יָמִים בָּאִים נְאֻם־יְהוָה וְנִבְנְתָה הָעִיר לַיהוָה מִמִּגְדַּל חֲנַנְאֵל
שַׁעַר הַפִּנָּה:

| Behold | הִנֵּה |
| the days are coming | יָמִים בָּאִים |
| **declares** the Lᴏʀᴅ | נְאֻם־יְהוָה |
| when the city **shall be rebuilt** | וְנִבְנְתָה הָעִיר |
| for the Lᴏʀᴅ | לַיהוָה |
| from the Tower of Hananel | מִמִּגְדַּל חֲנַנְאֵל |
| to the Corner **Gate** | שַׁעַר הַפִּנָּה |

So the king arose and **sat** (וַיֵּשֶׁב) in the **gate** (שַׁעַר). When **they told** (הִגִּידוּ) all the people, saying, "Behold, the king **is sitting** (יוֹשֵׁב) in the **gate** (שַׁעַר)," then all the people came before the king. Now Israel had fled, each to his tent. (NASB)

| נגד | to tell, announce, report | 371x |
|---|---|---|
| *nāgad* | | S5046 |

יָשַׁב  ➤  DAY 41        שַׁעַר  ➤  DAY 142

וַיָּקָם הַמֶּלֶךְ וַיֵּשֶׁב בַּשָּׁעַר וּלְכָל־הָעָם הִגִּידוּ לֵאמֹר הִנֵּה הַמֶּלֶךְ יוֹשֵׁב בַּשָּׁעַר וַיָּבֹא כָל־הָעָם לִפְנֵי הַמֶּלֶךְ וְיִשְׂרָאֵל נָס אִישׁ לְאֹהָלָיו:

| So the king arose | וַיָּקָם הַמֶּלֶךְ |
|---|---|
| and **sat** in the **gate** | וַיֵּשֶׁב בַּשָּׁעַר |
| When **they told** all the people, saying | וּלְכָל־הָעָם הִגִּידוּ לֵאמֹר |
| Behold, the king | הִנֵּה הַמֶּלֶךְ |
| **is sitting** in the **gate** | יוֹשֵׁב בַּשָּׁעַר |
| then all the people came | וַיָּבֹא כָל־הָעָם |
| before the king | לִפְנֵי הַמֶּלֶךְ |
| Now Israel had fled | וְיִשְׂרָאֵל נָס |
| each to his tent | אִישׁ לְאֹהָלָיו |

Then it was reported [lit., **they reported (וַיַּגִּידוּ)**] to Saul, "**Look (הִנֵּה)**, the troops are sinning against the Lᴏʀᴅ by eating with the **blood (דָּם)**." And he said, "You have dealt treacherously; roll a large stone before me here [lit., today]." (ɴʀsᴠ)

| דָּם | blood, bloodshed, bloodguilt | 361x |
|------|------------------------------|------|
| *dām* | | S1818 |

| הִנֵּה | ▷ | DAY 46 | נגד | ▷ | DAY 143 |
|--------|---|--------|------|---|---------|

וַיַּגִּידוּ לְשָׁאוּל לֵאמֹר הִנֵּה הָעָם חֹטִאים לַיהוָה לֶאֱכֹל עַל־הַדָּם
וַיֹּאמֶר בְּגַדְתֶּם גֹּלּוּ־אֵלַי הַיּוֹם אֶבֶן גְּדוֹלָה:

| Then it was reported [lit., **they reported**] to Saul | וַיַּגִּידוּ לְשָׁאוּל לֵאמֹר |
|---|---|
| **Look**, the troops | הִנֵּה הָעָם |
| are sinning against the Lᴏʀᴅ | חֹטִאים לַיהוָה |
| by eating with the **blood** | לֶאֱכֹל עַל־הַדָּם |
| And he said | וַיֹּאמֶר |
| You have dealt treacherously | בְּגַדְתֶּם |
| roll . . . before me | גֹּלּוּ־אֵלַי |
| a large stone | אֶבֶן גְּדוֹלָה |
| here [lit., today] | הַיּוֹם |

Thus says the LORD, "By this you shall know that I am the LORD: behold, with the staff that is in my hand **I** (אָנֹכִי) **will strike** (מַכֶּה) the water that is in the Nile, and it shall turn into **blood** (דָם)." (ESV)

| אָנֹכִי | I | | 359x |
|---|---|---|---|
| ʾānōḵî | | | S595 |

| נכה | ➤ | DAY 104 | | דָם | ➤ | DAY 144 |

כֹּה אָמַר יְהוָה בְּזֹאת תֵּדַע כִּי אֲנִי יְהוָה הִנֵּה אָנֹכִי מַכֶּה בַּמַּטֶּה אֲשֶׁר־בְּיָדִי עַל־הַמַּיִם אֲשֶׁר בַּיְאֹר וְנֶהֶפְכוּ לְדָם:

| Thus says the LORD | כֹּה אָמַר יְהוָה |
|---|---|
| By this you shall know | בְּזֹאת תֵּדַע |
| that I am the LORD | כִּי אֲנִי יְהוָה |
| behold . . . **I will strike** | הִנֵּה אָנֹכִי מַכֶּה |
| with the staff | בַּמַּטֶּה |
| that is in my hand | אֲשֶׁר־בְּיָדִי |
| the water | עַל־הַמַּיִם |
| that is in the Nile | אֲשֶׁר בַּיְאֹר |
| and it shall turn into **blood** | וְנֶהֶפְכוּ לְדָם |

Perhaps the house of Judah will hear all the **calamity** (רָעָה) which
**I** (אָנֹכִי) plan to bring on them, in order that every man will turn
from his **evil** (רָעָה) **way** (דַּרְכּוֹ); then I will forgive their iniquity
and their sin. (NASB)

| רַע | bad, evil | | 357x |
|-----|-----------|--|------|
| ra< | | | S7451 |

| דֶּרֶךְ | ▷ | DAY 78 | אָנֹכִי | ▷ | DAY 145 |

אוּלַי יִשְׁמְעוּ בֵּית יְהוּדָה אֵת כָּל־הָרָעָה אֲשֶׁר אָנֹכִי חֹשֵׁב לַעֲשׂוֹת
לָהֶם לְמַעַן יָשׁוּבוּ אִישׁ מִדַּרְכּוֹ הָרָעָה וְסָלַחְתִּי לַעֲוֹנָם וּלְחַטָּאתָם:

| Perhaps the house of Judah | אוּלַי . . . בֵּית יְהוּדָה |
|---|---|
| will hear | יִשְׁמְעוּ |
| all the **calamity** | אֵת כָּל־הָרָעָה |
| which **I** plan | אֲשֶׁר אָנֹכִי חֹשֵׁב |
| to bring on them | לַעֲשׂוֹת לָהֶם |
| in order that every man will turn | לְמַעַן יָשׁוּבוּ אִישׁ |
| from his **evil way** | מִדַּרְכּוֹ הָרָעָה |
| then I will forgive | וְסָלַחְתִּי |
| their iniquity and their sin | לַעֲוֹנָם וּלְחַטָּאתָם |

Jehoiakim was **twenty**-five (עֶשְׂרִים וְחָמֵשׁ) years old when he **became king** (מָלְכוֹ), and **he reigned** (מָלַךְ) in Jerusalem eleven years. He did **evil** (רַע) in the eyes of the LORD his God. (NIV)

| מלך | to reign, become king | 351x |
|---|---|---|
| *mālak* | | S4427 |

עֶשֶׂר   ➤   DAY 110      רַע   ➤   DAY 146

בֶּן־עֶשְׂרִים וְחָמֵשׁ שָׁנָה יְהוֹיָקִים בְּמָלְכוֹ וְאַחַת עֶשְׂרֵה שָׁנָה מָלַךְ בִּירוּשָׁלָםִ וַיַּעַשׂ הָרַע בְּעֵינֵי יְהוָה אֱלֹהָיו:

| | |
|---|---|
| Jehoiakim | יְהוֹיָקִים |
| was **twenty**-five years old | בֶּן־עֶשְׂרִים וְחָמֵשׁ שָׁנָה |
| when he **became king** | בְּמָלְכוֹ |
| and . . . eleven years | וְאַחַת עֶשְׂרֵה שָׁנָה |
| **he reigned** in Jerusalem | מָלַךְ בִּירוּשָׁלָםִ |
| He did **evil** | וַיַּעַשׂ הָרַע |
| in the eyes of the LORD his God | בְּעֵינֵי יְהוָה אֱלֹהָיו |

. . . then also my covenant with David my servant may be broken, so that he shall not have a son **to reign** (מֶלֶךְ) on his throne, and my covenant with the Levitical priests [lit., the **Levites** (לְוִים), the **priests** (כֹּהֲנִים)] my ministers. (ESV)

| לֵוִי | Levi, Levite | 350x |
|---|---|---|
| *lēvî* | | S3878 |

כֹּהֵן   ➤   DAY 71            מלך   ➤   DAY 147

גַּם־בְּרִיתִי תֻפַר אֶת־דָּוִד עַבְדִּי מִהְיוֹת־לוֹ בֵן מֹלֵךְ עַל־כִּסְאוֹ וְאֶת־הַלְוִים הַכֹּהֲנִים מְשָׁרְתָי:

| then also my covenant | גַּם־בְּרִיתִי |
|---|---|
| with David my servant | אֶת־דָּוִד עַבְדִּי |
| may be broken | תֻפַר |
| so that he shall not have | מִהְיוֹת־לוֹ |
| a son **to reign** | בֵן מֹלֵךְ |
| on his throne | עַל־כִּסְאוֹ |
| and my covenant with the Levitical priests [lit., the **Levites**, the **priests**] | וְאֶת־הַלְוִים הַכֹּהֲנִים |
| my ministers | מְשָׁרְתָי |

Then after that the **Levites** (לְוִיִּם) went in to perform their service
in the **tent** (אֹהֶל) of meeting before Aaron and before his sons;
just as the LORD **had commanded** (צִוָּה) Moses concerning the
**Levites** (לְוִיִּם), so they did to them. (NASB)

| אֹהֶל | tent, tabernacle | 349x |
|---|---|---|
| ʾōhel | | S168 |

צוה  ➤  DAY 108          לֵוִי  ➤  DAY 148

וְאַחֲרֵי־כֵן בָּאוּ הַלְוִיִּם לַעֲבֹד אֶת־עֲבֹדָתָם בְּאֹהֶל מוֹעֵד לִפְנֵי אַהֲרֹן
וְלִפְנֵי בָנָיו כַּאֲשֶׁר צִוָּה יְהוָה אֶת־מֹשֶׁה עַל־הַלְוִיִּם כֵּן עָשׂוּ לָהֶם:

| Then after that | וְאַחֲרֵי־כֵן |
|---|---|
| the **Levites** went in | בָּאוּ הַלְוִיִּם |
| to perform their service | לַעֲבֹד אֶת־עֲבֹדָתָם |
| in the **tent** of meeting | בְּאֹהֶל מוֹעֵד |
| before Aaron | לִפְנֵי אַהֲרֹן |
| and before his sons | וְלִפְנֵי בָנָיו |
| just as the LORD **had commanded** Moses | כַּאֲשֶׁר צִוָּה יְהוָה אֶת־מֹשֶׁה |
| concerning the **Levites** | עַל־הַלְוִיִּם |
| so they did to them | כֵּן עָשׂוּ לָהֶם |

Thus says the Lord: I am going to restore the fortunes of the **tents** (אָהֳלֵי) of Jacob (יַעֲקוֹב), and have compassion on his dwellings; the city **shall be rebuilt** (וְנִבְנְתָה) upon its mound, and the citadel set on its rightful site. (NRSV)

| יַעֲקֹב | Jacob | 349x |
|---|---|---|
| yaʿăqōv | | S3290 |

בנה   ➤ DAY 140        אֹהֶל   ➤ DAY 149

כֹּה אָמַר יְהוָה הִנְנִי־שָׁב שְׁבוּת אָהֳלֵי יַעֲקוֹב וּמִשְׁכְּנֹתָיו אֲרַחֵם וְנִבְנְתָה עִיר עַל־תִּלָּהּ וְאַרְמוֹן עַל־מִשְׁפָּטוֹ יֵשֵׁב׃

| | |
|---|---|
| Thus says the Lord | כֹּה אָמַר יְהוָה |
| I am going to restore | הִנְנִי־שָׁב |
| the fortunes of | שְׁבוּת |
| the **tents** of **Jacob** | אָהֳלֵי יַעֲקוֹב |
| and have compassion on his dwellings | וּמִשְׁכְּנֹתָיו אֲרַחֵם |
| the city **shall be rebuilt** | וְנִבְנְתָה עִיר |
| upon its mound | עַל־תִּלָּהּ |
| and the citadel set | וְאַרְמוֹן . . . יֵשֵׁב |
| on its rightful site | עַל־מִשְׁפָּטוֹ |

When **Jacob** (יַעֲקֹב) went to Egypt, your ancestors cried out to the
Lord, and he [lit., the Lord] sent them Moses and **Aaron** (אַהֲרֹן),
who led your ancestors out of Egypt and settled them in this **place**
(מָקוֹם). (CSB)

| **אַהֲרֹן** | Aaron | 347x |
| ʾahărōn | | S175 |

| מָקוֹם | ▹ DAY 134 | יַעֲקֹב | ▹ DAY 150 |

כַּאֲשֶׁר־בָּא יַעֲקֹב מִצְרַיִם וַיִּזְעֲקוּ אֲבוֹתֵיכֶם אֶל־יְהוָה וַיִּשְׁלַח יְהוָה
אֶת־מֹשֶׁה וְאֶת־אַהֲרֹן וַיּוֹצִיאוּ אֶת־אֲבֹתֵיכֶם מִמִּצְרַיִם וַיֹּשִׁבוּם
בַּמָּקוֹם הַזֶּה:

| When **Jacob** went to Egypt | כַּאֲשֶׁר־בָּא יַעֲקֹב מִצְרַיִם |
| your ancestors cried out | וַיִּזְעֲקוּ אֲבוֹתֵיכֶם |
| to the Lord | אֶל־יְהוָה |
| and he [lit., the Lord] sent them | וַיִּשְׁלַח יְהוָה |
| Moses and **Aaron** | אֶת־מֹשֶׁה וְאֶת־אַהֲרֹן |
| who led your ancestors | וַיּוֹצִיאוּ אֶת־אֲבֹתֵיכֶם |
| out of Egypt | מִמִּצְרַיִם |
| and settled them | וַיֹּשִׁבוּם |
| in this **place** | בַּמָּקוֹם הַזֶּה |

He will slaughter it on the north side of the **altar** (מִזְבֵּחַ) before
the LORD. **Aaron**'s (אַהֲרֹן) sons the priests will splatter its blood
against the altar **on all sides** (סָבִיב). (CSB)

| | | |
|---|---|---|
| סָבִיב | round about, environs | 338x |
| *sāvîv* | | S5439 |

מִזְבֵּחַ    ➤    DAY 133        אַהֲרֹן    ➤    DAY 151

וְשָׁחַט אֹתוֹ עַל יֶרֶךְ הַמִּזְבֵּחַ צָפֹנָה לִפְנֵי יְהוָה וְזָרְקוּ בְּנֵי אַהֲרֹן
הַכֹּהֲנִים אֶת־דָּמוֹ עַל־הַמִּזְבֵּחַ סָבִיב:

| | |
|---|---|
| He will slaughter it | וְשָׁחַט אֹתוֹ |
| on the north side | עַל יֶרֶךְ . . . צָפֹנָה |
| of the **altar** | הַמִּזְבֵּחַ |
| before the LORD | לִפְנֵי יְהוָה |
| **Aaron**'s sons the priests | בְּנֵי אַהֲרֹן הַכֹּהֲנִים |
| will splatter its blood | וְזָרְקוּ . . . אֶת־דָּמוֹ |
| against the altar | עַל־הַמִּזְבֵּחַ |
| **on all sides** | סָבִיב |

Ahaz was twenty **years** (שָׁנָה) old when **he became king** (מָלְכוֹ),
and **he remained king** (מָלַךְ) in Jerusalem for six**teen** (עֶשְׂרֵה)
**years** (שָׁנָה). He failed to do what was right in the LORD's eyes as
David his father had done. (MLB)

| עָשָׂר | -teen, -teenth | 337x |
|---|---|---|
| ʿāśār | | S6240 |

שָׁנָה    ➤   DAY 54        מלך    ➤    DAY 147

בֶּן־עֶשְׂרִים שָׁנָה אָחָז בְּמָלְכוֹ וְשֵׁשׁ־עֶשְׂרֵה שָׁנָה מָלַךְ בִּירוּשָׁלִָם
וְלֹא־עָשָׂה הַיָּשָׁר בְּעֵינֵי יְהוָה כְּדָוִיד אָבִיו:

| Ahaz | אָחָז |
|---|---|
| was twenty **years** old | בֶּן־עֶשְׂרִים שָׁנָה |
| when **he became king** | בְּמָלְכוֹ |
| and . . . for six**teen years** | וְשֵׁשׁ־עֶשְׂרֵה שָׁנָה |
| **he remained king** in Jerusalem | מָלַךְ בִּירוּשָׁלִָם |
| He failed to do | וְלֹא־עָשָׂה |
| what was right | הַיָּשָׁר |
| in the LORD's eyes | בְּעֵינֵי יְהוָה |
| as David his father had done | כְּדָוִיד אָבִיו |

As for Ishmael, I have heard you; behold, **I have blessed** (בֵּרַכְתִּי)
him and will make him fruitful and multiply him greatly. **He shall
father** (יוֹלִיד) twelve [lit., two-(and-)**ten** (עָשָׂר)] princes, and I
will make him into a great nation. (ESV)

| ברך | to bless, kneel | 330x |
|-----|-----------------|------|
| *bāraḵ* | | S1288 |

| יָלַד | ➤ | DAY 109 | עָשָׂר | ➤ | DAY 153 |
|-------|---|---------|--------|---|---------|

וּלְיִשְׁמָעֵאל שְׁמַעְתִּיךָ הִנֵּה בֵּרַכְתִּי אֹתוֹ וְהִפְרֵיתִי אֹתוֹ וְהִרְבֵּיתִי אֹתוֹ
בִּמְאֹד מְאֹד שְׁנֵים־עָשָׂר נְשִׂיאִם יוֹלִיד וּנְתַתִּיו לְגוֹי גָּדוֹל׃

| As for Ishmael | וּלְיִשְׁמָעֵאל |
|---|---|
| I have heard you | שְׁמַעְתִּיךָ |
| behold, **I have blessed** him | הִנֵּה בֵּרַכְתִּי אֹתוֹ |
| and will make him fruitful | וְהִפְרֵיתִי אֹתוֹ |
| and multiply him | וְהִרְבֵּיתִי אֹתוֹ |
| greatly | בִּמְאֹד מְאֹד |
| **He shall father** | יוֹלִיד |
| twelve [lit., two-(and-)**ten**] princes | שְׁנֵים־עָשָׂר נְשִׂיאִם |
| and I will make him | וּנְתַתִּיו |
| into a great nation | לְגוֹי גָּדוֹל |

Is there any seed left in the barn? Do the vine, the fig tree, the pomegranate, and the olive **tree** (עֵץ) still **yield** (נָשָׂא) nothing? From this day on **I will bless** (אֲבָרֵךְ) you. (NRSV)

| | | |
|---|---|---|
| עֵץ | tree, wood | 330x |
| ʿēṣ | | S6086 |

נשׂא ➤ DAY 81          ברך ➤ DAY 154

הֶעוֹד הַזֶּרַע בַּמְּגוּרָה וְעַד־הַגֶּפֶן וְהַתְּאֵנָה וְהָרִמּוֹן וְעֵץ הַזַּיִת לֹא נָשָׂא מִן־הַיּוֹם הַזֶּה אֲבָרֵךְ:

| | |
|---|---|
| Is there any seed left | הֶעוֹד הַזֶּרַע |
| in the barn? | בַּמְּגוּרָה |
| Do the vine | הַגֶּפֶן |
| the fig tree | וְהַתְּאֵנָה |
| the pomegranate | וְהָרִמּוֹן |
| and the olive **tree** | וְעֵץ הַזַּיִת |
| still **yield** nothing? | וְעַד־ . . . לֹא נָשָׂא |
| From this day on | מִן־הַיּוֹם הַזֶּה |
| **I will bless** you | אֲבָרֵךְ |

Any earthen **vessel** (כְלִי) that the one with the discharge touches shall be broken; and every **vessel** (כְּלִי) of **wood** (עֵץ) shall be rinsed in **water** (מָיִם). (NRSV)

| כְּלִי | utensil, vessel, weapon | 325x |
|---|---|---|
| kĕlî | | S3627 |

מַיִם  ➤  DAY 92      עֵץ  ➤  DAY 155

וּכְלִי־חֶרֶשׂ אֲשֶׁר־יִגַּע־בּוֹ הַזָּב יִשָּׁבֵר וְכָל־כְּלִי־עֵץ יִשָּׁטֵף בַּמָּיִם:

| Any earthen **vessel** | וּכְלִי־חֶרֶשׂ |
|---|---|
| that the one with the discharge | אֲשֶׁר־ . . . הַזָּב |
| touches | יִגַּע־בּוֹ |
| shall be broken | יִשָּׁבֵר |
| and every **vessel** of **wood** | וְכָל־כְּלִי־עֵץ |
| shall be rinsed | יִשָּׁטֵף |
| in **water** | בַּמָּיִם |

David said to Ahimelech, "Now is there not a spear **or (אוֹ)** a **sword (חֶרֶב)** on hand? For I brought neither my **sword (חַרְבִּי)** nor my **weapons (כְּלַי)** with me, because the king's matter was urgent." (NASB)

| אוֹ | or, if | | 321x |
|---|---|---|---|
| ʾô | | | S176 |

חֶרֶב ➤ DAY 128        כְּלִי ➤ DAY 156

וַיֹּאמֶר דָּוִד לַאֲחִימֶלֶךְ וְאִין יֶשׁ־פֹּה תַחַת־יָדְךָ חֲנִית אוֹ־**חֶרֶב** כִּי גַם־**חַרְבִּי** וְגַם־**כֵּלַי** לֹא־לָקַחְתִּי בְיָדִי כִּי־הָיָה דְבַר־הַמֶּלֶךְ נָחוּץ:

| David said to Ahimelech | וַיֹּאמֶר דָּוִד לַאֲחִימֶלֶךְ |
|---|---|
| Now is there not | וְאִין יֶשׁ־פֹּה |
| a spear **or** a **sword** | חֲנִית אוֹ־חֶרֶב |
| on hand? | תַחַת־יָדְךָ |
| For I brought neither my **sword** nor my **weapons** with me | כִּי גַם־חַרְבִּי וְגַם־כֵּלַי לֹא־לָקַחְתִּי בְיָדִי |
| because the king's matter | כִּי־ . . . דְבַר־הַמֶּלֶךְ |
| was urgent | הָיָה . . . נָחוּץ |

I adjure you, O daughters of **Jerusalem** (יְרוּשָׁלַ֫ם), by the gazelles
**or** (אוֹ) the does of the **field** (שָׂדֶה), that you not stir up or awaken
love until it pleases. (ESV)

| | | |
|---|---|---|
| **שָׂדֶה** | field | 321x |
| *śādê* | | S7704 |

| | | | | |
|---|---|---|---|---|
| יְרוּשָׁלַ֫ם | ⊳ | DAY 82 | אוֹ    ⊳    DAY 157 | |

הִשְׁבַּ֫עְתִּי אֶתְכֶם בְּנוֹת יְרוּשָׁלַ֫ם בִּצְבָא֔וֹת א֖וֹ בְּאַיְל֣וֹת הַשָּׂדֶ֑ה אִם־
תָּעִ֣ירוּ וְאִם־תְּע֧וֹרְר֛וּ אֶת־הָאַהֲבָ֖ה עַ֥ד שֶׁתֶּחְפָּֽץ׃

| | |
|---|---|
| I adjure you | הִשְׁבַּ֫עְתִּי אֶתְכֶם |
| O daughters of **Jerusalem** | בְּנוֹת יְרוּשָׁלַ֫ם |
| by the gazelles | בִּצְבָא֔וֹת |
| **or** the does of the **field** | א֖וֹ בְּאַיְל֣וֹת הַשָּׂדֶ֑ה |
| that you not stir up | אִם־תָּעִ֣ירוּ |
| or awaken | וְאִם־תְּע֧וֹרְר֛וּ |
| love | אֶת־הָאַהֲבָ֖ה |
| until it pleases | עַ֥ד שֶׁתֶּחְפָּֽץ |

And I will make for them a covenant on that day **with (עִם)** the beasts of the **field (שָׂדֶה)**, [and **with (עִם)**] the birds of the heavens, and the creeping things of the ground. And I will abolish the bow, the sword, and **war (מִלְחָמָה)** from the land. (ESV)

| מִלְחָמָה | battle, war | 319x |
|---|---|---|
| *milḥāmâ* | | S4421 |

עִם  ➤  DAY 47          שָׂדֶה  ➤  DAY 158

וְכָרַתִּי לָהֶם בְּרִית בַּיּוֹם הַהוּא עִם־חַיַּת הַשָּׂדֶה וְעִם־עוֹף הַשָּׁמַיִם
וְרֶמֶשׂ הָאֲדָמָה וְקֶשֶׁת וְחֶרֶב וּמִלְחָמָה אֶשְׁבּוֹר מִן־הָאָרֶץ

| | |
|---|---|
| And I will make for them a covenant | וְכָרַתִּי לָהֶם בְּרִית |
| on that day | בַּיּוֹם הַהוּא |
| **with** the beasts of the **field** | עִם־חַיַּת הַשָּׂדֶה |
| [and **with**] the birds of the heavens | וְעִם־עוֹף הַשָּׁמַיִם |
| and the creeping things of the ground | וְרֶמֶשׂ הָאֲדָמָה |
| And . . . the bow, the sword, and **war** | וְקֶשֶׁת וְחֶרֶב וּמִלְחָמָה |
| I will abolish | אֶשְׁבּוֹר |
| from the land | מִן־הָאָרֶץ |

When you go to **war** (מִלְחָמָה) against your enemies and see horses and chariots and an army greater than yours, do not **be afraid** (תִירָא) of them, because the LORD your God, who brought you up out of **Egypt** (מִצְרַיִם), will be with you. (NIV)

| יְרֵא | to fear | 318x |
| yārē' | | S3372 |

מִצְרַיִם ➤ DAY 80      מִלְחָמָה ➤ DAY 159

כִּי־תֵצֵא לַמִּלְחָמָה עַל־אֹיְבֶיךָ וְרָאִיתָ סוּס וָרֶכֶב עַם רַב מִמְּךָ לֹא
תִירָא מֵהֶם כִּי־יְהוָה אֱלֹהֶיךָ עִמָּךְ הַמַּעַלְךָ מֵאֶרֶץ מִצְרָיִם:

| When you go to **war** | כִּי־תֵצֵא לַמִּלְחָמָה |
| against your enemies | עַל־אֹיְבֶיךָ |
| and see | וְרָאִיתָ |
| horses and chariots | סוּס וָרֶכֶב |
| and an army greater than yours | עַם רַב מִמְּךָ |
| do not **be afraid** of them | לֹא תִירָא מֵהֶם |
| because the LORD your God | כִּי־יְהוָה אֱלֹהֶיךָ |
| who brought you up | הַמַּעַלְךָ |
| out of **Egypt** | מֵאֶרֶץ מִצְרָיִם |
| will be with you | עִמָּךְ |

Behold, **I** (אָנֹכִי) will send you Elijah the **prophet** (נָבִיא) before the coming of the great and **terrible** (נוֹרָא) day of the LORD. (MLB)

| נָבִיא | prophet | 317x |
|---|---|---|
| nāvî' | | S5030 |

אָנֹכִי ➤ DAY 145          ירא ➤ DAY 160

הִנֵּה אָנֹכִי שֹׁלֵחַ לָכֶם אֵת אֵלִיָּה הַנָּבִיא לִפְנֵי בּוֹא יוֹם יְהוָה הַגָּדוֹל וְהַנּוֹרָא:

| Behold | הִנֵּה |
|---|---|
| **I** will send you | אָנֹכִי שֹׁלֵחַ לָכֶם |
| Elijah | אֵת אֵלִיָּה |
| the **prophet** | הַנָּבִיא |
| before the coming of | לִפְנֵי בּוֹא |
| the . . . day of the LORD | יוֹם יְהוָה |
| great and **terrible** | הַגָּדוֹל וְהַנּוֹרָא |

And when **Saul** (שָׁאוּל) inquired of the Lord, the Lord did not **answer** (עָנָהוּ) him, either by dreams, or by Urim, or by **prophets** (נְבִיאִם). (ESV)

| עָנָה | to answer | 316x |
|---|---|---|
| ʿānâ | | S6030 |

שָׁאוּל ▷ DAY 131          נָבִיא ▷ DAY 161

וַיִּשְׁאַל שָׁאוּל בַּיהוָה וְלֹא עָנָהוּ יְהוָה גַּם בַּחֲלֹמוֹת גַּם בָּאוּרִים גַּם בַּנְּבִיאִם׃

| And when **Saul** inquired of the Lord | וַיִּשְׁאַל שָׁאוּל בַּיהוָה |
|---|---|
| the Lord did not **answer** him | וְלֹא עָנָהוּ יְהוָה |
| either by dreams | גַּם בַּחֲלֹמוֹת |
| or by Urim | גַּם בָּאוּרִים |
| or by **prophets** | גַּם בַּנְּבִיאִם |

The mind of the righteous ponders before **answering** (עֲנוֹת), but the **mouth** (פִּי) of the wicked pours forth **evil things** (רָעוֹת). (MLB)

| רָעָה | evil, wickedness | 311x |
| rāʿâ | | S7451 |

פֶּה ➤ DAY 106      עִנָה ➤ DAY 136

לֵב צַדִּיק יֶהְגֶּה לַעֲנוֹת וּפִי רְשָׁעִים יַבִּיעַ רָעוֹת:

| The mind of the righteous | לֵב צַדִּיק |
| ponders | יֶהְגֶּה |
| before **answering** | לַעֲנוֹת |
| but the **mouth** of the wicked | וּפִי רְשָׁעִים |
| pours forth | יַבִּיעַ |
| **evil things** | רָעוֹת |

Therefore thus says the Lᴏʀᴅ: behold, against this **family** (מִשְׁפָּחָה) I am devising **disaster** (רָעָה), from which you cannot remove your necks, and **you shall** not **walk** (תֵלְכוּ) haughtily, for it will be a time of **disaster** (רָעָה). (ESV)

| מִשְׁפָּחָה | family, clan | 304x |
|---|---|---|
| *mišpāḥâ* | | S4940 |

הלך  ▹  DAY 31     רָעָה  ▹  DAY 163

לָכֵן כֹּה אָמַר יְהוָה הִנְנִי חֹשֵׁב עַל־הַמִּשְׁפָּחָה הַזֹּאת רָעָה אֲשֶׁר לֹא־תָמִישׁוּ מִשָּׁם צַוְּארֹתֵיכֶם וְלֹא תֵלְכוּ רוֹמָה כִּי עֵת רָעָה הִיא:

| Therefore | לָכֵן |
|---|---|
| thus says the Lᴏʀᴅ | כֹּה אָמַר יְהוָה |
| behold, . . . I am devising **disaster** | הִנְנִי חֹשֵׁב . . . רָעָה |
| against this **family** | עַל־הַמִּשְׁפָּחָה הַזֹּאת |
| from which | אֲשֶׁר . . . מִשָּׁם |
| you cannot remove | לֹא־תָמִישׁוּ |
| your necks | צַוְּארֹתֵיכֶם |
| and **you shall** not **walk** | וְלֹא תֵלְכוּ |
| haughtily | רוֹמָה |
| for it will be | כִּי . . . הִיא |
| a time of **disaster** | עֵת רָעָה |

Only you **have I known** (יָדַעְתִּי) of all the **families** (מִשְׁפְּחוֹת) of the earth. Therefore **will I visit** (אֶפְקֹד) upon you all your iniquities. (MLB)

| | | |
|---|---|---|
| **פָּקַד** | to visit, take care of, punish | 304x |
| *pāqad* | | S6485 |

יָדַע    ▷    DAY 50          מִשְׁפָּחָה    ▷    DAY 164

רַק אֶתְכֶם יָדַעְתִּי מִכֹּל מִשְׁפְּחוֹת הָאֲדָמָה עַל־כֵּן אֶפְקֹד עֲלֵיכֶם אֵת כָּל־עֲוֹנֹתֵיכֶם׃

| | |
|---|---|
| Only you | רַק אֶתְכֶם |
| **have I known** | יָדַעְתִּי |
| of all the **families** of | מִכֹּל מִשְׁפְּחוֹת |
| the earth | הָאֲדָמָה |
| Therefore | עַל־כֵּן |
| **will I visit** upon you | אֶפְקֹד עֲלֵיכֶם |
| all your iniquities | אֵת כָּל־עֲוֹנֹתֵיכֶם |

Yet the men were **very** (מְאֹד) good to us, and we were not insulted, nor **did we miss** (פָּקַדְנוּ) anything as long as we went about with them, while we were in the **fields** (שָׂדֶה). (NASB)

| מְאֹד | much, very | 300x |
|---|---|---|
| *mĕ'ōd* | | S3966 |

שָׂדֶה　▷　DAY 158　　　　פקד　▷　DAY 165

וְהָאֲנָשִׁים טֹבִים לָנוּ מְאֹד וְלֹא הָכְלַמְנוּ וְלֹא־פָקַדְנוּ מְאוּמָה כָּל־יְמֵי
הִתְהַלַּכְנוּ אִתָּם בִּהְיוֹתֵנוּ בַּשָּׂדֶה:

| Yet the men | וְהָאֲנָשִׁים |
|---|---|
| were **very** good | טֹבִים . . . מְאֹד |
| to us | לָנוּ |
| and we were not insulted | וְלֹא הָכְלַמְנוּ |
| nor **did we miss** | וְלֹא־פָקַדְנוּ |
| anything | מְאוּמָה |
| as long as | כָּל־יְמֵי |
| we went about with them | הִתְהַלַּכְנוּ אִתָּם |
| while we were | בִּהְיוֹתֵנוּ |
| in the **fields** | בַּשָּׂדֶה |

But there was no **food** (לֶחֶם) in the entire **region** (אֶרֶץ), for the famine was **very** (מְאֹד) severe. The **land** (אֶרֶץ) of Egypt and the **land** (אֶרֶץ) of Canaan were exhausted by the famine. (CSB)

| לֶחֶם | bread, food | 299x |
|---|---|---|
| *leḥem* | | S3899 |

| אֶרֶץ | ➤ | DAY 23 | מְאֹד | ➤ | DAY 166 |
|---|---|---|---|---|---|

וְלֶחֶם אֵין בְּכָל־הָאָרֶץ כִּי־כָבֵד הָרָעָב מְאֹד וַתֵּלַהּ אֶרֶץ מִצְרַיִם
וְאֶרֶץ כְּנַעַן מִפְּנֵי הָרָעָב:

| But there was no **food** | וְלֶחֶם אֵין |
|---|---|
| in the entire **region** | בְּכָל־הָאָרֶץ |
| for the famine | כִּי־ . . . הָרָעָב |
| was **very** severe | כָבֵד . . . מְאֹד |
| The **land** of Egypt | אֶרֶץ מִצְרַיִם |
| and the **land** of Canaan | וְאֶרֶץ כְּנַעַן |
| were exhausted | וַתֵּלַהּ |
| by the famine | מִפְּנֵי הָרָעָב |

Then I lay prostrate before the Lᴏʀᴅ as before, forty days and forty nights. I neither ate **bread** (לֶחֶם) nor drank water, because of all the **sin** (חַטַּאתְכֶם) that you had committed, in doing what was **evil** (רַע) in the sight of the Lᴏʀᴅ to provoke him to anger. (ESV)

| חַטָּאת | sin, sin offering | 298x |
|---|---|---|
| ḥaṭṭā't | | S2403 |

רַע　▷　DAY 146　　　　　לֶחֶם　▷　DAY 167

וָאֶתְנַפַּל לִפְנֵי יְהוָה כָּרִאשֹׁנָה אַרְבָּעִים יוֹם וְאַרְבָּעִים לַיְלָה לֶחֶם לֹא
אָכַלְתִּי וּמַיִם לֹא שָׁתִיתִי עַל כָּל-**חַטַּאתְכֶם** אֲשֶׁר חֲטָאתֶם לַעֲשׂוֹת
הָ**רַע** בְּעֵינֵי יְהוָה לְהַכְעִיסוֹ:

| Then I lay prostrate before the Lᴏʀᴅ | וָאֶתְנַפַּל לִפְנֵי יְהוָה |
|---|---|
| as before | כָּרִאשֹׁנָה |
| forty days | אַרְבָּעִים יוֹם |
| and forty nights | וְאַרְבָּעִים לַיְלָה |
| I neither ate **bread** | לֶחֶם לֹא אָכַלְתִּי |
| nor drank water | וּמַיִם לֹא שָׁתִיתִי |
| because of all the **sin** | עַל כָּל-**חַטַּאתְכֶם** |
| that you had committed | אֲשֶׁר חֲטָאתֶם |
| in doing what was **evil** | לַעֲשׂוֹת הָ**רַע** |
| in the sight of the Lᴏʀᴅ | בְּעֵינֵי יְהוָה |
| to provoke him to anger | לְהַכְעִיסוֹ |

With it he touched my mouth and said, "See, **this** (זֶה) has touched your lips; your guilt **is taken away** (סָר) and your **sin** (חַטָּאתְךָ) atoned for." (NIV)

| סוּר | to turn aside, remove | 298x |
|---|---|---|
| *sûr* | | S5493 |

זֶה ➤ DAY 37      חַטָּאת ➤ DAY 168

וַיַּגַּע עַל־פִּי וַיֹּאמֶר הִנֵּה נָגַע זֶה עַל־שְׂפָתֶיךָ וְסָר עֲוֹנֶךָ וְחַטָּאתְךָ תְּכֻפָּר:

| With it he touched | וַיַּגַּע |
|---|---|
| my mouth | עַל־פִּי |
| and said | וַיֹּאמֶר |
| See | הִנֵּה |
| **this** has touched | נָגַע זֶה |
| your lips | עַל־שְׂפָתֶיךָ |
| your guilt | עֲוֹנֶךָ |
| **is taken away** | וְסָר |
| and your **sin** | וְחַטָּאתְךָ |
| atoned for | תְּכֻפָּר |

From the **time** (עֵת) that Amaziah **turned away** (סָר) from the
LORD, they conspired against him at Jerusalem; he fled to Lachish,
but **they sent** (וַיִּשְׁלְחוּ) after him to Lachish and assassinated him
there. (MLB)

| עֵת | time | 296x |
|---|---|---|
| ʿēt | | S6256 |

שׁלח   ➤   DAY 57        סוּר   ➤   DAY 169

וּמֵעֵת אֲשֶׁר־סָר אֲמַצְיָהוּ מֵאַחֲרֵי יְהוָה וַיִּקְשְׁרוּ עָלָיו קֶשֶׁר בִּירוּשָׁלַם
וַיָּנָס לָכִישָׁה וַיִּשְׁלְחוּ אַחֲרָיו לָכִישָׁה וַיְמִיתֻהוּ שָׁם:

| From the **time** that | וּמֵעֵת אֲשֶׁר־ |
|---|---|
| Amaziah **turned away** | סָר אֲמַצְיָהוּ |
| from the LORD | מֵאַחֲרֵי יְהוָה |
| they conspired | וַיִּקְשְׁרוּ . . . קֶשֶׁר |
| against him at Jerusalem | עָלָיו . . . בִּירוּשָׁלַם |
| he fled to Lachish | וַיָּנָס לָכִישָׁה |
| but **they sent** after him | וַיִּשְׁלְחוּ אַחֲרָיו |
| to Lachish | לָכִישָׁה |
| and assassinated him | וַיְמִיתֻהוּ |
| there | שָׁם |

At that **time** (עֵת) **Solomon** (שְׁלֹמֹה) held the festival for **seven**
(שִׁבְעַת) days, and all Israel with him, a very great congregation,
from Lebo-hamath to the Wadi of Egypt. (NRSV)

| שְׁלֹמֹה | Solomon | 293x |
|---|---|---|
| šĕlōmô | | S8010 |

שֶׁבַע  ➤  DAY 113          עֵת  ➤  DAY 170

וַיַּעַשׂ שְׁלֹמֹה אֶת־הֶחָג בָּעֵת הַהִיא שִׁבְעַת יָמִים וְכָל־יִשְׂרָאֵל עִמּוֹ
קָהָל גָּדוֹל מְאֹד מִלְּבוֹא חֲמָת עַד־נַחַל מִצְרָיִם:

| | |
|---|---|
| At that **time** | בָּעֵת הַהִיא |
| **Solomon** held | וַיַּעַשׂ שְׁלֹמֹה |
| the festival | אֶת־הֶחָג |
| for **seven** days | שִׁבְעַת יָמִים |
| and all Israel with him | וְכָל־יִשְׂרָאֵל עִמּוֹ |
| a very great congregation | קָהָל גָּדוֹל מְאֹד |
| from Lebo-hamath | מִלְּבוֹא חֲמָת |
| to the Wadi of Egypt | עַד־נַחַל מִצְרָיִם |

And Adonijah **was afraid** (יָרֵא) of **Solomon** (שְׁלֹמֹה), and he
arose, went and **took hold** (וַיַּחֲזֵק) of the horns of the altar. (NASB)

| חֲזַק | to be strong, courageous; to overpower | 290x |
|---|---|---|
| ḥāzaq | | S2388 |

יָרֵא    ➤    DAY 160        שְׁלֹמֹה    ➤    DAY 171

וַאֲדֹנִיָּהוּ יָרֵא מִפְּנֵי שְׁלֹמֹה וַיָּקָם וַיֵּלֶךְ וַיַּחֲזֵק בְּקַרְנוֹת הַמִּזְבֵּחַ:

| And Adonijah | וַאֲדֹנִיָּהוּ |
|---|---|
| **was afraid** | יָרֵא |
| of **Solomon** | מִפְּנֵי שְׁלֹמֹה |
| and he arose | וַיָּקָם |
| went | וַיֵּלֶךְ |
| and **took hold** | וַיַּחֲזֵק |
| of the horns of | בְּקַרְנוֹת |
| the altar | הַמִּזְבֵּחַ |

Then Samson called to the LORD and said, "Lord GOD, remember me and **strengthen** (חַזְּקֵנִי) me only this once, O God, so that with this one act of revenge I may pay back the **Philistines** (פְּלִשְׁתִּים) for my **two** (שְׁתֵי) eyes." (NRSV)

| פְּלִשְׁתִּי | Philistine | 290x |
|---|---|---|
| pĕlištî | | S6430 |

שְׁנַיִם   ➤   DAY 67      חזק   ➤   DAY 172

וַיִּקְרָא שִׁמְשׁוֹן אֶל־יְהוָה וַיֹּאמַר אֲדֹנָי יֱהֹוִה זָכְרֵנִי נָא וְחַזְּקֵנִי נָא אַךְ
הַפַּעַם הַזֶּה הָאֱלֹהִים וְאִנָּקְמָה נְקַם־אַחַת מִשְּׁתֵי עֵינַי מִפְּלִשְׁתִּים:

| Then Samson called | וַיִּקְרָא שִׁמְשׁוֹן |
|---|---|
| to the LORD | אֶל־יְהוָה |
| and said | וַיֹּאמַר |
| Lord GOD | אֲדֹנָי יֱהֹוִה |
| remember me | זָכְרֵנִי נָא |
| and **strengthen** me | וְחַזְּקֵנִי נָא |
| only this once | אַךְ הַפַּעַם הַזֶּה |
| O God | הָאֱלֹהִים |
| so that . . . I may pay back the **Philistines** | וְאִנָּקְמָה . . . מִפְּלִשְׁתִּים |
| with this one act of revenge | נְקַם־אַחַת |
| for my **two** eyes | מִשְּׁתֵי עֵינַי |

So they made [lit., **they cut** (וַיִּכְרְתוּ)] a covenant at Beersheba. Then Abimelech and Phicol the **commander** (שַׂר) of his army rose up and returned to the land of the **Philistines** (פְּלִשְׁתִּים). (ESV)

| כרת | to cut (down), destroy | 289x |
|-----|------------------------|------|
| *kārat* | | S3772 |

שַׂר ➤ DAY 125          פְּלִשְׁתִּי ➤ DAY 173

וַיִּכְרְתוּ בְרִית בִּבְאֵר שָׁבַע וַיָּקָם אֲבִימֶלֶךְ וּפִיכֹל שַׂר־צְבָאוֹ וַיָּשֻׁבוּ אֶל־אֶרֶץ פְּלִשְׁתִּים:

| | |
|---|---|
| So they made [lit., **they cut**] a covenant | וַיִּכְרְתוּ בְרִית |
| at Beersheba | בִּבְאֵר שָׁבַע |
| Then . . . rose up | וַיָּקָם |
| Abimelech and Phicol | אֲבִימֶלֶךְ וּפִיכֹל |
| the **commander** of his army | שַׂר־צְבָאוֹ |
| and returned | וַיָּשֻׁבוּ |
| to the land of | אֶל־אֶרֶץ |
| the **Philistines** | פְּלִשְׁתִּים |

Now Nahash the Ammonite **came up** (וַיַּעַל) and besieged Jabesh-gilead; and all the men of Jabesh said to Nahash, "Make [lit., **cut** (כְּרָת־)] a covenant with us and **we will serve** (נַעַבְדֶךָ) you." (NASB)

| עָבַד | to work, do, make, serve | 289x |
|---|---|---|
| ʿāvad | | S5647 |

עָלָה    ➤   DAY 52       כרת    ➤   DAY 174

וַיַּעַל נָחָשׁ הָעַמּוֹנִי וַיִּחַן עַל־יָבֵשׁ גִּלְעָד וַיֹּאמְרוּ כָּל־אַנְשֵׁי יָבֵישׁ אֶל־
נָחָשׁ כְּרָת־לָנוּ בְרִית וְנַעַבְדֶךָ:

| | |
|---|---|
| Now . . . **came up** | וַיַּעַל |
| Nahash the Ammonite | נָחָשׁ הָעַמּוֹנִי |
| and besieged | וַיִּחַן עַל־ |
| Jabesh-gilead | יָבֵשׁ גִּלְעָד |
| and . . . said to Nahash | וַיֹּאמְרוּ . . . אֶל־נָחָשׁ |
| all the men of Jabesh | כָּל־אַנְשֵׁי יָבֵישׁ |
| Make [lit., **cut**] a covenant with us | כְּרָת־לָנוּ בְרִית |
| and **we will serve** you | וְנַעַבְדֶךָ |

**You have** not **brought** (הֵבֵיאתָ) me your sheep for **burnt
offerings** (עֹלֹתֶיךָ), or honored me with your sacrifices. **I have** not
**burdened** (הֶעֱבַדְתִּיךָ) you with offerings, or wearied you with
frankincense. (NRSV)

| עֹלָה | burnt offering | 287x |
|---|---|---|
| ʿōlâ | | S5930 |

בוֹא  ▷  DAY 20          עבד  ▷  DAY 175

לֹא־הֵבֵיאתָ לִּי שֵׂה עֹלֹתֶיךָ וּזְבָחֶיךָ לֹא כִבַּדְתָּנִי לֹא הֶעֱבַדְתִּיךָ
בְּמִנְחָה וְלֹא הוֹגַעְתִּיךָ בִּלְבוֹנָה:

| | |
|---|---|
| **You have** not **brought** me | לֹא־הֵבֵיאתָ לִּי |
| your sheep for **burnt offerings** | שֵׂה עֹלֹתֶיךָ |
| or honored me | לֹא כִבַּדְתָּנִי |
| with your sacrifices | וּזְבָחֶיךָ |
| **I have** not **burdened** you | לֹא הֶעֱבַדְתִּיךָ |
| with offerings | בְּמִנְחָה |
| or wearied you | וְלֹא הוֹגַעְתִּיךָ |
| with frankincense | בִּלְבוֹנָה |

To Zedekiah king of Judah **I spoke** (דִּבַּרְתִּי) in like manner [lit.,
according to all these words]: "Bring your necks under the yoke of
the king of Babylon, and **serve** (עִבְדוּ) him and his people and **live**
(חֲיוּ)." (ESV)

| חיה | to live | 284x |
|---|---|---|
| ḥāyâ | | S2421 |

דבר  ➤  DAY 39          עבד  ➤  DAY 175

וְאֶל־צִדְקִיָּה מֶלֶךְ־יְהוּדָה דִּבַּרְתִּי כְּכָל־הַדְּבָרִים הָאֵלֶּה לֵאמֹר הָבִיאוּ
אֶת־צַוְּארֵיכֶם בְּעֹל מֶלֶךְ־בָּבֶל וְעִבְדוּ אֹתוֹ וְעַמּוֹ וִחְיוּ:

| | |
|---|---|
| To Zedekiah | וְאֶל־צִדְקִיָּה |
| king of Judah | מֶלֶךְ־יְהוּדָה |
| **I spoke** | דִּבַּרְתִּי . . . לֵאמֹר |
| in like manner [lit., according to all these words] | כְּכָל־הַדְּבָרִים הָאֵלֶּה |
| Bring | הָבִיאוּ |
| your necks | אֶת־צַוְּארֵיכֶם |
| under the yoke of | בְּעֹל |
| the king of Babylon | מֶלֶךְ־בָּבֶל |
| and **serve** | וְעִבְדוּ |
| him and his people | אֹתוֹ וְעַמּוֹ |
| and **live** | וִחְיוּ |

Though I walk in the midst of trouble, **you preserve** my **life** (תְּחַיֵּנִי). You stretch out your **hand** (יָדֶךָ) against the anger of my **foes** (אֹיְבַי); with your right hand you save me. (NIV)

| אֹיֵב | enemy, adversary | 284x |
|---|---|---|
| ᵓōyēv | | S341 |

יָד  ▷  DAY 30       חיה  ▷  DAY 177

אִם־אֵלֵךְ בְּקֶרֶב צָרָה תְּחַיֵּנִי עַל אַף אֹיְבַי תִּשְׁלַח יָדֶךָ וְתוֹשִׁיעֵנִי יְמִינֶךָ:

| Though I walk | אִם־אֵלֵךְ |
|---|---|
| in the midst of trouble | בְּקֶרֶב צָרָה |
| **you preserve** my **life** | תְּחַיֵּנִי |
| You stretch out your **hand** | תִּשְׁלַח יָדֶךָ |
| against the anger of | עַל אַף |
| my **foes** | אֹיְבַי |
| with your right hand | יְמִינֶךָ |
| you save me | וְתוֹשִׁיעֵנִי |

I will bring the **sword** (חֶרֶב) against you, executing vengeance for the **covenant** (בְּרִית); and if you withdraw within your cities, I will send pestilence among you, and you shall be delivered into **enemy** (אֹיֵב) hands. (NRSV)

| בְּרִית | covenant | 284x |
|---|---|---|
| *běrît* | | S1285 |

חֶרֶב ➤ DAY 128     אֹיֵב ➤ DAY 178

וְהֵבֵאתִי עֲלֵיכֶם חֶרֶב נֹקֶמֶת נְקַם־בְּרִית וְנֶאֱסַפְתֶּם אֶל־עָרֵיכֶם וְשִׁלַּחְתִּי דֶבֶר בְּתוֹכְכֶם וְנִתַּתֶּם בְּיַד־אוֹיֵב:

| I will bring the **sword** | וְהֵבֵאתִי . . . חֶרֶב |
|---|---|
| against you | עֲלֵיכֶם |
| executing vengeance for | נֹקֶמֶת נְקַם־ |
| the **covenant** | בְּרִית |
| and if you withdraw | וְנֶאֱסַפְתֶּם |
| within your cities | אֶל־עָרֵיכֶם |
| I will send pestilence | וְשִׁלַּחְתִּי דֶבֶר |
| among you | בְּתוֹכְכֶם |
| and you shall be delivered | וְנִתַּתֶּם |
| into **enemy** hands | בְּיַד־אוֹיֵב |

They slaughtered the Passover lamb on the fourteenth day of the second **month** (חֹדֶשׁ). The priests and the **Levites** (לְוִיִּם) were ashamed and consecrated themselves and brought **burnt offerings** (עֹלוֹת) to the temple of the LORD. (NIV)

| חֹדֶשׁ | month, new moon | 284x |
|---|---|---|
| ḥōdeš | | S2320 |

לֵוִי ➤ DAY 148          עֹלָה ➤ DAY 176

וַיִּשְׁחֲטוּ הַפֶּסַח בְּאַרְבָּעָה עָשָׂר לַחֹדֶשׁ הַשֵּׁנִי וְהַכֹּהֲנִים וְהַלְוִיִּם נִכְלְמוּ וַיִּתְקַדָּשׁוּ וַיָּבִיאוּ עֹלוֹת בֵּית יְהוָה:

| They slaughtered | וַיִּשְׁחֲטוּ |
|---|---|
| the Passover lamb | הַפֶּסַח |
| on the fourteenth day | בְּאַרְבָּעָה עָשָׂר |
| of the second **month** | לַחֹדֶשׁ הַשֵּׁנִי |
| The priests and the **Levites** | וְהַכֹּהֲנִים וְהַלְוִיִּם |
| were ashamed | נִכְלְמוּ |
| and consecrated themselves | וַיִּתְקַדָּשׁוּ |
| and brought | וַיָּבִיאוּ |
| **burnt offerings** | עֹלוֹת |
| to the temple of the LORD | בֵּית יְהוָה |

And they commanded the people, saying, "When you see the ark of the **covenant** (בְּרִית) of the Lᴏʀᴅ your God with the Levitical priests carrying it, then **you** (אַתֶּם) shall set out from your **place** (מִקּוֹמְכֶם) and go after it." (NASB)

| | | |
|---|---|---|
| אַתֶּם | you (masc pl) | 283x |
| ʾattem | | S859 |

מָקוֹם   ▷   DAY 134       בְּרִית   ▷   DAY 179

וַיְצַוּוּ אֶת־הָעָם לֵאמֹר כִּרְאוֹתְכֶם אֵת אֲרוֹן בְּרִית־יְהוָה אֱלֹהֵיכֶם וְהַכֹּהֲנִים הַלְוִיִּם נֹשְׂאִים אֹתוֹ וְאַתֶּם תִּסְעוּ מִמְּקוֹמְכֶם וַהֲלַכְתֶּם אַחֲרָיו:

| | |
|---|---|
| And they commanded the people, saying | וַיְצַוּוּ אֶת־הָעָם לֵאמֹר |
| When you see | כִּרְאוֹתְכֶם |
| the ark of the **covenant** of | אֵת אֲרוֹן בְּרִית־ |
| the Lᴏʀᴅ your God | יְהוָה אֱלֹהֵיכֶם |
| with the Levitical priests | וְהַכֹּהֲנִים הַלְוִיִּם |
| carrying it | נֹשְׂאִים אֹתוֹ |
| then **you** shall set out | וְאַתֶּם תִּסְעוּ |
| from your **place** | מִמְּקוֹמְכֶם |
| and go after it | וַהֲלַכְתֶּם אַחֲרָיו |

They shall perform duties for you and for the whole tent. But **they must** not **approach** (יִקְרָבוּ) either the **utensils** (כְּלֵי) of the sanctuary or the altar, otherwise both they and **you** (אַתֶּם) will die. (NRSV)

| קָרַב *qārav* | to approach; bring near | 280x S7126 |
| --- | --- | --- |

כְּלֵי ◁ DAY 156     אַתֶּם ◁ DAY 181

וְשָׁמְרוּ מִשְׁמַרְתְּךָ וּמִשְׁמֶרֶת כָּל־הָאֹהֶל אַךְ אֶל־כְּלֵי הַקֹּדֶשׁ וְאֶל־הַמִּזְבֵּחַ לֹא יִקְרָבוּ וְלֹא־יָמֻתוּ גַם־הֵם גַּם־אַתֶּם׃

| They shall perform duties for you | וְשָׁמְרוּ מִשְׁמַרְתְּךָ |
| --- | --- |
| and for the whole tent | וּמִשְׁמֶרֶת כָּל־הָאֹהֶל |
| But **they must** not **approach** | אַךְ . . . לֹא יִקְרָבוּ |
| either the **utensils** of the sanctuary | אֶל־כְּלֵי הַקֹּדֶשׁ |
| or the altar | וְאֶל־הַמִּזְבֵּחַ |
| otherwise . . . will die | וְלֹא־יָמֻתוּ |
| both they | גַם־הֵם |
| and **you** | גַּם־אַתֶּם |

As soon as **he came near** (קָרַב) the camp and saw the calf and the dancing, Moses' **anger** (אַף) burned hot, and he threw the tablets from his hands and broke them **at the foot of** (תַּחַת) the mountain. (NRSV)

| אַף | nose, face; anger | 277x |
|---|---|---|
| ᵓaf | | S639 |

תַּחַת ▷ DAY 101　　　　קרב ▷ DAY 182

וַיְהִי כַּאֲשֶׁר קָרַב אֶל־הַמַּחֲנֶה וַיַּרְא אֶת־הָעֵגֶל וּמְחֹלֹת וַיִּחַר־אַף
מֹשֶׁה וַיַּשְׁלֵךְ מִיָּדָיו אֶת־הַלֻּחֹת וַיְשַׁבֵּר אֹתָם תַּחַת הָהָר:

| As soon as | וַיְהִי כַּאֲשֶׁר |
|---|---|
| **he came near** the camp | קָרַב אֶל־הַמַּחֲנֶה |
| and saw | וַיַּרְא |
| the calf | אֶת־הָעֵגֶל |
| and the dancing | וּמְחֹלֹת |
| Moses' **anger** burned hot | וַיִּחַר־אַף מֹשֶׁה |
| and he threw the tablets | וַיַּשְׁלֵךְ . . . אֶת־הַלֻּחֹת |
| from his hands | מִיָּדָיו |
| and broke them | וַיְשַׁבֵּר אֹתָם |
| **at the foot of** the mountain | תַּחַת הָהָר |

But **six** (שֵׁשׁ) hundred turned and fled toward the wilderness to the rock of Rimmon, and **remained** (וַיֵּשְׁבוּ) at the rock of Rimmon for four **months** (חֳדָשִׁים). (NRSV)

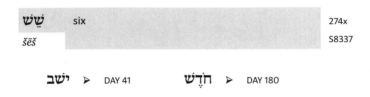

| שֵׁשׁ | six | 274x |
|------|-----|------|
| šēš | | S8337 |

| יָשַׁב | ▷ | DAY 41 | | חֹדֶשׁ | ▷ | DAY 180 |

וַיִּפְנוּ וַיָּנֻסוּ הַמִּדְבָּרָה אֶל־סֶלַע הָרִמּוֹן שֵׁשׁ מֵאוֹת אִישׁ וַיֵּשְׁבוּ בְּסֶלַע רִמּוֹן אַרְבָּעָה חֳדָשִׁים:

| But . . . turned | וַיִּפְנוּ |
|---|---|
| **six** hundred | שֵׁשׁ מֵאוֹת אִישׁ |
| and fled | וַיָּנֻסוּ |
| toward the wilderness | הַמִּדְבָּרָה |
| to the rock of Rimmon | אֶל־סֶלַע הָרִמּוֹן |
| and **remained** | וַיֵּשְׁבוּ |
| at the rock of Rimmon | בְּסֶלַע רִמּוֹן |
| for four **months** | אַרְבָּעָה חֳדָשִׁים |

**Pharaoh** (פַּרְעֹה) **removed** (וַיָּסַר) his signet ring from his hand
and put it on Joseph's hand, clothed him with fine linen garments,
and placed a **gold** (זָהָב) chain around his neck. (CSB)

| פַּרְעֹה | Pharaoh | 274x |
|---|---|---|
| par'ô | | S6547 |

| זָהָב | ▷ DAY 136 | סוּר | ▷ DAY 169 |
|---|---|---|---|

וַיָּסַר פַּרְעֹה אֶת־טַבַּעְתּוֹ מֵעַל יָדוֹ וַיִּתֵּן אֹתָהּ עַל־יַד יוֹסֵף וַיַּלְבֵּשׁ
אֹתוֹ בִּגְדֵי־שֵׁשׁ וַיָּשֶׂם רְבִד הַזָּהָב עַל־צַוָּארוֹ:

| **Pharaoh removed** | וַיָּסַר פַּרְעֹה |
|---|---|
| his signet ring | אֶת־טַבַּעְתּוֹ |
| from his hand | מֵעַל יָדוֹ |
| and put it | וַיִּתֵּן אֹתָהּ |
| on Joseph's hand | עַל־יַד יוֹסֵף |
| clothed him | וַיַּלְבֵּשׁ אֹתוֹ |
| with fine linen garments | בִּגְדֵי־שֵׁשׁ |
| and placed | וַיָּשֶׂם |
| a **gold** chain | רְבִד הַזָּהָב |
| around his neck | עַל־צַוָּארוֹ |

So Joseph went in and **told** (וַיַּגֵּד) Pharaoh (פַּרְעֹה), "My father and my brothers, with their **flocks** (צֹאנָם) and herds and all that they possess, have come from the land of Canaan. They are now in the land of Goshen." (ESV)

| צֹאן | sheep, flock | 274x |
|---|---|---|
| *ṣōʾn* | | S6629 |

נגד ➤ DAY 143      **פַּרְעֹה** ➤ DAY 185

וַיָּבֹא יוֹסֵף וַיַּגֵּד לְפַרְעֹה וַיֹּאמֶר אָבִי וְאַחַי וְצֹאנָם וּבְקָרָם וְכָל־אֲשֶׁר לָהֶם בָּאוּ מֵאֶרֶץ כְּנָעַן וְהִנָּם בְּאֶרֶץ גֹּשֶׁן:

| So Joseph went in | וַיָּבֹא יוֹסֵף |
|---|---|
| and **told Pharaoh** | וַיַּגֵּד לְפַרְעֹה וַיֹּאמֶר |
| My father and my brothers | אָבִי וְאַחַי |
| with their **flocks** and herds | וְצֹאנָם וּבְקָרָם |
| and all that they possess | וְכָל־אֲשֶׁר לָהֶם |
| have come | בָּאוּ |
| from the land of Canaan | מֵאֶרֶץ כְּנָעַן |
| They are now | וְהִנָּם |
| in the land of Goshen | בְּאֶרֶץ גֹּשֶׁן |

As he looked, he saw a well in the **field** (שָׂדֶה) and three flocks
of **sheep** (צֹאן) lying there beside it; for out of that well the flocks
were watered. The **stone** (אֶבֶן) on the well's mouth was large.
(NRSV)

| | | | |
|---|---|---|---|
| אֶבֶן | stone | | 272x |
| ʾeven | | | S68 |

שָׂדֶה  ▷  DAY 158        צֹאן  ▷  DAY 186

וַיַּרְא וְהִנֵּה בְאֵר בַּשָּׂדֶה וְהִנֵּה־שָׁם שְׁלֹשָׁה עֶדְרֵי־צֹאן רֹבְצִים עָלֶיהָ
כִּי מִן־הַבְּאֵר הַהִוא יַשְׁקוּ הָעֲדָרִים וְהָאֶבֶן גְּדֹלָה עַל־פִּי הַבְּאֵר:

| As he looked, he saw | וַיַּרְא וְהִנֵּה |
|---|---|
| a well in the **field** | בְאֵר בַּשָּׂדֶה |
| and . . . lying there beside it | וְהִנֵּה־שָׁם . . . רֹבְצִים עָלֶיהָ |
| three flocks of **sheep** | שְׁלֹשָׁה עֶדְרֵי־צֹאן |
| for out of that well | כִּי מִן־הַבְּאֵר הַהִוא |
| the flocks were watered | יַשְׁקוּ הָעֲדָרִים |
| The **stone** . . . was large | וְהָאֶבֶן גְּדֹלָה |
| on the well's mouth | עַל־פִּי הַבְּאֵר |

A full and fair **weight** (אֶבֶן) you shall have, a full and fair measure
you shall have, **that** (לְמַעַן) your **days** (יָמֶיךָ) may be long in the
land that the LORD your God is giving you. (ESV)

| לְמַעַן | in order that, for the sake of | 272x |
|---|---|---|
| lĕma'an | | S4616 |

יוֹם   ➤   DAY 24      אֶבֶן   ➤   DAY 187

אֶבֶן שְׁלֵמָה וָצֶדֶק יִהְיֶה־לָּךְ אֵיפָה שְׁלֵמָה וָצֶדֶק יִהְיֶה־לָּךְ לְמַעַן
יַאֲרִיכוּ יָמֶיךָ עַל הָאֲדָמָה אֲשֶׁר־יְהוָה אֱלֹהֶיךָ נֹתֵן לָךְ:

| A . . . **weight** | אֶבֶן |
|---|---|
| full and fair | שְׁלֵמָה וָצֶדֶק |
| you shall have | יִהְיֶה־לָּךְ |
| a . . . measure | אֵיפָה |
| full and fair | שְׁלֵמָה וָצֶדֶק |
| you shall have | יִהְיֶה־לָּךְ |
| **that** your **days** | לְמַעַן . . . יָמֶיךָ |
| may be long | יַאֲרִיכוּ |
| in the land | עַל הָאֲדָמָה |
| that the LORD your God | אֲשֶׁר־יְהוָה אֱלֹהֶיךָ |
| is giving you | נֹתֵן לָךְ |

Reuben further said to them, "Shed no blood. Throw him into this pit that is in the **wilderness** (מִדְבָּר), but do not lay hands on him"—**that** (לְמַעַן) he might rescue him out of their hands, **to restore** (הֲשִׁיבוֹ) him to his father. (NASB)

| | | |
|---|---|---|
| **מִדְבָּר** | desert, wilderness | 271x |
| *midbār* | | S4057 |

**שׁוּב** ➤ DAY 44        **לְמַעַן** ➤ DAY 188

וַיֹּאמֶר אֲלֵהֶם רְאוּבֵן אַל־תִּשְׁפְּכוּ־דָם הַשְׁלִיכוּ אֹתוֹ אֶל־הַבּוֹר הַזֶּה
אֲשֶׁר בַּמִּדְבָּר וְיָד אַל־תִּשְׁלְחוּ־בוֹ לְמַעַן הַצִּיל אֹתוֹ מִיָּדָם לַהֲשִׁיבוֹ
אֶל־אָבִיו:

| | |
|---|---|
| Reuben further said to them | וַיֹּאמֶר אֲלֵהֶם רְאוּבֵן |
| Shed no blood | אַל־תִּשְׁפְּכוּ־דָם |
| Throw him | הַשְׁלִיכוּ אֹתוֹ |
| into this pit | אֶל־הַבּוֹר הַזֶּה |
| that is in the **wilderness** | אֲשֶׁר בַּמִּדְבָּר |
| but do not lay hands on him | וְיָד אַל־תִּשְׁלְחוּ־בוֹ |
| **that** he might rescue him | לְמַעַן הַצִּיל אֹתוֹ |
| out of their hands | מִיָּדָם |
| **to restore** him | לַהֲשִׁיבוֹ |
| to his father | אֶל־אָבִיו |

Would that we had died by the hand of the Lord in the land of
Egypt, when we sat by the **meat** (בָּשָׂר) pots and ate bread to the
full, for **you have brought** us **out** (הוֹצֵאתֶם) into this **wilderness**
(מִדְבָּר) to kill this whole assembly with hunger. (ESV)

| | | |
|---|---|---|
| בָּשָׂר | flesh, meat | 270x |
| *bāśār* | | S1320 |

יָצָא ▷ DAY 43 מִדְבָּר ▷ DAY 189

מִי־יִתֵּן מוּתֵנוּ בְיַד־יְהוָה בְּאֶרֶץ מִצְרַיִם בְּשִׁבְתֵּנוּ עַל־סִיר הַבָּשָׂר
בְּאָכְלֵנוּ לֶחֶם לָשֹׂבַע כִּי־**הוֹצֵאתֶם** אֹתָנוּ אֶל־הַמִּדְבָּר הַזֶּה לְהָמִית
אֶת־כָּל־הַקָּהָל הַזֶּה בָּרָעָב:

| | |
|---|---|
| Would that we had died | מִי־יִתֵּן מוּתֵנוּ |
| by the hand of the Lord | בְיַד־יְהוָה |
| in the land of Egypt | בְּאֶרֶץ מִצְרַיִם |
| when we sat by | בְּשִׁבְתֵּנוּ עַל־ |
| the **meat** pots | סִיר הַבָּשָׂר |
| and ate bread | בְּאָכְלֵנוּ לֶחֶם |
| to the full | לָשֹׂבַע |
| for **you have brought** us **out** | כִּי־**הוֹצֵאתֶם** אֹתָנוּ |
| into this **wilderness** | אֶל־הַמִּדְבָּר הַזֶּה |
| to kill . . . with hunger | לְהָמִית . . . בָּרָעָב |
| this whole assembly | אֶת־כָּל־הַקָּהָל הַזֶּה |

The clamor will resound to the ends of the earth, for the Lord has an indictment against the **nations** (גּוֹיִם); he is entering into judgment with all **flesh** (בָּשָׂר), and the **wicked** (רְשָׁעִים) he will put to the sword, declares the Lord. (ESV)

| רָשָׁע | wicked, guilty | 264x |
|---|---|---|
| rāšāʿ | | S7563 |

גּוֹי   ▷   DAY 95      בָּשָׂר   ▷   DAY 190

בָּא שָׁאוֹן עַד־קְצֵה הָאָרֶץ כִּי רִיב לַיהוָה בַּגּוֹיִם נִשְׁפָּט הוּא לְכָל־
בָּשָׂר הָרְשָׁעִים נְתָנָם לַחֶרֶב נְאֻם־יְהוָה:

| The clamor will resound | בָּא שָׁאוֹן |
|---|---|
| to the ends of the earth | עַד־קְצֵה הָאָרֶץ |
| for the Lord has an indictment | כִּי רִיב לַיהוָה |
| against the **nations** | בַּגּוֹיִם |
| he is entering into judgment | נִשְׁפָּט הוּא |
| with all **flesh** | לְכָל־בָּשָׂר |
| and the **wicked** | הָרְשָׁעִים |
| he will put to the sword | נְתָנָם לַחֶרֶב |
| declares the Lord | נְאֻם־יְהוָה |

**I will strengthen** (וְחִזַּקְתִּי) the arms of the king of **Babylon** (בָּבֶל), and put my sword in his hand; but I will break the arms of **Pharaoh** (פַּרְעֹה), and he will groan before him with the groans of one mortally wounded. (NRSV)

| בָּבֶל | Babylon | 262x |
|---|---|---|
| *bāvel* | | S894 |

חָזַק  ▷  DAY 172      פַּרְעֹה  ▷  DAY 185

וְחִזַּקְתִּי אֶת־זְרֹעוֹת מֶלֶךְ בָּבֶל וְנָתַתִּי אֶת־חַרְבִּי בְּיָדוֹ וְשָׁבַרְתִּי אֶת־
זְרֹעוֹת פַּרְעֹה וְנָאַק נַאֲקוֹת חָלָל לְפָנָיו:

| I will strengthen | וְחִזַּקְתִּי |
|---|---|
| the arms of | אֶת־זְרֹעוֹת |
| the king of **Babylon** | מֶלֶךְ בָּבֶל |
| and put my sword | וְנָתַתִּי אֶת־חַרְבִּי |
| in his hand | בְּיָדוֹ |
| but I will break | וְשָׁבַרְתִּי |
| the arms of **Pharaoh** | אֶת־זְרֹעוֹת פַּרְעֹה |
| and he will groan | וְנָאַק |
| before him | לְפָנָיו |
| with the groans of | נַאֲקוֹת |
| one mortally wounded | חָלָל |

As I **live** (חַי), declares the Lord God, surely in the place where the king dwells who made him king, whose oath he despised, and whose **covenant** (בְּרִיתוֹ) with him he broke, in **Babylon** (בָּבֶל) he shall die. (ESV)

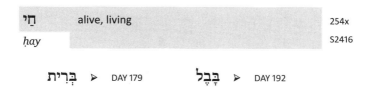

| חַי | alive, living | 254x |
|-----|---------------|------|
| ḥay | | S2416 |

בְּרִית　　▷　DAY 179　　　　בָּבֶל　　▷　DAY 192

חַי־אָנִי נְאֻם אֲדֹנָי יְהוִה אִם־לֹא בִּמְקוֹם הַמֶּלֶךְ הַמַּמְלִיךְ אֹתוֹ אֲשֶׁר
בָּזָה אֶת־אָלָתוֹ וַאֲשֶׁר הֵפֵר אֶת־בְּרִיתוֹ אִתּוֹ בְּתוֹךְ־בָּבֶל יָמוּת:

| As I **live** | חַי־אָנִי |
|---|---|
| declares the Lord God | נְאֻם אֲדֹנָי יְהוִה |
| surely | אִם־לֹא |
| in the place where the king dwells | בִּמְקוֹם הַמֶּלֶךְ |
| who made him king | הַמַּמְלִיךְ אֹתוֹ |
| whose oath | אֲשֶׁר . . . אֶת־אָלָתוֹ |
| he despised | בָּזָה |
| and whose **covenant** with him | וַאֲשֶׁר . . . אֶת־בְּרִיתוֹ אִתּוֹ |
| he broke | הֵפֵר |
| in **Babylon** he shall die | בְּתוֹךְ־בָּבֶל יָמוּת |

**So** (כֵּן), then, when ambassadors from the princes of **Babylon** (בָּבֶל) were sent to him to enquire about the sign which had occurred in the land, God left him to test him, to find out all that was in his **heart** (לִבָבוֹ). (MLB)

| לֵבָב | heart, mind | 252x |
|---|---|---|
| *lēvāv* | | S3824 |

כֵּן    ➤    DAY 75        בָּבֶל    ➤    DAY 192

וְכֵן בִּמְלִיצֵי שָׂרֵי בָּבֶל הַמְשַׁלְּחִים עָלָיו לִדְרשׁ הַמּוֹפֵת אֲשֶׁר הָיָה בָאָרֶץ עֲזָבוֹ הָאֱלֹהִים לְנַסּוֹתוֹ לָדַעַת כָּל־בִּלְבָבוֹ:

| | |
|---|---|
| **So**, then | וְכֵן |
| when ambassadors from the princes of **Babylon** | בִּמְלִיצֵי שָׂרֵי בָּבֶל |
| were sent to him | הַמְשַׁלְּחִים עָלָיו |
| to enquire about | לִדְרשׁ |
| the sign | הַמּוֹפֵת |
| which had occurred in the land | אֲשֶׁר הָיָה בָאָרֶץ |
| God left him | עֲזָבוֹ הָאֱלֹהִים |
| to test him | לְנַסּוֹתוֹ |
| to find out | לָדַעַת |
| all that was in his **heart** | כָּל־בִּלְבָבוֹ |

Every daughter who comes into possession of an inheritance of any **tribe** (מַטּוֹת) of the sons of Israel shall be wife to one of the **family** (מִשְׁפַּחַת) of the tribe of her father, **so that** (לְמַעַן) the sons of Israel each may possess the inheritance of his fathers. (NASB)

| מַטֶּה | rod, staff, tribe | 252x |
|---|---|---|
| *maṭṭê* | | S4294 |

מִשְׁפָּחָה   ▷   DAY 164         לְמַעַן   ▷   DAY 188

וְכָל־בַּת יֹרֶשֶׁת נַחֲלָה מִמַּטּוֹת בְּנֵי יִשְׂרָאֵל לְאֶחָד מִמִּשְׁפַּחַת מַטֵּה אָבִיהָ תִּהְיֶה לְאִשָּׁה לְמַעַן יִירְשׁוּ בְּנֵי יִשְׂרָאֵל אִישׁ נַחֲלַת אֲבֹתָיו:

| Every daughter | וְכָל־בַּת |
|---|---|
| who comes into possession of | יֹרֶשֶׁת |
| an inheritance of any **tribe** of | נַחֲלָה מִמַּטּוֹת |
| the sons of Israel | בְּנֵי יִשְׂרָאֵל |
| shall be wife | תִּהְיֶה לְאִשָּׁה |
| to one of the **family** of | לְאֶחָד מִמִּשְׁפַּחַת |
| the tribe of her father | מַטֵּה אָבִיהָ |
| **so that** the sons of Israel | לְמַעַן . . . בְּנֵי יִשְׂרָאֵל |
| each may possess | יִירְשׁוּ . . . אִישׁ |
| the inheritance of his fathers | נַחֲלַת אֲבֹתָיו |

Then King David rose to his **feet** (רַגְלָיו) and said, "Hear me, my brothers and my people. I myself had in **mind** (לְבָבִי) to build a temple as a resting place for the ark of the Lᴏʀᴅ's **covenant** (בְּרִית) and for the footstool of our God." (MLB)

| רֶגֶל | foot, sole, leg | 251x |
|---|---|---|
| *regel* | | S7272 |

בְּרִית ▸ DAY 179          לֵבָב ▸ DAY 194

וַיָּקָם דָּוִיד הַמֶּלֶךְ עַל־רַגְלָיו וַיֹּאמֶר שְׁמָעוּנִי אַחַי וְעַמִּי אֲנִי עִם־לְבָבִי
לִבְנוֹת בֵּית מְנוּחָה לַאֲרוֹן בְּרִית־יְהוָה וְלַהֲדֹם רַגְלֵי אֱלֹהֵינוּ

| Then King David rose | וַיָּקָם דָּוִיד הַמֶּלֶךְ |
|---|---|
| to his **feet** | עַל־**רַגְלָיו** |
| and said | וַיֹּאמֶר |
| Hear me | שְׁמָעוּנִי |
| my brothers and my people | אַחַי וְעַמִּי |
| I myself had in **mind** | אֲנִי עִם־**לְבָבִי** |
| to build a temple as a resting place | לִבְנוֹת בֵּית מְנוּחָה |
| for the ark of the Lᴏʀᴅ's **covenant** | לַאֲרוֹן **בְּרִית**־יְהוָה |
| and for the footstool of our God | וְלַהֲדֹם **רַגְלֵי** אֱלֹהֵינוּ |

And Moses swore on that day, saying, "Surely the land on which your **foot** (רַגְלְךָ) has trodden shall be an inheritance for you and your children forever [lit., to **eternity** (עוֹלָם)], because you have wholeheartedly followed [lit., **gone fully** (מִלֵּאתָ) after] the LORD my God." (NRSV)

| מלא | to be full, fill; fulfill | 251x |
|---|---|---|
| *mālēʾ* | | S4390 |

עוֹלָם   ➤   DAY 119         רֶגֶל   ➤   DAY 196

וַיִּשָּׁבַע מֹשֶׁה בַּיּוֹם הַהוּא לֵאמֹר אִם־לֹא הָאָרֶץ אֲשֶׁר דָּרְכָה **רַגְלְךָ**
בָּהּ לְךָ תִהְיֶה לְנַחֲלָה וּלְבָנֶיךָ עַד־**עוֹלָם** כִּי **מִלֵּאתָ** אַחֲרֵי יְהוָה אֱלֹהָי:

| | |
|---|---|
| And Moses swore . . . , saying | וַיִּשָּׁבַע מֹשֶׁה . . . לֵאמֹר |
| on that day | בַּיּוֹם הַהוּא |
| Surely | אִם־לֹא |
| the land on which | הָאָרֶץ אֲשֶׁר . . . בָּהּ |
| your **foot** has trodden | דָּרְכָה **רַגְלְךָ** |
| shall be an inheritance | תִהְיֶה לְנַחֲלָה |
| for you and your children | לְךָ . . . וּלְבָנֶיךָ |
| forever [lit., to **eternity**] | עַד־**עוֹלָם** |
| because you have wholeheartedly followed [lit., **gone fully** after] | כִּי **מִלֵּאתָ** אַחֲרֵי |
| the LORD my God | יְהוָה אֱלֹהָי |

And the foundations [lit., **pivots (אַמּוֹת)**] of the thresholds shook at the **voice (קוֹל)** of him who called, and the house **was filled (יִמָּלֵא)** with smoke. (ESV)

| אַמָּה | cubit, (door) pivot | 250x |
|---|---|---|
| ʾammâ | | S520 |

קוֹל   ➤   DAY 103          מלא   ➤   DAY 197

וַיָּנֻעוּ אַמּוֹת הַסִּפִּים מִקּוֹל הַקּוֹרֵא וְהַבַּיִת יִמָּלֵא עָשָׁן׃

| And . . . shook | וַיָּנֻעוּ |
| the foundations [lit., **pivots**] of | אַמּוֹת |
| the thresholds | הַסִּפִּים |
| at the **voice** of | מִקּוֹל |
| him who called | הַקּוֹרֵא |
| and the house | וְהַבַּיִת |
| **was filled** | יִמָּלֵא |
| with smoke | עָשָׁן |

He loves righteousness and **justice** (מִשְׁפָּט); the earth **is full of** (מָלְאָה) the Lord's **lovingkindness** (חֶסֶד). (MLB)

| חֶסֶד | faithfulness, kindness, mercy | 249x |
| --- | --- | --- |
| *ḥesed* | | S2617 |

מִשְׁפָּט ➤ DAY 123          מלא ➤ DAY 197

אֹהֵב צְדָקָה וּמִשְׁפָּט חֶסֶד יְהוָה מָלְאָה הָאָרֶץ:

| He loves | אֹהֵב |
| --- | --- |
| righteousness | צְדָקָה |
| and **justice** | וּמִשְׁפָּט |
| the earth | הָאָרֶץ |
| **is full of** | מָלְאָה |
| the Lord's **lovingkindness** | חֶסֶד יְהוָה |

But [he] overthrew **Pharaoh** (פַּרְעֹה) and his **army** (חֵילוֹ) in the
Red Sea, for his **steadfast love** (חַסְדּוֹ) endures forever. (NRSV)

| חַיִל | valor, strength, virtue, army, wealth | 245x |
|---|---|---|
| *ḥayil* | | S2428 |

פַּרְעֹה　　➤　DAY 185　　　　　חֶסֶד　　➤　DAY 199

וַיְנַעֵר פַּרְעֹה וְחֵילוֹ בְיַם־סוּף כִּי לְעוֹלָם חַסְדּוֹ:

| But [he] overthrew | וַיְנַעֵר |
|---|---|
| **Pharaoh** | פַּרְעֹה |
| and his **army** | וְחֵילוֹ |
| in the Red Sea | בְיַם־סוּף |
| for | כִּי |
| his **steadfast love** | חַסְדּוֹ |
| endures forever | לְעוֹלָם |

Your **wealth** (חֵילְךָ) and your treasures will I give for spoil, without price, for all your **sins** (חַטֹּאותֶיךָ), throughout all your **territory** (גְּבוּלֶיךָ). (MLB)

| גְּבוּל | boundary, territory | 241x |
|---|---|---|
| *gĕvûl* | | S1366 |

חַטָּאת ▷ DAY 168　　　　חַיִל ▷ DAY 200

חֵילְךָ וְאוֹצְרוֹתֶיךָ לָבַז אֶתֵּן לֹא בִמְחִיר וּבְכָל־חַטֹּאותֶיךָ
וּבְכָל־גְּבוּלֶיךָ:

| Your **wealth** | חֵילְךָ |
|---|---|
| and your treasures | וְאוֹצְרוֹתֶיךָ |
| will I give | אֶתֵּן |
| for spoil | לָבַז |
| without price | לֹא בִמְחִיר |
| for all your **sins** | וּבְכָל־חַטֹּאותֶיךָ |
| throughout all your **territory** | וּבְכָל־גְּבוּלֶיךָ |

Then Absalom commanded his **servants** (נְעָרָיו), "Mark when Amnon's heart is merry with wine, and when I say to you, 'Strike Amnon,' then kill him. Do not **fear** (תִּירָאוּ); have I not commanded you? Be courageous and be valiant [lit., sons of **valor** (חָיִל)]." (ESV)

| נַעַר | boy, servant, young man | | 240x |
|---|---|---|---|
| *naʿar* | | | S5288 |

יָרֵא ➤ DAY 160          חַיִל ➤ DAY 200

וַיְצַו אַבְשָׁלוֹם אֶת־נְעָרָיו לֵאמֹר רְאוּ נָא כְּטוֹב לֵב־אַמְנוֹן בַּיַּיִן וְאָמַרְתִּי אֲלֵיכֶם הַכּוּ אֶת־אַמְנוֹן וַהֲמִתֶּם אֹתוֹ אַל־תִּירָאוּ הֲלוֹא כִּי אָנֹכִי צִוִּיתִי אֶתְכֶם חִזְקוּ וִהְיוּ לִבְנֵי־חָיִל:

| Then Absalom commanded his **servants** | וַיְצַו אַבְשָׁלוֹם אֶת־נְעָרָיו לֵאמֹר |
|---|---|
| Mark | רְאוּ נָא |
| when Amnon's heart is merry with wine | כְּטוֹב לֵב־אַמְנוֹן בַּיַּיִן |
| and when I say to you | וְאָמַרְתִּי אֲלֵיכֶם |
| Strike Amnon | הַכּוּ אֶת־אַמְנוֹן |
| then kill him | וַהֲמִתֶּם אֹתוֹ |
| Do not **fear** | אַל־תִּירָאוּ |
| have I not commanded you? | הֲלוֹא כִּי אָנֹכִי צִוִּיתִי אֶתְכֶם |
| Be courageous | חִזְקוּ |
| and be valiant [lit., sons of **valor**] | וִהְיוּ לִבְנֵי־חָיִל |

No more shall there be in it an infant that lives but a few days,
or an old person who does not live out a lifetime [lit., **complete
(יְמַלֵּא)** his days]; for one who dies at a hundred years will be
considered a **youth (נַעַר)**, and one who **falls short (חוֹטֵא)** of a
hundred will be considered accursed. (NRSV)

| חטא | to sin, miss the mark | 239x |
|---|---|---|
| ḥāṭāʾ | | S2398 |

מלא  ▷  DAY 197          נַעַר  ▷  DAY 202

לֹא־יִהְיֶה מִשָּׁם עוֹד עוּל יָמִים וְזָקֵן אֲשֶׁר לֹא־יְמַלֵּא אֶת־יָמָיו כִּי
הַנַּעַר בֶּן־מֵאָה שָׁנָה יָמוּת וְהַחוֹטֵא בֶּן־מֵאָה שָׁנָה יְקֻלָּל:

| No more shall there be in it | לֹא־יִהְיֶה מִשָּׁם עוֹד |
|---|---|
| an infant that lives but a few days | עוּל יָמִים |
| or an old person who | וְזָקֵן אֲשֶׁר |
| does not live out a lifetime [lit., **complete** his days] | לֹא־יְמַלֵּא אֶת־יָמָיו |
| for one who dies | כִּי . . . יָמוּת |
| at a hundred years | בֶּן־מֵאָה שָׁנָה |
| will be considered a **youth** | הַנַּעַר |
| and one who **falls short** of | וְהַחוֹטֵא |
| a hundred | בֶּן־מֵאָה שָׁנָה |
| will be considered accursed | יְקֻלָּל |

But they fell on their faces and said, "O **God** (אֵל), God of the spirits of all **flesh** (בָּשָׂר), when one man **sins** (יֶחֱטָא), will You be angry with the entire congregation?" (NASB)

| אֵל | God, god | 237x |
|---|---|---|
| ʾēl | | S410 |

| בָּשָׂר | ➤ | DAY 190 | | חטא | ➤ | DAY 203 |
|---|---|---|---|---|---|---|

וַיִּפְּלוּ עַל־פְּנֵיהֶם וַיֹּאמְרוּ אֵל אֱלֹהֵי הָרוּחֹת לְכָל־בָּשָׂר הָאִישׁ אֶחָד
יֶחֱטָא וְעַל כָּל־הָעֵדָה תִּקְצֹף׃

| But they fell | וַיִּפְּלוּ |
|---|---|
| on their faces | עַל־פְּנֵיהֶם |
| and said | וַיֹּאמְרוּ |
| O **God** | אֵל |
| God of the spirits | אֱלֹהֵי הָרוּחֹת |
| of all **flesh** | לְכָל־בָּשָׂר |
| when one man **sins** | הָאִישׁ אֶחָד יֶחֱטָא |
| will You be angry | תִּקְצֹף |
| with the entire congregation? | וְעַל כָּל־הָעֵדָה |

For to us a child **is born** (יֻלַּד), to us a son is given, and the government will be on his shoulders. And he will be called Wonderful Counselor, Mighty **God** (אֵל), Everlasting Father, Prince of **Peace** (שָׁלוֹם). (NIV)

| שָׁלוֹם | peace, welfare | 237x |
|---|---|---|
| *šālôm* | | S7965 |

ילד ➤ DAY 109　　　　אֵל ➤ DAY 204

כִּי־יֶלֶד יֻלַּד־לָנוּ בֵּן נִתַּן־לָנוּ וַתְּהִי הַמִּשְׂרָה עַל־שִׁכְמוֹ וַיִּקְרָא שְׁמוֹ פֶּלֶא יוֹעֵץ אֵל גִּבּוֹר אֲבִיעַד שַׂר־שָׁלוֹם:

| For to us | כִּי־ . . . לָנוּ |
|---|---|
| a child **is born** | יֶלֶד יֻלַּד־ |
| to us a son is given | בֵּן נִתַּן־לָנוּ |
| and the government will be | וַתְּהִי הַמִּשְׂרָה |
| on his shoulders | עַל־שִׁכְמוֹ |
| And he will be called | וַיִּקְרָא שְׁמוֹ |
| Wonderful Counselor | פֶּלֶא יוֹעֵץ |
| Mighty **God** | אֵל גִּבּוֹר |
| Everlasting Father | אֲבִיעַד |
| Prince of **Peace** | שַׂר־שָׁלוֹם |

O Lord, you will ordain **peace** (שָׁלוֹם) for us, for **indeed** (גַּם), all
that we have done [lit., our **deeds** (מַעֲשֵׂינוּ)], you have done for
us. (NRSV)

| מַעֲשֶׂה | deed, action, work, product | 235x |
| --- | --- | --- |
| ma‘ăśê | | S4639 |

גַּם ➤ DAY 66　　　　　שָׁלוֹם ➤ DAY 205

יְהוָה תִּשְׁפֹּת שָׁלוֹם לָנוּ כִּי גַּם כָּל־מַעֲשֵׂינוּ פָּעַלְתָּ לָּנוּ׃

| O Lord | יְהוָה |
| --- | --- |
| you will ordain | תִּשְׁפֹּת |
| **peace** | שָׁלוֹם |
| for us | לָנוּ |
| for **indeed** | כִּי גַּם |
| all that we have done [lit., our **deeds**] | כָּל־מַעֲשֵׂינוּ |
| you have done | פָּעַלְתָּ |
| for us | לָּנוּ |

And after all that has come upon us for our evil **deeds** (מַעֲשֵׂינוּ)
and for our great guilt, seeing that you, our God, have punished
us less than our **iniquities** (עֲוֺנֵנוּ) deserved and have given us
such a remnant as **this** (זֹאת), . . . (ESV)

| עָוֺן | iniquity, guilt, punishment | 233x |
|---|---|---|
| ʿāvōn | | S5771 |

זֹאת ▷ DAY 86　　　מַעֲשֶׂה ▷ DAY 206

וְאַחֲרֵי כָּל־הַבָּא עָלֵינוּ בְּמַעֲשֵׂינוּ הָרָעִים וּבְאַשְׁמָתֵנוּ הַגְּדֹלָה כִּי
אַתָּה אֱלֹהֵינוּ חָשַׂכְתָּ לְמַטָּה מֵעֲוֺנֵנוּ וְנָתַתָּה לָּנוּ פְּלֵיטָה כָּזֹאת:

| | |
|---|---|
| And after all | וְאַחֲרֵי כָּל־ |
| that has come upon us | הַבָּא עָלֵינוּ |
| for our evil **deeds** | בְּמַעֲשֵׂינוּ הָרָעִים |
| and for our great guilt | וּבְאַשְׁמָתֵנוּ הַגְּדֹלָה |
| seeing that you, our God | כִּי אַתָּה אֱלֹהֵינוּ |
| have punished us | חָשַׂכְתָּ |
| less | לְמַטָּה |
| than our **iniquities** deserved | מֵעֲוֺנֵנוּ |
| and have given us | וְנָתַתָּה לָּנוּ |
| such . . . as **this** | כָּזֹאת |
| a remnant | פְּלֵיטָה |

Prepare slaughter for his sons because of the **guilt** (עָוֹן) of their fathers, lest they rise and **possess** (וְיָרְשׁוּ) the earth, and **fill** (וּמָלְאוּ) the face of the world with cities. (ESV)

| | | |
|---|---|---|
| **יָרַשׁ** | to (dis)possess | 232x |
| *yāraš* | | S3423 |

**מלא** ➤ DAY 197     **עָוֹן** ➤ DAY 207

הָכִינוּ לְבָנָיו מַטְבֵּחַ בַּעֲוֹן אֲבוֹתָם בַּל־יָקֻמוּ וְיָרְשׁוּ אָרֶץ וּמָלְאוּ פְנֵי־תֵבֵל עָרִים:

| | |
|---|---|
| Prepare slaughter | הָכִינוּ . . . מַטְבֵּחַ |
| for his sons | לְבָנָיו |
| because of the **guilt** of | בַּעֲוֹן |
| their fathers | אֲבוֹתָם |
| lest they rise | בַּל־יָקֻמוּ |
| and **possess** the earth | וְיָרְשׁוּ אָרֶץ |
| and **fill** | וּמָלְאוּ |
| the face of the world | פְנֵי־תֵבֵל |
| with cities | עָרִים |

Mordecai the Jew was second only to King Ahasuerus. He was **famous** (גָּדוֹל) among the Jews and esteemed by many of his relatives. He continued to pursue prosperity for his people and to speak for the **well-being** (שָׁלוֹם) of all his **descendants** (זַרְעוֹ). (CSB)

| | | |
|---|---|---|
| זֶרַע | seed, descendant(s) | 229x |
| *zeraʿ* | | S2233 |

גָּדוֹל    ➤    DAY 99        שָׁלוֹם    ➤    DAY 205

כִּי מָרְדֳּכַי הַיְּהוּדִי מִשְׁנֶה לַמֶּלֶךְ אֲחַשְׁוֵרוֹשׁ וְגָדוֹל לַיְּהוּדִים וְרָצוּי
לְרֹב אֶחָיו דֹּרֵשׁ טוֹב לְעַמּוֹ וְדֹבֵר שָׁלוֹם לְכָל־זַרְעוֹ:

| | |
|---|---|
| Mordecai the Jew | כִּי מָרְדֳּכַי הַיְּהוּדִי |
| was second only | מִשְׁנֶה |
| to King Ahasuerus | לַמֶּלֶךְ אֲחַשְׁוֵרוֹשׁ |
| He was **famous** among the Jews | וְגָדוֹל לַיְּהוּדִים |
| and highly esteemed | וְרָצוּי |
| by many of his relatives | לְרֹב אֶחָיו |
| He continued to pursue prosperity | דֹּרֵשׁ טוֹב |
| for his people | לְעַמּוֹ |
| and to speak for the **well-being** | וְדֹבֵר שָׁלוֹם |
| of all his **descendants** | לְכָל־זַרְעוֹ |

Indeed I will greatly bless you, and **I will greatly multiply** (הַרְבָּה אַרְבֶּה) your **seed** (זַרְעֲךָ) as the stars of the heavens and as the sand which is on the seashore; and your **seed** (זַרְעֲךָ) **shall possess** (יִרַשׁ) the gate of their enemies. (NASB)

| רבה | to be many, great; increase | 229x |
|-----|------------------------------|------|
| *rāvâ* | | S7235 |

ירשׁ  ▷  DAY 208          זֶרַע  ▷  DAY 209

כִּי־בָרֵךְ אֲבָרֶכְךָ וְהַרְבָּה אַרְבֶּה אֶת־זַרְעֲךָ כְּכוֹכְבֵי הַשָּׁמַיִם וְכַחוֹל אֲשֶׁר עַל־שְׂפַת הַיָּם וְיִרַשׁ זַרְעֲךָ אֵת שַׁעַר אֹיְבָיו:

| Indeed | כִּי־ |
|--------|-------|
| I will greatly bless you | בָרֵךְ אֲבָרֶכְךָ |
| and **I will greatly multiply** | וְהַרְבָּה אַרְבֶּה |
| your **seed** | אֶת־זַרְעֲךָ |
| as the stars of the heavens | כְּכוֹכְבֵי הַשָּׁמַיִם |
| and as the sand which | וְכַחוֹל אֲשֶׁר |
| is on the seashore | עַל־שְׂפַת הַיָּם |
| and your **seed shall possess** | וְיִרַשׁ זַרְעֲךָ |
| the gate of their enemies | אֵת שַׁעַר אֹיְבָיו |

That **night** (לַיְלָה) the LORD appeared to him and said, "I am the
God of your father Abraham. . . . I will bless you and **will increase
the number of** (וְהִרְבֵּיתִי) your **descendants** (זַרְעֶךָ) for the sake of
my servant Abraham." (NIV)

לַיְלָה          night                                           227x
*laylâ*                                                         S3915

זֶרַע     ➤    DAY 209          רבה     ➤    DAY 210


וַיֵּרָא אֵלָיו יְהוָה בַּלַּיְלָה הַהוּא וַיֹּאמֶר אָנֹכִי אֱלֹהֵי אַבְרָהָם אָבִיךָ
בַּעֲבוּר אַבְרָהָם עַבְדִּי: . . . וּבֵרַכְתִּיךָ וְהִרְבֵּיתִי אֶת־זַרְעֲךָ

| | |
|---|---|
| That **night** | בַּלַּיְלָה הַהוּא |
| the LORD appeared to him | וַיֵּרָא אֵלָיו יְהוָה |
| and said | וַיֹּאמֶר |
| I am the God of | אָנֹכִי אֱלֹהֵי |
| your father Abraham. . . . | אַבְרָהָם אָבִיךָ . . . |
| I will bless you | וּבֵרַכְתִּיךָ |
| and **will increase the number of** your **descendants** | וְהִרְבֵּיתִי אֶת־זַרְעֲךָ |
| for the sake of | בַּעֲבוּר |
| my servant Abraham | אַבְרָהָם עַבְדִּי |

My soul yearns for you in the **night** (לַיְלָה), my spirit within [lit., in the **midst** (קִרְבִּי) of] me earnestly seeks you. For when your **judgments** (מִשְׁפָּטֶיךָ) are in the earth, the inhabitants of the world learn righteousness. (NRSV)

| קֶרֶב | inward part, center, midst | 227x |
|---|---|---|
| *qerev* | | S7130 |

מִשְׁפָּט    ⊳    DAY 123      לַיְלָה    ⊳    DAY 211

נַפְשִׁי אִוִּיתִיךָ בַּלַּיְלָה אַף־רוּחִי בְקִרְבִּי אֲשַׁחֲרֶךָּ כִּי כַּאֲשֶׁר מִשְׁפָּטֶיךָ
לָאָרֶץ צֶדֶק לָמְדוּ יֹשְׁבֵי תֵבֵל:

| | |
|---|---|
| My soul | נַפְשִׁי |
| yearns for you | אִוִּיתִיךָ |
| in the **night** | בַּלַּיְלָה |
| my spirit within [lit., in the **midst** of] me | אַף־רוּחִי בְקִרְבִּי |
| earnestly seeks you | אֲשַׁחֲרֶךָּ |
| For when | כִּי כַּאֲשֶׁר |
| your **judgments** | מִשְׁפָּטֶיךָ |
| are in the earth | לָאָרֶץ |
| the inhabitants of the world | יֹשְׁבֵי תֵבֵל |
| learn | לָמְדוּ |
| righteousness | צֶדֶק |

On my bed by **night** (לֵילוֹת) **I sought** (בִּקַּשְׁתִּי) him whom my soul loves; **I sought** (בִּקַּשְׁתִּיו) him, but **found** (מְצָאתִיו) him not. (ESV)

| בקש | to seek, inquire, request | 225x |
|---|---|---|
| *bāqaš* | | S1245 |

**מצא**  ➤  DAY 117          **לַיְלָה**  ➤  DAY 211

עַל־מִשְׁכָּבִי בַּלֵּילוֹת בִּקַּשְׁתִּי אֵת שֶׁאָהֲבָה נַפְשִׁי בִּקַּשְׁתִּיו וְלֹא מְצָאתִיו:

| On my bed | עַל־מִשְׁכָּבִי |
|---|---|
| by **night** | בַּלֵּילוֹת |
| **I sought** | בִּקַּשְׁתִּי |
| him whom my soul loves | אֵת שֶׁאָהֲבָה נַפְשִׁי |
| **I sought** him | בִּקַּשְׁתִּיו |
| but **found** him not | וְלֹא מְצָאתִיו |

Yet **she increased** (וַתַּרְבֶּה) her whoring, **remembering** (לִזְכֹּר)
the days of her youth, when she played the whore in the land of
**Egypt** (מִצְרָיִם). (ESV)

| זכר | to remember, mention | 225x |
|---|---|---|
| *zāḵar* | | S2142 |

מִצְרַיִם   ➤   DAY 80      רבה   ➤   DAY 210

וַתַּרְבֶּה אֶת־תַּזְנוּתֶיהָ לִזְכֹּר אֶת־יְמֵי נְעוּרֶיהָ אֲשֶׁר זָנְתָה בְּאֶרֶץ
מִצְרָיִם:

| | |
|---|---|
| Yet **she increased** | וַתַּרְבֶּה |
| her whoring | אֶת־תַּזְנוּתֶיהָ |
| **remembering** | לִזְכֹּר |
| the days of her youth | אֶת־יְמֵי נְעוּרֶיהָ |
| when | אֲשֶׁר |
| she played the whore | זָנְתָה |
| in the land of **Egypt** | בְּאֶרֶץ מִצְרָיִם |

Now when the plot **was investigated** (וַיְבֻקַּשׁ) and found to be so, they were both hanged on a **gallows** (עֵץ); and **it was written** (וַיִּכָּתֵב) in the Book of the Chronicles in the king's presence. (NASB)

| כתב | to write | 225x |
|---|---|---|
| *kātav* | | S3789 |

עֵץ  ➤  DAY 155          בקשׁ  ➤  DAY 213

וַיְבֻקַּשׁ הַדָּבָר וַיִּמָּצֵא וַיִּתָּלוּ שְׁנֵיהֶם עַל־עֵץ וַיִּכָּתֵב בְּסֵפֶר דִּבְרֵי הַיָּמִים לִפְנֵי הַמֶּלֶךְ:

| Now when the plot **was investigated** | וַיְבֻקַּשׁ הַדָּבָר |
|---|---|
| and found to be so | וַיִּמָּצֵא |
| they were both hanged | וַיִּתָּלוּ שְׁנֵיהֶם |
| on a **gallows** | עַל־עֵץ |
| and **it was written** | וַיִּכָּתֵב |
| in the Book of the Chronicles | בְּסֵפֶר דִּבְרֵי הַיָּמִים |
| in the king's presence | לִפְנֵי הַמֶּלֶךְ |

Therefore when the LORD your God has given you rest from all your enemies **around** (סָבִיב) you, in the land that the LORD your God is giving you for an **inheritance** (נַחֲלָה) to **possess** (רִשְׁתָּהּ), . . . (ESV)

| נַחֲלָה | inheritance | 223x |
|---|---|---|
| naḥălâ | | S5159 |

סָבִיב   ➤   DAY 152      יָרַשׁ   ➤   DAY 208

וְהָיָה בְּהָנִיחַ יְהוָה אֱלֹהֶיךָ לְךָ מִכָּל־אֹיְבֶיךָ מִסָּבִיב בָּאָרֶץ אֲשֶׁר יְהוָה־אֱלֹהֶיךָ נֹתֵן לְךָ נַחֲלָה לְרִשְׁתָּהּ

| | |
|---|---|
| Therefore when the LORD your God has given you rest | וְהָיָה בְּהָנִיחַ יְהוָה אֱלֹהֶיךָ לְךָ |
| from all your enemies | מִכָּל־אֹיְבֶיךָ |
| **around** you | מִסָּבִיב |
| in the land that | בָּאָרֶץ אֲשֶׁר |
| the LORD your God | יְהוָה־אֱלֹהֶיךָ |
| is giving you | נֹתֵן לְךָ |
| for an **inheritance** to **possess** | נַחֲלָה לְרִשְׁתָּהּ |

To the sons of Levi, behold, I have given all the tithe in Israel for an **inheritance** (נַחֲלָה), in return for their service which they **perform** (עֹבְדִים), the service of the tent of **meeting** (מוֹעֵד). (NASB)

| מוֹעֵד | appointed time, feast, meeting, assembly | 223x |
|---|---|---|
| mōʻēd | | S4150 |

עֹבֵד   ➤   DAY 175       נַחֲלָה   ➤   DAY 216

וְלִבְנֵי לֵוִי הִנֵּה נָתַתִּי כָּל־מַעֲשֵׂר בְּיִשְׂרָאֵל לְנַחֲלָה חֵלֶף עֲבֹדָתָם אֲשֶׁר־הֵם עֹבְדִים אֶת־עֲבֹדַת אֹהֶל מוֹעֵד:

| To the sons of Levi | וְלִבְנֵי לֵוִי |
|---|---|
| behold, I have given | הִנֵּה נָתַתִּי |
| all the tithe | כָּל־מַעֲשֵׂר |
| in Israel | בְּיִשְׂרָאֵל |
| for an **inheritance** | לְנַחֲלָה |
| in return for | חֵלֶף |
| their service | עֲבֹדָתָם |
| which they **perform** | אֲשֶׁר־הֵם עֹבְדִים |
| the service of | אֶת־עֲבֹדַת |
| the tent of **meeting** | אֹהֶל מוֹעֵד |

The Lord said to Moses, "Come up to me on the mountain, and wait there; and I will give you the tablets of **stone** (אֶבֶן), with the **law** (תּוֹרָה) and the commandment, which **I have written** (כָּתַבְתִּי) for their instruction." (NRSV)

| תּוֹרָה | law, teaching, instruction | 223x |
|---|---|---|
| *tôrâ* | | S8451 |

אֶבֶן ➤ DAY 187          כתב ➤ DAY 215

וַיֹּ֨אמֶר יְהוָ֜ה אֶל־מֹשֶׁ֗ה עֲלֵ֥ה אֵלַ֛י הָהָ֖רָה וֶהְיֵה־שָׁ֑ם וְאֶתְּנָ֨ה לְךָ֜ אֶת־
לֻחֹ֣ת הָאֶ֗בֶן וְהַתּוֹרָה֙ וְהַמִּצְוָ֔ה אֲשֶׁ֥ר כָּתַ֖בְתִּי לְהוֹרֹתָֽם׃

| The Lord said | וַיֹּ֨אמֶר יְהוָ֜ה |
|---|---|
| to Moses | אֶל־מֹשֶׁ֗ה |
| Come up to me | עֲלֵ֥ה אֵלַ֛י |
| on the mountain | הָהָ֖רָה |
| and wait there | וֶהְיֵה־שָׁ֑ם |
| and I will give you | וְאֶתְּנָ֨ה לְךָ֜ |
| the tablets of **stone** | אֶת־לֻחֹ֣ת הָאֶ֗בֶן |
| with the **law** | וְהַתּוֹרָה֙ |
| and the commandment | וְהַמִּצְוָ֔ה |
| which **I have written** | אֲשֶׁ֥ר כָּתַ֖בְתִּי |
| for their instruction | לְהוֹרֹתָֽם |

And I will not cause the **feet** (רֶגֶל) of Israel to wander anymore out of the **land** (אֲדָמָה) that I gave to their fathers, if only they will be careful to do according to all that I have commanded them, and according to all the **Law** (תּוֹרָה) . . . (ESV)

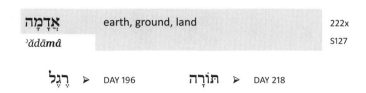

| | | |
|---|---|---|
| אֲדָמָה | earth, ground, land | 222x |
| ʾădāmâ | | S127 |

| רֶגֶל | ➤ DAY 196 | תּוֹרָה | ➤ DAY 218 |

וְלֹא אֹסִיף לְהָנִיד רֶגֶל יִשְׂרָאֵל מִן־הָאֲדָמָה אֲשֶׁר נָתַתִּי לַאֲבוֹתָם רַק
אִם־יִשְׁמְרוּ לַעֲשׂוֹת כְּכֹל אֲשֶׁר צִוִּיתִים וּלְכָל־הַתּוֹרָה

| And I will not . . . anymore | וְלֹא אֹסִיף |
|---|---|
| cause . . . to wander | לְהָנִיד |
| the **feet** of Israel | רֶגֶל יִשְׂרָאֵל |
| out of the **land** that | מִן־הָאֲדָמָה אֲשֶׁר |
| I gave to their fathers | נָתַתִּי לַאֲבוֹתָם |
| if only | רַק אִם־ |
| they will be careful to do | יִשְׁמְרוּ לַעֲשׂוֹת |
| according to all that | כְּכֹל אֲשֶׁר |
| I have commanded them | צִוִּיתִים |
| and according to all the **Law** | וּלְכָל־הַתּוֹרָה |

Honor your father and your **mother** (אִמֶּךָ), **that** (לְמַעַן) your days
may be long in the **land** (אֲדָמָה) that the LORD your God is giving
you. (ESV)

| | | | |
|---|---|---|---|
| אֵם | mother | | 220x |
| ʾēm | | | S517 |

לְמַעַן  ➤  DAY 188          אֲדָמָה  ➤  DAY 219

כַּבֵּד אֶת־אָבִיךָ וְאֶת־אִמֶּךָ לְמַעַן יַאֲרִכוּן יָמֶיךָ עַל הָאֲדָמָה אֲשֶׁר־
יְהוָה אֱלֹהֶיךָ נֹתֵן לָךְ:

| | |
|---|---|
| Honor | כַּבֵּד |
| your father | אֶת־אָבִיךָ |
| and your **mother** | וְאֶת־אִמֶּךָ |
| **that** your days | לְמַעַן . . . יָמֶיךָ |
| may be long | יַאֲרִכוּן |
| in the **land** | עַל הָאֲדָמָה |
| that the LORD your God | אֲשֶׁר־יְהוָה אֱלֹהֶיךָ |
| is giving you | נֹתֵן לָךְ |

He who practices deceit shall not stay in [the **midst (קֶרֶב)** of] my home; he who habitually tells lies **shall** not **be secure (יִכּוֹן)** in my **sight (עֵינָי)**. (MLB)

| כוּן | to stand firm, establish, prepare, determine | 219x |
|---|---|---|
| kûn | | S3559 |

עַיִן ➤ DAY 51　　　　קֶרֶב ➤ DAY 212

לֹא־יֵשֵׁב בְּקֶרֶב בֵּיתִי עֹשֵׂה רְמִיָּה דֹּבֵר שְׁקָרִים לֹא־יִכּוֹן לְנֶגֶד עֵינָי:

| He who practices | עֹשֵׂה |
|---|---|
| deceit | רְמִיָּה |
| shall not stay | לֹא־יֵשֵׁב |
| in [the **midst** of] my home | בְּקֶרֶב בֵּיתִי |
| he who habitually tells | דֹּבֵר |
| lies | שְׁקָרִים |
| **shall** not **be secure** | לֹא־יִכּוֹן |
| in my **sight** | לְנֶגֶד עֵינָי |

So **Joshua** (יְהוֹשֻׁעַ) called the twelve [lit., two-(and-)**ten** (עָשָׂר)] men whom **he had appointed** (הֵכִין) from the sons of Israel, one man from each tribe. (NASB)

| | | |
|---|---|---|
| **יְהוֹשֻׁעַ** | Joshua | 218x |
| yĕhôšûaʿ | | S3091 |

עָשָׂר  ➤  DAY 153         כון  ➤  DAY 221

וַיִּקְרָא יְהוֹשֻׁעַ אֶל־שְׁנֵים הֶעָשָׂר אִישׁ אֲשֶׁר הֵכִין מִבְּנֵי יִשְׂרָאֵל אִישׁ־
אֶחָד אִישׁ־אֶחָד מִשָּׁבֶט:

| | |
|---|---|
| So **Joshua** called | וַיִּקְרָא יְהוֹשֻׁעַ |
| the twelve [lit., two-(and-)**ten**] | אֶל־שְׁנֵים הֶעָשָׂר |
| men | אִישׁ |
| whom **he had appointed** | אֲשֶׁר הֵכִין |
| from the sons of Israel | מִבְּנֵי יִשְׂרָאֵל |
| one man from each tribe | אִישׁ־אֶחָד אִישׁ־אֶחָד מִשָּׁבֶט |

Now **Joshua** (וִיהוֹשֻׁעַ) was dressed in filthy **clothes** (בְּגָדִים) as **he stood** (עֹמֵד) before the angel. (NIV)

| בֶּגֶד | garment, clothing | 217x |
|---|---|---|
| *beged* | | S899 |

עמד    ➢    DAY 100       יְהוֹשֻׁעַ    ➢    DAY 222

וִיהוֹשֻׁעַ הָיָה לָבֻשׁ בְּגָדִים צוֹאִים וְעֹמֵד לִפְנֵי הַמַּלְאָךְ:

| Now **Joshua** | וִיהוֹשֻׁעַ |
|---|---|
| was dressed | הָיָה לָבֻשׁ |
| in filthy **clothes** | בְּגָדִים צוֹאִים |
| as **he stood** | וְעֹמֵד |
| before the angel | לִפְנֵי הַמַּלְאָךְ |

So he went and **got** (וַיִּקַּח) them and brought them to his **mother** (אִמּוֹ), and she [lit., his **mother** (אִמּוֹ)] prepared some tasty food, just the way his father **liked** (אָהֵב) it. (NIV)

| אהב | to love | 217x |
|---|---|---|
| ʾāhav | | S157 |

לקח ➤ DAY 49      אֵם ➤ DAY 220

וַיֵּלֶךְ וַיִּקַּח וַיָּבֵא לְאִמּוֹ וַתַּעַשׂ אִמּוֹ מַטְעַמִּים כַּאֲשֶׁר אָהֵב אָבִיו:

| So he went | וַיֵּלֶךְ |
|---|---|
| and **got** them | וַיִּקַּח |
| and brought them | וַיָּבֵא |
| to his **mother** | לְאִמּוֹ |
| and she [lit., his **mother**] prepared | וַתַּעַשׂ אִמּוֹ |
| some tasty food | מַטְעַמִּים |
| just the way | כַּאֲשֶׁר |
| his father **liked** it | אָהֵב אָבִיו |

They were there with David for **three** (שְׁלוֹשָׁה) days, eating and **drinking** (שׁוֹתִים), for their kindred **had provided** (הֵכִינוּ) for them. (NRSV)

| שׁתה שָׁתָה | to drink | 217x |
|---|---|---|
| šātâ | | S8354 |

שָׁלֹשׁ ➤ DAY 85     כּוּן ➤ DAY 221

וַיִּהְיוּ־שָׁם עִם־דָּוִיד יָמִים שְׁלוֹשָׁה אֹכְלִים וְשׁוֹתִים כִּי־הֵכִינוּ לָהֶם אֲחֵיהֶם:

| They were there | וַיִּהְיוּ־שָׁם |
|---|---|
| with David | עִם־דָּוִיד |
| for **three** days | יָמִים שְׁלוֹשָׁה |
| eating | אֹכְלִים |
| and **drinking** | וְשׁוֹתִים |
| for their kindred | כִּי־ . . . אֲחֵיהֶם |
| **had provided** for them | הֵכִינוּ לָהֶם |

On pledged **garments** (בְּגָדִים) **they stretch out** (יַטּוּ) beside every altar; wine bought with fines **they drink** (יִשְׁתּוּ) in the house of their god. (MLB)

| | | |
|---|---|---|
| נטה | to stretch out, bend, turn | 216x |
| nāṭâ | | S5186 |

בֶּגֶד ➤ DAY 223          שׁתה ➤ DAY 225

וְעַל־בְּגָדִים חֲבֻלִים יַטּוּ אֵצֶל כָּל־מִזְבֵּחַ וְיֵין עֲנוּשִׁים יִשְׁתּוּ בֵּית
אֱלֹהֵיהֶם:

| | |
|---|---|
| On | וְעַל־ |
| pledged **garments** | בְּגָדִים חֲבֻלִים |
| **they stretch out** | יַטּוּ |
| beside | אֵצֶל |
| every altar | כָּל־מִזְבֵּחַ |
| wine bought with fines | וְיֵין עֲנוּשִׁים |
| **they drink** | יִשְׁתּוּ |
| in the house of their god | בֵּית אֱלֹהֵיהֶם |

For we are slaves; yet in our bondage our God **has** not **forsaken** (עֲזָבָנוּ) us, but **has extended** (וַיֵּט) lovingkindness (חֶסֶד) to us in the sight of the kings of Persia, to give us reviving to raise up the house of our God. (NASB)

| עָזַב | to leave, forsake | 215x |
|---|---|---|
| *ʿāzav* | | S5800 |

חֶסֶד ➤ DAY 199    נטה ➤ DAY 226

כִּי־עֲבָדִים אֲנַחְנוּ וּבְעַבְדֻתֵנוּ לֹא עֲזָבָנוּ אֱלֹהֵינוּ וַיֵּט־עָלֵינוּ חֶסֶד לִפְנֵי מַלְכֵי פָרַס לָתֶת־לָנוּ מִחְיָה לְרוֹמֵם אֶת־בֵּית אֱלֹהֵינוּ

| For we are slaves | כִּי־עֲבָדִים אֲנַחְנוּ |
|---|---|
| yet in our bondage | וּבְעַבְדֻתֵנוּ |
| our God | אֱלֹהֵינוּ |
| **has** not **forsaken** us | לֹא עֲזָבָנוּ |
| but **has extended** **lovingkindness** to us | וַיֵּט־עָלֵינוּ חֶסֶד |
| in the sight of the kings of Persia | לִפְנֵי מַלְכֵי פָרַס |
| to give us | לָתֶת־לָנוּ |
| reviving | מִחְיָה |
| to raise up | לְרוֹמֵם |
| the house of our God | אֶת־בֵּית אֱלֹהֵינוּ |

Therefore they arose and fled in the twilight, and **left** (וַיַּעַזְבוּ)
their **tents** (אָהֳלֵיהֶם) and their horses and their donkeys, even the
**camp** (מַחֲנֶה) just as it was, and fled for their life. (NASB)

| מַחֲנֶה | camp, encampment, army | 215x |
|---|---|---|
| maḥănê | | S4264 |

אֹהֶל ◁ ➤ DAY 149          עזב ➤ DAY 227

וַיָּקוּמוּ וַיָּנוּסוּ בַנֶּשֶׁף וַיַּעַזְבוּ אֶת־אָהֳלֵיהֶם וְאֶת־סוּסֵיהֶם וְאֶת־
חֲמֹרֵיהֶם הַמַּחֲנֶה כַּאֲשֶׁר־הִיא וַיָּנֻסוּ אֶל־נַפְשָׁם׃

| Therefore they arose | וַיָּקוּמוּ |
|---|---|
| and fled | וַיָּנוּסוּ |
| in the twilight | בַנֶּשֶׁף |
| and **left** | וַיַּעַזְבוּ |
| their **tents** | אֶת־אָהֳלֵיהֶם |
| and their horses | וְאֶת־סוּסֵיהֶם |
| and their donkeys | וְאֶת־חֲמֹרֵיהֶם |
| even the **camp** | הַמַּחֲנֶה |
| just as it was | כַּאֲשֶׁר־הִיא |
| and fled | וַיָּנֻסוּ |
| for their life | אֶל־נַפְשָׁם |

I will no longer [lit., **will** not **continue** (אוֹסִיף) to] drive out before them any of the nations **Joshua** (יְהוֹשֻׁעַ) **left** (עָזַב) when he died. (NIV)

| | | |
|---|---|---|
| **יסף** | to add, continue | 214x |
| *yāsaf* | | S3254 |

| יְהוֹשֻׁעַ | ➤ DAY 222 | עָזַב | ➤ DAY 227 |
|---|---|---|---|

גַּם־אֲנִי לֹא אוֹסִיף לְהוֹרִישׁ אִישׁ מִפְּנֵיהֶם מִן־הַגּוֹיִם אֲשֶׁר־עָזַב יְהוֹשֻׁעַ וַיָּמֹת:

| I | גַּם־אֲנִי |
|---|---|
| will no longer [lit., **will** not **continue** to] drive out | לֹא אוֹסִיף לְהוֹרִישׁ |
| before them | מִפְּנֵיהֶם |
| any of the nations | אִישׁ . . . מִן־הַגּוֹיִם |
| **Joshua left** | אֲשֶׁר־עָזַב יְהוֹשֻׁעַ |
| when he died | וַיָּמֹת |

May God do so to the **enemies** (אֹיְבֵי) of David, and more also [lit., and thus **may he do further** (יֹסִיף)], if by **morning** (בֹּקֶר) I leave as much as one male [lit., one who urinates against a wall] of any who belong to him. (NASB)

| | | |
|---|---|---|
| **בֹּקֶר**     morning | | 214x |
| *bōqer* | | S1242 |

אֹיֵב   ▷   DAY 178          יסף   ▷   DAY 229

כֹּה־יַעֲשֶׂה אֱלֹהִים לְאֹיְבֵי דָוִד וְכֹה יֹסִיף אִם־אַשְׁאִיר מִכָּל־אֲשֶׁר־לֹו עַד־הַבֹּקֶר מַשְׁתִּין בְּקִיר:

| | |
|---|---|
| May God do so | כֹּה־יַעֲשֶׂה אֱלֹהִים |
| to the **enemies** of David | לְאֹיְבֵי דָוִד |
| and more also [lit., and thus **may he do further**] | וְכֹה יֹסִיף |
| if . . . I leave | אִם־אַשְׁאִיר |
| by **morning** | עַד־הַבֹּקֶר |
| as much as one male [lit., one who urinates against a wall] | מַשְׁתִּין בְּקִיר |
| of any who belong to him | מִכָּל־אֲשֶׁר־לֹו |

And **she called** (וַתִּקְרָא) his name **Joseph** (יוֹסֵף), saying, "**May** the
LORD **add** (יֹסֵף) to me another son!" (ESV)

| יוֹסֵף | Joseph | 213x |
|---|---|---|
| yôsēf | | S3130 |

קְרָא ➤ DAY 76     יסף ➤ DAY 229

וַתִּקְרָא אֶת־שְׁמוֹ יוֹסֵף לֵאמֹר יֹסֵף יְהוָה לִי בֵּן אַחֵר:

| And **she called** | וַתִּקְרָא |
|---|---|
| his name | אֶת־שְׁמוֹ |
| **Joseph** | יוֹסֵף |
| saying | לֵאמֹר |
| **May** the LORD **add** to me | יֹסֵף יְהוָה לִי |
| another son! | בֵּן אַחֵר |

Saul sent **messengers** (מַלְאָכִים) to David's house to keep watch over him, planning to kill him in the **morning** (בֹּקֶר). David's **wife** (אִשְׁתּוֹ) Michal told him, "If you do not save your life tonight, tomorrow you will be killed." (NRSV)

| מַלְאָךְ | angel, messenger | 213x |
|---|---|---|
| mal'āḵ | | S4397 |

| אִשָּׁה | ➤ | DAY 64 | | בֹּקֶר | ➤ | DAY 230 |
|---|---|---|---|---|---|---|

וַיִּשְׁלַח שָׁאוּל מַלְאָכִים אֶל־בֵּית דָּוִד לְשָׁמְרוֹ וְלַהֲמִיתוֹ בַּבֹּקֶר וַתַּגֵּד לְדָוִד מִיכַל אִשְׁתּוֹ לֵאמֹר אִם־אֵינְךָ מְמַלֵּט אֶת־נַפְשְׁךָ הַלַּיְלָה מָחָר אַתָּה מוּמָת:

| Saul sent **messengers** | וַיִּשְׁלַח שָׁאוּל מַלְאָכִים |
|---|---|
| to David's house | אֶל־בֵּית דָּוִד |
| to keep watch over him | לְשָׁמְרוֹ |
| planning to kill him | וְלַהֲמִיתוֹ |
| in the **morning** | בַּבֹּקֶר |
| David's **wife** Michal told him | וַתַּגֵּד לְדָוִד מִיכַל אִשְׁתּוֹ לֵאמֹר |
| If you do not save your life | אִם־אֵינְךָ מְמַלֵּט אֶת־נַפְשְׁךָ |
| tonight | הַלַּיְלָה |
| tomorrow | מָחָר |
| you will be killed | אַתָּה מוּמָת |

Because the Lord your God walks in the midst of your **camp**
(מַחֲנֶךָ), **to deliver** (הַצִּילְךָ) you and to give up your **enemies**
(אֹיְבֶיךָ) before you, therefore your **camp** (מַחֲנֶיךָ) must be holy.
(ESV)

| נצל | to deliver | 213x |
|---|---|---|
| *nāṣal* | | S5337 |

אֹיֵב ➤ DAY 178　　　　　מַחֲנֶה ➤ DAY 228

כִּי יְהוָה אֱלֹהֶיךָ מִתְהַלֵּךְ בְּקֶרֶב מַחֲנֶךָ לְהַצִּילְךָ וְלָתֵת אֹיְבֶיךָ לְפָנֶיךָ
וְהָיָה מַחֲנֶיךָ קָדוֹשׁ

| Because | כִּי |
|---|---|
| the Lord your God | יְהוָה אֱלֹהֶיךָ |
| walks | מִתְהַלֵּךְ |
| in the midst of your **camp** | בְּקֶרֶב מַחֲנֶךָ |
| **to deliver** you | לְהַצִּילְךָ |
| and to give up your **enemies** | וְלָתֵת אֹיְבֶיךָ |
| before you | לְפָנֶיךָ |
| therefore your **camp** must be holy | וְהָיָה מַחֲנֶיךָ קָדוֹשׁ |

So David sent **messengers** (מַלְאָכִים) and **took** (וַיִּקָּחֶהָ) her, and she came to him, and **he lay** (וַיִּשְׁכַּב) with her. (Now she had been purifying herself from her uncleanness.) Then she returned to her house. (ESV)

| שָׁכַב<br>*šāḵav* | to lie down | 213x<br>S7901 |
| --- | --- | --- |

לָקַח    ▷    DAY 49       מַלְאָךְ    ▷    DAY 232

וַיִּשְׁלַח דָּוִד מַלְאָכִים וַיִּקָּחֶהָ וַתָּבוֹא אֵלָיו וַיִּשְׁכַּב עִמָּהּ וְהִיא מִתְקַדֶּשֶׁת מִטֻּמְאָתָהּ וַתָּשָׁב אֶל־בֵּיתָהּ:

| So David sent | וַיִּשְׁלַח דָּוִד |
| --- | --- |
| **messengers** | מַלְאָכִים |
| and **took** her | וַיִּקָּחֶהָ |
| and she came to him | וַתָּבוֹא אֵלָיו |
| and **he lay** with her | וַיִּשְׁכַּב עִמָּהּ |
| Now she had been purifying herself | וְהִיא מִתְקַדֶּשֶׁת |
| from her uncleanness | מִטֻּמְאָתָהּ |
| Then she returned | וַתָּשָׁב |
| to her house | אֶל־בֵּיתָהּ |

So **they prepared** (וַיָּכִינוּ) the **present** (מִנְחָה) for **Joseph**'s (יוֹסֵף) coming at noon; for they had heard that they were to eat a meal there. (NASB)

| מִנְחָה | gift, offering | 211x |
|---|---|---|
| minḥâ | | S4503 |

כון ➤ DAY 221   יוֹסֵף ➤ DAY 231

וַיָּכִינוּ אֶת־הַמִּנְחָה עַד־בּוֹא יוֹסֵף בַּצׇּהֳרָיִם כִּי שָׁמְעוּ כִּי־שָׁם יֹאכְלוּ לָחֶם:

| So **they prepared** | וַיָּכִינוּ |
|---|---|
| the **present** | אֶת־הַמִּנְחָה |
| for **Joseph**'s coming | עַד־בּוֹא יוֹסֵף |
| at noon | בַּצׇּהֳרָיִם |
| for they had heard that | כִּי שָׁמְעוּ כִּי־ |
| they were to eat a meal | יֹאכְלוּ לָחֶם |
| there | שָׁם |

Though they fast, I will not hear their cry, and though they offer
**burnt offering** (עֹלָה) and **grain offering** (מִנְחָה), I will not accept
them. But I **will consume** (מְכַלֶּה) them by the sword, by famine,
and by pestilence. (ESV)

| כלה | to cease, perish; complete, destroy | 208x |
|---|---|---|
| kālâ | | S3615 |

עֹלָה  ➤  DAY 176          מִנְחָה  ➤  DAY 235

כִּי יָצֻמוּ אֵינֶנִּי שֹׁמֵעַ אֶל־רִנָּתָם וְכִי יַעֲלוּ עֹלָה וּמִנְחָה אֵינֶנִּי רֹצָם כִּי
בַּחֶרֶב וּבָרָעָב וּבַדֶּבֶר אָנֹכִי מְכַלֶּה אוֹתָם:

| Though they fast | כִּי יָצֻמוּ |
|---|---|
| I will not hear their cry | אֵינֶנִּי שֹׁמֵעַ אֶל־רִנָּתָם |
| and though they offer | וְכִי יַעֲלוּ |
| **burnt offering** | עֹלָה |
| and **grain offering** | וּמִנְחָה |
| I will not accept them | אֵינֶנִּי רֹצָם |
| But I **will consume** them | כִּי . . . אָנֹכִי מְכַלֶּה אוֹתָם |
| by the sword | בַּחֶרֶב |
| by famine | וּבָרָעָב |
| and by pestilence | וּבַדֶּבֶר |

Many are the **afflictions** (רָעוֹת) of the **righteous** (צַדִּיק), but the
LORD **delivers** (יַצִּילֶנּוּ) him out of them all. (ESV)

| צַדִּיק | righteous | 206x |
|---|---|---|
| ṣaddîq | | S6662 |

רָעָה  ▷  DAY 163          נצל  ▷  DAY 233

רַבּוֹת רָעוֹת צַדִּיק וּמִכֻּלָּם יַצִּילֶנּוּ יְהוָה:

| Many | רַבּוֹת |
|---|---|
| are the **afflictions** of | רָעוֹת |
| the **righteous** | צַדִּיק |
| but . . . out of them all | וּמִכֻּלָּם |
| the LORD | יְהוָה |
| **delivers** him | יַצִּילֶנּוּ |

Rejoice **greatly** (מְאֹד), daughter of Zion! Shout, daughter of Jerusalem! Behold, your King shall come to you, **righteous** (צַדִּיק) and **victorious** (נוֹשָׁע), humble and riding on a donkey, on a colt, the foal of a donkey. (MLB)

| ישׁע | to save, deliver | 205x |
|---|---|---|
| yāšaʿ | | S3467 |

| מְאֹד | ➤ | DAY 166 | | צַדִּיק | ➤ | DAY 237 |
|---|---|---|---|---|---|---|

גִּילִי מְאֹד בַּת־צִיּוֹן הָרִיעִי בַּת יְרוּשָׁלַם הִנֵּה מַלְכֵּךְ יָבוֹא לָךְ צַדִּיק וְנוֹשָׁע הוּא עָנִי וְרֹכֵב עַל־חֲמוֹר וְעַל־עַיִר בֶּן־אֲתֹנוֹת:

| Rejoice **greatly** | גִּילִי מְאֹד |
|---|---|
| daughter of Zion! | בַּת־צִיּוֹן |
| Shout | הָרִיעִי |
| daughter of Jerusalem! | בַּת יְרוּשָׁלַם |
| Behold | הִנֵּה |
| your King shall come to you | מַלְכֵּךְ יָבוֹא לָךְ |
| **righteous** and **victorious** | צַדִּיק וְנוֹשָׁע הוּא |
| humble | עָנִי |
| and riding on a donkey | וְרֹכֵב עַל־חֲמוֹר |
| on a colt | וְעַל־עַיִר |
| the foal of a donkey | בֶּן־אֲתֹנוֹת |

**For** (כִּי) the LORD is our **judge** (שֹׁפְטֵנוּ), the LORD is our lawgiver,
the LORD is our King; He **will save** (יוֹשִׁיעֵנוּ) us. (MLB)

| שׁפט<br>*šāfaṭ* | to judge | 204x<br>S8199 |

כִּי  ➤  DAY 15        יָשַׁע  ➤  DAY 238

כִּי יְהוָה שֹׁפְטֵנוּ יְהוָה מְחֹקְקֵנוּ יְהוָה מַלְכֵּנוּ הוּא יוֹשִׁיעֵנוּ׃

| For | כִּי |
| the LORD | יְהוָה |
| is our **judge** | שֹׁפְטֵנוּ |
| the LORD | יְהוָה |
| is our lawgiver | מְחֹקְקֵנוּ |
| the LORD | יְהוָה |
| is our King | מַלְכֵּנוּ |
| He | הוּא |
| **will save** us | יוֹשִׁיעֵנוּ |

As soon as he mentioned the **ark** (אֲרוֹן) of God, Eli [lit., he] fell over backward from his seat by the side of the **gate** (שַׁעַר), and his neck was broken and he died, for the man was old and heavy. He **had judged** (שָׁפַט) Israel forty years. (ESV)

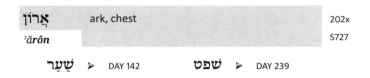

| | | |
|---|---|---|
| **אֲרוֹן** | ark, chest | 202x |
| ʾărôn | | S727 |

שַׁעַר ➤ DAY 142          שָׁפַט ➤ DAY 239

וַיְהִי כְּהַזְכִּירוֹ אֶת־אֲרוֹן הָאֱלֹהִים וַיִּפֹּל מֵעַל־הַכִּסֵּא אֲחֹרַנִּית בְּעַד יַד הַשַּׁעַר וַתִּשָּׁבֵר מַפְרַקְתּוֹ וַיָּמֹת כִּי־זָקֵן הָאִישׁ וְכָבֵד וְהוּא שָׁפַט אֶת־יִשְׂרָאֵל אַרְבָּעִים שָׁנָה:

| | |
|---|---|
| As soon as he mentioned | וַיְהִי כְּהַזְכִּירוֹ |
| the **ark** of God | אֶת־אֲרוֹן הָאֱלֹהִים |
| Eli [lit., he] fell over backward | וַיִּפֹּל אֲחֹרַנִּית |
| from his seat | מֵעַל־הַכִּסֵּא |
| by the side of the **gate** | בְּעַד יַד הַשַּׁעַר |
| and his neck was broken | וַתִּשָּׁבֵר מַפְרַקְתּוֹ |
| and he died | וַיָּמֹת |
| for the man was old and heavy | כִּי־זָקֵן הָאִישׁ וְכָבֵד |
| He **had judged** Israel | וְהוּא שָׁפַט אֶת־יִשְׂרָאֵל |
| forty years | אַרְבָּעִים שָׁנָה |

So they sent and **gathered** (וַיַּאַסְפוּ) together all the lords of the
**Philistines** (פְלִשְׁתִּים) and said, "What shall we do with the **ark**
(אֲרוֹן) of the God of Israel?" They answered, "Let the **ark** (אֲרוֹן)
of the God of Israel be brought around to Gath." (ESV)

| אסף | to gather, glean | 200x |
|---|---|---|
| ᵓāsaf | | S622 |

פְּלִשְׁתִּי   ➤   DAY 173          אֲרוֹן   ➤   DAY 240

וַיִּשְׁלְחוּ וַיַּאַסְפוּ אֶת־כָּל־סַרְנֵי פְלִשְׁתִּים אֲלֵיהֶם וַיֹּאמְרוּ מַה־נַּעֲשֶׂה
לַאֲרוֹן אֱלֹהֵי יִשְׂרָאֵל וַיֹּאמְרוּ יִסֹּב אֲרוֹן אֱלֹהֵי יִשְׂרָאֵל

| | |
|---|---|
| So they sent | וַיִּשְׁלְחוּ |
| and **gathered** together | וַיַּאַסְפוּ . . . אֲלֵיהֶם |
| all the lords of the **Philistines** | אֶת־כָּל־סַרְנֵי פְלִשְׁתִּים |
| and said | וַיֹּאמְרוּ |
| What shall we do | מַה־נַּעֲשֶׂה |
| with the **ark** of the God of Israel? | לַאֲרוֹן אֱלֹהֵי יִשְׂרָאֵל |
| They answered | וַיֹּאמְרוּ |
| Let . . . be brought around | יִסֹּב |
| the **ark** of the God of Israel | אֲרוֹן אֱלֹהֵי יִשְׂרָאֵל |
| to Gath | גַּת |

Then your light will break forth like the dawn, and your healing will quickly appear; then your righteousness **will go** (וְהָלַךְ) before you, and the **glory** (כְּבוֹד) of the LORD will be your rear guard [lit., **will gather** (יַאַסְפֶךָ) you]. (NIV)

| | | |
|---|---|---|
| כָּבוֹד | glory, splendor | 200x |
| *kāvôd* | | S3519 |

הלך    ➤    DAY 31      אסף    ➤    DAY 241

אָז יִבָּקַע כַּשַּׁחַר אוֹרֶךָ וַאֲרֻכָתְךָ מְהֵרָה תִצְמָח וְהָלַךְ לְפָנֶיךָ צִדְקֶךָ
כְּבוֹד יְהוָה יַאַסְפֶךָ:

| | |
|---|---|
| Then your light | אָז . . . אוֹרֶךָ |
| will break forth | יִבָּקַע |
| like the dawn | כַּשַּׁחַר |
| and your healing | וַאֲרֻכָתְךָ |
| will . . . appear | תִצְמָח |
| quickly | מְהֵרָה |
| then your righteousness **will go** before you | וְהָלַךְ לְפָנֶיךָ צִדְקֶךָ |
| and the **glory** of the LORD | כְּבוֹד יְהוָה |
| will be your rear guard [lit., **will gather** you] | יַאַסְפֶךָ |

The LORD **is exalted** (רָם) over all the **nations** (גּוֹיִם), his **glory** (כְּבוֹדוֹ) above the heavens. (NIV)

| רוּם | to be high; raise, exalt | 196x |
| --- | --- | --- |
| *rûm* | | S7311 |

גּוֹי ➤ DAY 95          כָּבוֹד ➤ DAY 242

רָם עַל־כָּל־גּוֹיִם יְהוָה עַל הַשָּׁמַיִם כְּבוֹדוֹ:

| The LORD | יְהוָה |
| --- | --- |
| **is exalted** | רָם |
| over all the **nations** | עַל־כָּל־גּוֹיִם |
| his **glory** | כְּבוֹדוֹ |
| above the heavens | עַל הַשָּׁמַיִם |

And while my **glory** (כְּבֹדִי) **passes by** (עֲבֹר) I will put you in a cleft of the rock, and I will cover you with my **hand** (כַּפִּי) until I **have passed by** (עָבְרִי). (NRSV)

| כַּף | palm, hand, sole | 195x |
|------|------------------|------|
| *kaf* | | S3709 |

עבר ➤ DAY 97          כָּבוֹד ➤ DAY 242

וְהָיָה בַּעֲבֹר כְּבֹדִי וְשַׂמְתִּיךָ בְּנִקְרַת הַצּוּר וְשַׂכֹּתִי כַפִּי עָלֶיךָ
עַד־עָבְרִי:

| And while my **glory passes by** | וְהָיָה בַּעֲבֹר כְּבֹדִי |
|---|---|
| I will put you | וְשַׂמְתִּיךָ |
| in a cleft of | בְּנִקְרַת |
| the rock | הַצּוּר |
| and I will cover you | וְשַׂכֹּתִי . . . עָלֶיךָ |
| with my **hand** | כַפִּי |
| until I **have passed by** | עַד־עָבְרִי |

When **he saw** (וַיַּרְא) that **he had** not **prevailed** (יָכֹל) against him, he touched the **socket** (כַף) of his thigh; so the **socket** (כַּף) of Jacob's thigh was dislocated while he wrestled with him. (NASB)

| יָכֹל | to be able | 194x |
|---|---|---|
| *yāḵal* | | S3201 |

רָאָה   ▷  DAY 34        כַּף  ▷  DAY 244

וַיַּרְא כִּי לֹא יָכֹל לוֹ וַיִּגַּע בְּכַף־יְרֵכוֹ וַתֵּקַע כַּף־יֶרֶךְ יַעֲקֹב בְּהֵאָבְקוֹ עִמּוֹ:

| When **he saw** that | וַיַּרְא כִּי |
|---|---|
| **he had** not **prevailed** against him | לֹא יָכֹל לוֹ |
| he touched | וַיִּגַּע |
| the **socket** of his thigh | בְּכַף־יְרֵכוֹ |
| so . . . was dislocated | וַתֵּקַע |
| the **socket** of Jacob's thigh | כַּף־יֶרֶךְ יַעֲקֹב |
| while he wrestled with him | בְּהֵאָבְקוֹ עִמּוֹ |

Then the **priest** (כֹּהֵן) will take some of the one-third quart of **olive oil** (שֶׁמֶן) and pour it into his [lit., the **priest's** (כֹּהֵן)] left **palm** (כַּף). (CSB)

| | שֶׁמֶן |
|---|---|
| oil | |
| šemen | 193x |
| | S8081 |

כֹּהֵן　▷　DAY 71　　　　כַּף　▷　DAY 244

וְלָקַח הַכֹּהֵן מִלֹּג הַשֶּׁמֶן וְיָצַק עַל־כַּף הַכֹּהֵן הַשְּׂמָאלִית:

| Then the **priest** will take | וְלָקַח הַכֹּהֵן |
|---|---|
| some of the one-third quart of | מִלֹּג |
| **olive oil** | הַשֶּׁמֶן |
| and pour it | וְיָצַק |
| into his [lit., the **priest's**] left **palm** | עַל־כַּף הַכֹּהֵן הַשְּׂמָאלִית |

**Oil** (שֶׁמֶן) and incense bring joy to the heart, and the sweetness of a **friend** (רֵעֵהוּ) is better than **self**-counsel (עֲצַת־נָפֶשׁ). (CSB)

| רֵעַ | companion, friend, neighbor | 191x |
|---|---|---|
| *rēaᶜ* | | S7453 |

נֶפֶשׁ   ➤   DAY 69         שֶׁמֶן   ➤   DAY 246

שֶׁמֶן וּקְטֹרֶת יְשַׂמַּח־לֵב וּמֶתֶק רֵעֵהוּ מֵעֲצַת־נָפֶשׁ׃

| | |
|---|---|
| Oil | שֶׁמֶן |
| and incense | וּקְטֹרֶת |
| bring joy to | יְשַׂמַּח־ |
| the heart | לֵב |
| and the sweetness of | וּמֶתֶק |
| a **friend** | רֵעֵהוּ |
| is better than **self**-counsel | מֵעֲצַת־נָפֶשׁ |

Then the **glory** (כְּבוֹד) of the LORD **rose up** (וַיָּרָם) from the
cherub to the threshold of the house; the house was filled with the
cloud, and the **court** (חָצֵר) was full of the brightness of the **glory**
(כְּבוֹד) of the LORD. (NRSV)

| | | |
|---|---|---|
| חָצֵר | courtyard | 191x |
| ḥāṣēr | | S2691 |

כְּבוֹד  ➢  DAY 242          רום  ➢  DAY 243

וַיָּרָם כְּבוֹד־יְהוָה מֵעַל הַכְּרוּב עַל מִפְתַּן הַבָּיִת וַיִּמָּלֵא הַבַּיִת אֶת־
הֶעָנָן וְהֶחָצֵר מָלְאָה אֶת־נֹגַהּ כְּבוֹד יְהוָה:

| Then the **glory** of the LORD **rose up** | וַיָּרָם כְּבוֹד־יְהוָה |
|---|---|
| from the cherub | מֵעַל הַכְּרוּב |
| to the threshold of the house | עַל מִפְתַּן הַבָּיִת |
| the house was filled | וַיִּמָּלֵא הַבַּיִת |
| with the cloud | אֶת־הֶעָנָן |
| and the **court** was full of | וְהֶחָצֵר מָלְאָה |
| the brightness of | אֶת־נֹגַהּ |
| the **glory** of the LORD | כְּבוֹד יְהוָה |

If a man gives to his **neighbor** (רֵעֵהוּ) a donkey or an ox or a sheep or any **beast** (בְּהֵמָה) to keep safe, and **it dies** (וּמֵת) or is injured or is driven away, without anyone seeing it, . . . (ESV)

| בְּהֵמָה | cattle, beast | 190x |
|---|---|---|
| *běhēmâ* | | S929 |

| מוּת | ➤ | DAY 58 | | רֵעַ | ➤ | DAY 247 |

כִּי־יִתֵּן אִישׁ אֶל־רֵעֵהוּ חֲמוֹר אוֹ־שׁוֹר אוֹ־שֶׂה וְכָל־בְּהֵמָה לִשְׁמֹר וּמֵת אוֹ־נִשְׁבַּר אוֹ־נִשְׁבָּה אֵין רֹאֶה:

| If a man gives | כִּי־יִתֵּן אִישׁ |
|---|---|
| to his **neighbor** | אֶל־רֵעֵהוּ |
| a donkey | חֲמוֹר |
| or an ox | אוֹ־שׁוֹר |
| or a sheep | אוֹ־שֶׂה |
| or any **beast** | וְכָל־בְּהֵמָה |
| to keep safe | לִשְׁמֹר |
| and **it dies** | וּמֵת |
| or is injured | אוֹ־נִשְׁבַּר |
| or is driven away | אוֹ־נִשְׁבָּה |
| without anyone seeing it | אֵין רֹאֶה |

Joshua **assembled** (וַיֶּאֱסֹף) all the **tribes** (שִׁבְטֵי) of Israel at Shechem and summoned Israel's elders, leaders, **judges** (שֹׁפְטָיו), and officers, and they presented themselves before God. (CSB)

| שֵׁבֶט | tribe, rod | 190x |
|---|---|---|
| *šēveṭ* | | S7626 |

שׁפט    ➤    DAY 239        אסף    ➤    DAY 241

וַיֶּאֱסֹף יְהוֹשֻׁעַ אֶת־כָּל־שִׁבְטֵי יִשְׂרָאֵל שְׁכֶמָה וַיִּקְרָא לְזִקְנֵי יִשְׂרָאֵל
וּלְרָאשָׁיו וּלְשֹׁפְטָיו וּלְשֹׁטְרָיו וַיִּתְיַצְּבוּ לִפְנֵי הָאֱלֹהִים:

| Joshua **assembled** | וַיֶּאֱסֹף יְהוֹשֻׁעַ |
|---|---|
| all the **tribes** of Israel | אֶת־כָּל־שִׁבְטֵי יִשְׂרָאֵל |
| at Shechem | שְׁכֶמָה |
| and summoned | וַיִּקְרָא |
| Israel's elders | לְזִקְנֵי יִשְׂרָאֵל |
| leaders | וּלְרָאשָׁיו |
| **judges** | וּלְשֹׁפְטָיו |
| and officers | וּלְשֹׁטְרָיו |
| and they presented themselves | וַיִּתְיַצְּבוּ |
| before God | לִפְנֵי הָאֱלֹהִים |

So they went to the king in the **court** (חָצֵרָה), but they had deposited the scroll in the chamber of Elishama the scribe, and **they reported** (וַיַּגִּידוּ) all the words to [lit., in the **ears** (אָזְנֵי) of] the king. (NASB)

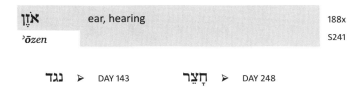

| | |
|---|---|
| אֹזֶן | ear, hearing     188x |
| ʾōzen | S241 |

נגד   ➤   DAY 143          חָצֵר   ➤   DAY 248

וַיָּבֹאוּ אֶל־הַמֶּלֶךְ חָצֵרָה וְאֶת־הַמְּגִלָּה הִפְקִדוּ בְּלִשְׁכַּת אֱלִישָׁמָע
הַסֹּפֵר וַיַּגִּידוּ בְּאָזְנֵי הַמֶּלֶךְ אֵת כָּל־הַדְּבָרִים:

| So they went | וַיָּבֹאוּ |
|---|---|
| to the king | אֶל־הַמֶּלֶךְ |
| in the **court** | חָצֵרָה |
| but . . . the scroll | וְאֶת־הַמְּגִלָּה |
| they had deposited | הִפְקִדוּ |
| in the chamber of | בְּלִשְׁכַּת |
| Elishama the scribe | אֱלִישָׁמָע הַסֹּפֵר |
| and **they reported** | וַיַּגִּידוּ |
| all the words | אֵת כָּל־הַדְּבָרִים |
| to [lit., in the **ears** of] the king | בְּאָזְנֵי הַמֶּלֶךְ |

For you, O LORD of **hosts** (צְבָאוֹת), the God of Israel, have made this revelation to [lit., **uncovered** (גָּלִיתָה) the **ear** (אֹזֶן) of] your servant, saying, "I will build you a house." (ESV)

| גלה | to reveal; go into exile | 187x |
|---|---|---|
| *gālâ* | | S1540 |

צָבָא ➤ DAY 114　　　　אֹזֶן ➤ DAY 251

כִּי־אַתָּה יְהוָה צְבָאוֹת אֱלֹהֵי יִשְׂרָאֵל גָּלִיתָה אֶת־אֹזֶן עַבְדְּךָ לֵאמֹר בַּיִת אֶבְנֶה־לָּךְ

| For you | כִּי־אַתָּה |
|---|---|
| O LORD of **hosts** | יְהוָה צְבָאוֹת |
| the God of Israel | אֱלֹהֵי יִשְׂרָאֵל |
| have made this revelation to [lit., **uncovered** the **ear** of] your servant | גָּלִיתָה אֶת־אֹזֶן עַבְדְּךָ |
| saying | לֵאמֹר |
| I will build you a house | בַּיִת אֶבְנֶה־לָּךְ |

So all Israel was enrolled by genealogies; and these are written in
the **Book** (סֵפֶר) of the Kings of Israel. And Judah **was taken into
exile** (הָגְלוּ) in **Babylon** (בְּבֶל) because of their unfaithfulness.
(NRSV)

| סֵפֶר | scroll, book | 187x |
|-------|--------------|------|
| *sēfer* | | S5612 |

בְּבֶל  ➤  DAY 192        גלה  ➤  DAY 252

וְכָל־יִשְׂרָאֵל הִתְיַחְשׂוּ וְהִנָּם כְּתוּבִים עַל־סֵפֶר מַלְכֵי יִשְׂרָאֵל וִיהוּדָה
הָגְלוּ לְבָבֶל בְּמַעֲלָם:

| So all Israel | וְכָל־יִשְׂרָאֵל |
|---|---|
| was enrolled by genealogies | הִתְיַחְשׂוּ |
| and these are written | וְהִנָּם כְּתוּבִים |
| in the **Book** of | עַל־סֵפֶר |
| the Kings of Israel | מַלְכֵי יִשְׂרָאֵל |
| And Judah | וִיהוּדָה |
| **was taken into exile** | הָגְלוּ |
| in **Babylon** | לְבָבֶל |
| because of their unfaithfulness | בְּמַעֲלָם |

The Lord will make you abound in prosperity, in the fruit of your womb, in the fruit of your **livestock** (בְּהֶמְתְּךָ), and in the fruit of your **ground** (אַדְמָתֶךָ) in the **land** (אֲדָמָה) that the Lord **swore** (נִשְׁבַּע) to your ancestors to give you. (NRSV)

| שׁבע | to swear an oath | 186x |
|---|---|---|
| šāvaʿ | | S7650 |

אֲדָמָה ➢ DAY 219     בְּהֵמָה ➢ DAY 249

וְהוֹתִרְךָ יְהוָה לְטוֹבָה בִּפְרִי בִטְנְךָ וּבִפְרִי בְהַמְתְּךָ וּבִפְרִי אַדְמָתֶךָ עַל הָאֲדָמָה אֲשֶׁר נִשְׁבַּע יְהוָה לַאֲבֹתֶיךָ לָתֶת לָךְ:

| The Lord will make you abound | וְהוֹתִרְךָ יְהוָה |
|---|---|
| in prosperity | לְטוֹבָה |
| in the fruit of your womb | בִּפְרִי בִטְנְךָ |
| in the fruit of your **livestock** | וּבִפְרִי בְהַמְתְּךָ |
| and in the fruit of your **ground** | וּבִפְרִי אַדְמָתֶךָ |
| in the **land** | עַל הָאֲדָמָה |
| that the Lord **swore** | אֲשֶׁר נִשְׁבַּע יְהוָה |
| to your ancestors | לַאֲבֹתֶיךָ |
| to give you | לָתֶת לָךְ |

"I will cut off the inhabitants from Ashdod, and him who holds the **scepter** (שֵׁבֶט) from Ashkelon; **I will turn** (וַהֲשִׁיבוֹתִי) my hand against Ekron, and the remnant of the Philistines **shall perish** (וְאָבְדוּ)," says the Lord GOD. (ESV)

| אבד | to wander, perish; destroy | 185x |
|---|---|---|
| ʾāvad | | S6 |

שׁוּב   ➤   DAY 44       שֵׁבֶט   ➤   DAY 250

וְהִכְרַתִּי יוֹשֵׁב מֵאַשְׁדּוֹד וְתוֹמֵךְ שֵׁבֶט מֵאַשְׁקְלוֹן וַהֲשִׁיבוֹתִי יָדִי עַל־
עֶקְרוֹן וְאָבְדוּ שְׁאֵרִית פְּלִשְׁתִּים אָמַר אֲדֹנָי יְהוִה:

| I will cut off | וְהִכְרַתִּי |
|---|---|
| the inhabitants | יוֹשֵׁב |
| from Ashdod | מֵאַשְׁדּוֹד |
| and him who holds | וְתוֹמֵךְ |
| the **scepter** | שֵׁבֶט |
| from Ashkelon | מֵאַשְׁקְלוֹן |
| **I will turn** | וַהֲשִׁיבוֹתִי |
| my hand | יָדִי |
| against Ekron | עַל־עֶקְרוֹן |
| and . . . **shall perish** | וְאָבְדוּ |
| the remnant of the Philistines | שְׁאֵרִית פְּלִשְׁתִּים |
| says the Lord GOD | אָמַר אֲדֹנָי יְהוִה |

I have strayed like a **lost** (אָבַד) sheep. **Seek** (בַּקֵּשׁ) your servant,
for I have not forgotten your **commands** (מִצְוֺתֶיךָ). (NIV)

| מִצְוָה | commandment | 184x |
|---|---|---|
| miṣvâ | | S4687 |

בַּקֵּשׁ   ➤   DAY 213      אָבַד   ➤   DAY 255

תָּעִיתִי כְּשֶׂה אֹבֵד בַּקֵּשׁ עַבְדְּךָ כִּי מִצְוֺתֶיךָ לֹא שָׁכָחְתִּי׃

| I have strayed | תָּעִיתִי |
|---|---|
| like a **lost** sheep | כְּשֶׂה אֹבֵד |
| **Seek** | בַּקֵּשׁ |
| your servant | עַבְדְּךָ |
| for | כִּי |
| I have not forgotten | לֹא שָׁכָחְתִּי |
| your **commands** | מִצְוֺתֶיךָ |

And they set aside the burnt offerings that they might distribute them according to the groupings of the fathers' houses of the lay people, **to offer** (הַקְרִיב) to the Lord, as it is written in the **Book** (סֵפֶר) of Moses. And so they did with the **bulls** (בָּקָר). (ESV)

| | | |
|---|---|---|
| **בָּקָר** | cattle | 183x |
| *bāqār* | | S1241 |

קרב  ▷  DAY 182          סֵפֶר  ▷  DAY 253

וַיָּסִירוּ הָעֹלָה לְתִתָּם לְמִפְלַגּוֹת לְבֵית־אָבוֹת לִבְנֵי הָעָם לְהַקְרִיב
לַיהוָה כַּכָּתוּב בְּסֵפֶר מֹשֶׁה וְכֵן לַבָּקָר:

| | |
|---|---|
| And they set aside | וַיָּסִירוּ |
| the burnt offerings | הָעֹלָה |
| that they might distribute them | לְתִתָּם |
| according to the groupings | לְמִפְלַגּוֹת |
| of the fathers' houses | לְבֵית־אָבוֹת |
| of the lay people | לִבְנֵי הָעָם |
| **to offer** to the Lord | לְהַקְרִיב לַיהוָה |
| as it is written | כַּכָּתוּב |
| in the **Book** of Moses | בְּסֵפֶר מֹשֶׁה |
| And so they did | וְכֵן |
| with the **bulls** | לַבָּקָר |

These are the **commands** (מִצְוֹת) and ordinances the LORD
**commanded** (צִוָּה) the Israelites through Moses in the plains of
Moab by the **Jordan** (יַרְדֵּן) across from Jericho. (CSB)

| יַרְדֵּן | Jordan | 183x |
|---|---|---|
| *yardēn* | | S3383 |

צָוָה ➤ DAY 108          מִצְוָה ➤ DAY 256

אֵלֶּה הַמִּצְוֹת וְהַמִּשְׁפָּטִים אֲשֶׁר צִוָּה יְהוָה בְּיַד־מֹשֶׁה אֶל־בְּנֵי
יִשְׂרָאֵל בְּעַרְבֹת מוֹאָב עַל יַרְדֵּן יְרֵחוֹ:

| These | אֵלֶּה |
|---|---|
| are the **commands** | הַמִּצְוֹת |
| and ordinances | וְהַמִּשְׁפָּטִים |
| the LORD **commanded** | אֲשֶׁר צִוָּה יְהוָה |
| the Israelites | אֶל־בְּנֵי יִשְׂרָאֵל |
| through Moses | בְּיַד־מֹשֶׁה |
| in the plains of Moab | בְּעַרְבֹת מוֹאָב |
| by the **Jordan** | עַל יַרְדֵּן |
| across from Jericho | יְרֵחוֹ |

But there will be no gloom for her who was in anguish. In the
**former** (רִאשׁוֹן) time he brought into contempt the **land** (אַרְצָה)
of Zebulun and the **land** (אַרְצָה) of Naphtali, but in the latter
time he has made glorious the way of the sea, the land beyond the
**Jordan** (יַרְדֵּן), Galilee of the nations. (ESV)

| רִאשׁוֹן | first, former | 182x |
|---|---|---|
| ri'šôn | | S7223 |

אֶרֶץ    ▷   DAY 23      יַרְדֵּן   ▷   DAY 258

כִּי לֹא מוּעָף לַאֲשֶׁר מוּצָק לָהּ כָּעֵת הָרִאשׁוֹן הֵקַל אַרְצָה זְבֻלוּן
וְאַרְצָה נַפְתָּלִי וְהָאַחֲרוֹן הִכְבִּיד דֶּרֶךְ הַיָּם עֵבֶר הַיַּרְדֵּן גְּלִיל הַגּוֹיִם:

| But there will be no gloom | כִּי לֹא מוּעָף |
|---|---|
| for her who was in anguish | לַאֲשֶׁר מוּצָק לָהּ |
| In the **former** time | כָּעֵת הָרִאשׁוֹן |
| he brought into contempt | הֵקַל |
| the **land** of Zebulun | אַרְצָה זְבֻלוּן |
| and the **land** of Naphtali | וְאַרְצָה נַפְתָּלִי |
| but in the latter time | וְהָאַחֲרוֹן |
| he has made glorious | הִכְבִּיד |
| the way of the sea | דֶּרֶךְ הַיָּם |
| the land beyond the **Jordan** | עֵבֶר הַיַּרְדֵּן |
| Galilee of the nations | גְּלִיל הַגּוֹיִם |

When I heal Israel, the iniquity of **Ephraim** (אֶפְרַיִם) and the
**crimes** (רָעוֹת) of Samaria **will be exposed** (וְנִגְלָה). For they
practice fraud; a thief breaks in; a raiding party pillages outside.
(CSB)

| אֶפְרַיִם | Ephraim | 180x |
|---|---|---|
| *'efrayim* | | S669 |

רָעָה ▷ DAY 163        גלה ▷ DAY 252

כְּרָפְאִי לְיִשְׂרָאֵל וְנִגְלָה עֲוֹן אֶפְרַיִם וְרָעוֹת שֹׁמְרוֹן כִּי פָעֲלוּ שָׁקֶר
וְגַנָּב יָבוֹא פָּשַׁט גְּדוּד בַּחוּץ׃

| When I heal Israel | כְּרָפְאִי לְיִשְׂרָאֵל |
|---|---|
| the iniquity of **Ephraim** | עֲוֹן אֶפְרַיִם |
| and the **crimes** of Samaria | וְרָעוֹת שֹׁמְרוֹן |
| **will be exposed** | וְנִגְלָה |
| For | כִּי |
| they practice fraud | פָעֲלוּ שָׁקֶר |
| a thief breaks in | וְגַנָּב יָבוֹא |
| a raiding party | גְּדוּד |
| pillages outside | פָּשַׁט . . . בַּחוּץ |

For Heshbon was the **city** (עִיר) of Sihon, king of the Amorites,
who had fought against the **former** (רִאשׁוֹן) king of **Moab** (מוֹאָב)
and had taken all his land out of his hand, as far as the Arnon.
(NASB)

| מוֹאָב | Moab | 180x |
| mô'āv | | S4124 |

עִיר ▷ DAY 40     רִאשׁוֹן ▷ DAY 259

כִּי חֶשְׁבּוֹן עִיר סִיחֹן מֶלֶךְ הָאֱמֹרִי הִוא וְהוּא נִלְחַם בְּמֶלֶךְ מוֹאָב
הָרִאשׁוֹן וַיִּקַּח אֶת־כָּל־אַרְצוֹ מִיָּדוֹ עַד־אַרְנֹן׃

| For Heshbon | כִּי חֶשְׁבּוֹן |
| was the **city** of Sihon | עִיר סִיחֹן . . . הִוא |
| king of the Amorites | מֶלֶךְ הָאֱמֹרִי |
| who had fought | וְהוּא נִלְחַם |
| against the **former** king of **Moab** | בְּמֶלֶךְ מוֹאָב הָרִאשׁוֹן |
| and had taken | וַיִּקַּח |
| all his land | אֶת־כָּל־אַרְצוֹ |
| out of his hand | מִיָּדוֹ |
| as far as the Arnon | עַד־אַרְנֹן |

And **Moab** (מוֹאָב) said to the **elders** (זִקְנֵי) of Midian, "This horde will now lick up all that is **around** (סְבִיבֹתֵינוּ) us, as an ox licks up the grass of the field." Now Balak son of Zippor was king of **Moab** (מוֹאָב) at that time. (NRSV)

| זָקֵן | old | | 179x |
| *zāqēn* | | | S2205 |

סָבִיב ➤ DAY 152     מוֹאָב ➤ DAY 261

וַיֹּאמֶר מוֹאָב אֶל־זִקְנֵי מִדְיָן עַתָּה יְלַחֲכוּ הַקָּהָל אֶת־כָּל־סְבִיבֹתֵינוּ
כִּלְחֹךְ הַשּׁוֹר אֵת יֶרֶק הַשָּׂדֶה וּבָלָק בֶּן־צִפּוֹר מֶלֶךְ לְמוֹאָב בָּעֵת
הַהִוא׃

| And **Moab** said | וַיֹּאמֶר מוֹאָב |
| to the **elders** of Midian | אֶל־זִקְנֵי מִדְיָן |
| This horde will . . . lick up | יְלַחֲכוּ הַקָּהָל |
| now | עַתָּה |
| all that is **around** us | אֶת־כָּל־סְבִיבֹתֵינוּ |
| as an ox licks up | כִּלְחֹךְ הַשּׁוֹר |
| the grass of the field | אֵת יֶרֶק הַשָּׂדֶה |
| Now Balak son of Zippor | וּבָלָק בֶּן־צִפּוֹר |
| was king of **Moab** | מֶלֶךְ לְמוֹאָב |
| at that time | בָּעֵת הַהִוא |

**He deprives** (מֵסִיר) of **speech** (שָׂפָה) those who are trusted, and takes away the discernment of the **elders** (זְקֵנִים). (NRSV)

| שָׂפָה | lip, language, edge | 178x |
|---|---|---|
| *śāfâ* | | S8193 |

סוּר ➤ DAY 169　　　　　זָקֵן ➤ DAY 262

מֵסִיר שָׂפָה לְנֶאֱמָנִים וְטַעַם זְקֵנִים יִקָּח׃

| He deprives | מֵסִיר |
|---|---|
| of **speech** | שָׂפָה |
| those who are trusted | לְנֶאֱמָנִים |
| and . . . the discernment of | וְטַעַם |
| the **elders** | זְקֵנִים |
| takes away | יִקָּח |

Absalom said to Hushai, "Is this your **loyalty** (חַסְדְּךָ) to your **friend** (רֵעֶךָ)? **Why** (לָמָה) did you not go with your **friend** (רֵעֶךָ)?" (NASB)

| לָמָה | why? | 178x |
|---|---|---|
| *lāmmâ* | | S4100 |

חֶסֶד  ➤  DAY 199          רֵעַ  ➤  DAY 247

וַיֹּאמֶר אַבְשָׁלוֹם אֶל־חוּשַׁי זֶה חַסְדְּךָ אֶת־רֵעֶךָ לָמָה לֹא־הָלַכְתָּ אֶת־רֵעֶךָ:

| Absalom said | וַיֹּאמֶר אַבְשָׁלוֹם |
|---|---|
| to Hushai | אֶל־חוּשַׁי |
| Is this | זֶה |
| your **loyalty** | חַסְדְּךָ |
| to your **friend**? | אֶת־רֵעֶךָ |
| **Why** | לָמָה |
| did you not go | לֹא־הָלַכְתָּ |
| with your **friend**? | אֶת־רֵעֶךָ |

Then the Lord said to **Abraham** (אַבְרָהָם), "**Why** (לָמָּה) did Sarah laugh and say, '**Will I** really **have a child** (אֵלֵד), now that I am old?'" (NIV)

| אַבְרָהָם | Abraham | 175x |
|---|---|---|
| ʾavrāhām | | S85 |

יֶלֶד   ➤   DAY 109       לָמָּה   ➤   DAY 264

וַיֹּאמֶר יְהוָה אֶל־אַבְרָהָם לָמָּה זֶּה צָחֲקָה שָׂרָה לֵאמֹר הַאַף אֻמְנָם אֵלֵד וַאֲנִי זָקַנְתִּי:

| Then the Lord said | וַיֹּאמֶר יְהוָה |
|---|---|
| to **Abraham** | אֶל־אַבְרָהָם |
| **Why** | לָמָּה זֶּה |
| did Sarah laugh | צָחֲקָה שָׂרָה |
| and say | לֵאמֹר |
| **Will I** really **have a child** | הַאַף אֻמְנָם אֵלֵד |
| now that I am old? | וַאֲנִי זָקַנְתִּי |

Then **he asked** (וַיִּשְׁאַל) them about their welfare, and said, "Is your **old** (זָקֵן) father well, of whom you spoke? Is he still **alive** (חָי)?" (NASB)

| שָׁאַל | to ask, inquire, request, demand | 175x |
|---|---|---|
| šāʾal | | S7592 |

חַי   ➤   DAY 193       זָקֵן   ➤   DAY 262

וַיִּשְׁאַל לָהֶם לְשָׁלוֹם וַיֹּאמֶר הֲשָׁלוֹם אֲבִיכֶם הַזָּקֵן אֲשֶׁר אֲמַרְתֶּם
הַעוֹדֶנּוּ חָי:

| Then **he asked** them | וַיִּשְׁאַל לָהֶם |
|---|---|
| about their welfare | לְשָׁלוֹם |
| and said | וַיֹּאמֶר |
| Is your **old** father well | הֲשָׁלוֹם אֲבִיכֶם הַזָּקֵן |
| of whom | אֲשֶׁר |
| you spoke? | אֲמַרְתֶּם |
| Is he still | הַעוֹדֶנּוּ |
| **alive?** | חָי |

Then Jethro, Moses's father-in-law, brought a burnt offering and **sacrifices** (זְבָחִים) to God, and Aaron came with all the **elders** (זִקְנֵי) of Israel to eat a **meal** (לֶחֶם) with Moses's father-in-law in God's presence. (CSB)

| זֶבַח | sacrifice | 174x |
|---|---|---|
| zevaḥ | | S2077 |

לֶחֶם  ➤  DAY 167        זָקֵן  ➤  DAY 262

וַיִּקַּח יִתְרוֹ חֹתֵן מֹשֶׁה עֹלָה וּזְבָחִים לֵאלֹהִים וַיָּבֹא אַהֲרֹן וְכֹל זִקְנֵי יִשְׂרָאֵל לֶאֱכָל־לֶחֶם עִם־חֹתֵן מֹשֶׁה לִפְנֵי הָאֱלֹהִים׃

| Then Jethro . . . brought | וַיִּקַּח יִתְרוֹ |
|---|---|
| Moses's father-in-law | חֹתֵן מֹשֶׁה |
| a burnt offering | עֹלָה |
| and **sacrifices** | וּזְבָחִים |
| to God | לֵאלֹהִים |
| and Aaron came | וַיָּבֹא אַהֲרֹן |
| with all the **elders** of Israel | וְכֹל זִקְנֵי יִשְׂרָאֵל |
| to eat a **meal** | לֶאֱכָל־לֶחֶם |
| with Moses's father-in-law | עִם־חֹתֵן מֹשֶׁה |
| in God's presence | לִפְנֵי הָאֱלֹהִים |

"You shall say, 'It is a Passover **sacrifice** (זֶבַח) to the Lord who passed over the houses of the sons of Israel in Egypt when He smote the Egyptians, but **spared** (הִצִּיל) our homes.'" And the people bowed low and **worshiped** (וַיִּשְׁתַּחֲוּוּ). (NASB)

| חוה | to bow down, worship | 173x |
|---|---|---|
| ḥāvâ | | S7812 |

נצל   ▷   DAY 233       זֶבַח   ▷   DAY 267

וַאֲמַרְתֶּם זֶבַח־פֶּסַח הוּא לַיהוָה אֲשֶׁר פָּסַח עַל־בָּתֵּי בְנֵי־יִשְׂרָאֵל
בְּמִצְרַיִם בְּנָגְפּוֹ אֶת־מִצְרַיִם וְאֶת־בָּתֵּינוּ הִצִּיל וַיִּקֹּד הָעָם וַיִּשְׁתַּחֲוּוּ׃

| | |
|---|---|
| You shall say | וַאֲמַרְתֶּם |
| It is a Passover **sacrifice** | זֶבַח־פֶּסַח הוּא |
| to the Lord | לַיהוָה |
| who passed over the houses of the sons of Israel | אֲשֶׁר פָּסַח עַל־בָּתֵּי בְנֵי־יִשְׂרָאֵל |
| in Egypt | בְּמִצְרַיִם |
| when He smote | בְּנָגְפּוֹ |
| the Egyptians | אֶת־מִצְרַיִם |
| but . . . our homes | וְאֶת־בָּתֵּינוּ |
| **spared** | הִצִּיל |
| And the people bowed low | וַיִּקֹּד הָעָם |
| and **worshiped** | וַיִּשְׁתַּחֲוּוּ |

Kings shall see and stand up, princes, and **they shall prostrate themselves** (יִשְׁתַּחֲוּוּ), **because of** (לְמַעַן) the Lord, who is faithful, the Holy One of Israel, who **has chosen** (וַיִּבְחָרֶךָּ) you. (NRSV)

| בחר | to choose, select, test | 172x |
|---|---|---|
| *bāḥar* | | S977 |

לְמַעַן ➤ DAY 188　　　　חוה ➤ DAY 268

מְלָכִים יִרְאוּ וָקָמוּ שָׂרִים וְיִשְׁתַּחֲוּוּ לְמַעַן יְהוָה אֲשֶׁר נֶאֱמָן קְדֹשׁ
יִשְׂרָאֵל וַיִּבְחָרֶךָּ׃

| Kings shall see | מְלָכִים יִרְאוּ |
|---|---|
| and stand up | וָקָמוּ |
| princes | שָׂרִים |
| and **they shall prostrate themselves** | וְיִשְׁתַּחֲוּוּ |
| **because of** the Lord | לְמַעַן יְהוָה |
| who is faithful | אֲשֶׁר נֶאֱמָן |
| the Holy One of Israel | קְדֹשׁ יִשְׂרָאֵל |
| who **has chosen** you | וַיִּבְחָרֶךָּ |

And **Abraham** (אַבְרָהָם) lifted up his eyes and looked, and behold, behind him was a **ram** (אַיִל), caught in a thicket by his horns. And **Abraham** (אַבְרָהָם) went and took the **ram** (אַיִל) and offered it up as a **burnt offering** (עֹלָה) instead of his son. (ESV)

| אַיִל | chief, mighty man, ram; oak | 171x |
|---|---|---|
| ʾayil | | S352 |

עֹלָה   ➤   DAY 176       אַבְרָהָם   ➤   DAY 265

וַיִּשָּׂא אַבְרָהָם אֶת־עֵינָיו וַיַּרְא וְהִנֵּה־אַיִל אַחַר נֶאֱחַז בַּסְּבַךְ בְּקַרְנָיו
וַיֵּלֶךְ אַבְרָהָם וַיִּקַּח אֶת־הָאַיִל וַיַּעֲלֵהוּ לְעֹלָה תַּחַת בְּנוֹ:

| And **Abraham** lifted up | וַיִּשָּׂא אַבְרָהָם |
|---|---|
| his eyes | אֶת־עֵינָיו |
| and looked | וַיַּרְא |
| and behold | וְהִנֵּה־ |
| behind him was a **ram** | אַיִל אַחַר |
| caught in a thicket | נֶאֱחַז בַּסְּבַךְ |
| by his horns | בְּקַרְנָיו |
| And **Abraham** went | וַיֵּלֶךְ אַבְרָהָם |
| and took the **ram** | וַיִּקַּח אֶת־הָאַיִל |
| and offered it up | וַיַּעֲלֵהוּ |
| as a **burnt offering** | לְעֹלָה |
| instead of his son | תַּחַת בְּנוֹ |

Moses said to Joshua, "**Choose** (בְּחַר) some men for us and go out, **fight** (הִלָּחֵם) with Amalek. Tomorrow I will stand on the top of the hill with the **staff** (מַטֵּה) of God in my hand." (NRSV)

| | | |
|---|---|---|
| **לחם** | to fight | 171x |
| *lāḥam* | | S3898 |

מַטֵּה ➤ DAY 195          בחר ➤ DAY 269

וַיֹּאמֶר מֹשֶׁה אֶל־יְהוֹשֻׁעַ בְּחַר־לָנוּ אֲנָשִׁים וְצֵא הִלָּחֵם בַּעֲמָלֵק מָחָר
אָנֹכִי נִצָּב עַל־רֹאשׁ הַגִּבְעָה וּמַטֵּה הָאֱלֹהִים בְּיָדִי:

| | |
|---|---|
| Moses said | וַיֹּאמֶר מֹשֶׁה |
| to Joshua | אֶל־יְהוֹשֻׁעַ |
| **Choose** . . . for us | בְּחַר־לָנוּ |
| some men | אֲנָשִׁים |
| and go out | וְצֵא |
| **fight** with Amalek | הִלָּחֵם בַּעֲמָלֵק |
| Tomorrow | מָחָר |
| I will stand | אָנֹכִי נִצָּב |
| on the top of the hill | עַל־רֹאשׁ הַגִּבְעָה |
| with the **staff** of God | וּמַטֵּה הָאֱלֹהִים |
| in my hand | בְּיָדִי |

Wisdom is found on the **lips** (שְׂפָתֵי) of the **discerning** (נָבוֹן), but a **rod** (שֵׁבֶט) is for the back of the one who lacks sense. (CSB)

| בִּין | to understand, have insight | 171x |
|---|---|---|
| *bîn* | | S995 |

שֵׁבֶט ➤ DAY 250                    שָׂפָה ➤ DAY 263

בִּשְׂפָתֵי נָבוֹן תִּמָּצֵא חָכְמָה וְשֵׁבֶט לְגֵו חֲסַר־לֵב׃

| Wisdom | חָכְמָה |
|---|---|
| is found | תִּמָּצֵא |
| on the **lips** of | בִּשְׂפָתֵי |
| the **discerning** | נָבוֹן |
| but a **rod** | וְשֵׁבֶט |
| is for the back of | לְגֵו |
| the one who lacks | חֲסַר־ |
| sense | לֵב |

Now this is what you shall do to them **to consecrate (קַדֵּשׁ)** them to minister as priests to Me: take one young bull [, a son of the **herd (בָּקָר)**,] and two **rams (אֵילִם)** without blemish. (NASB)

| קָדַשׁ | to be holy; consecrate | 171x |
|---|---|---|
| *qādaš* | | S6942 |

בָּקָר    ▶    DAY 257        אַיִל    ▶    DAY 270

וְזֶה הַדָּבָר אֲשֶׁר־תַּעֲשֶׂה לָהֶם לְקַדֵּשׁ אֹתָם לְכַהֵן לִי לְקַח פַּר אֶחָד בֶּן־בָּקָר וְאֵילִם שְׁנַיִם תְּמִימִם:

| | |
|---|---|
| Now this is what | וְזֶה הַדָּבָר אֲשֶׁר־ |
| you shall do to them | תַּעֲשֶׂה לָהֶם |
| **to consecrate** them | לְקַדֵּשׁ אֹתָם |
| to minister as priests | לְכַהֵן |
| to Me | לִי |
| take | לְקַח |
| one young bull | פַּר אֶחָד |
| [, a son of the **herd**,] | בֶּן־בָּקָר |
| and two **rams** | וְאֵילִם שְׁנַיִם |
| without blemish | תְּמִימִם |

**He acted wisely** (וַיָּבֶן) and distributed some of his sons through all the territories of Judah and **Benjamin** (בִּנְיָמִן) to all the fortified cities, and he gave them food in abundance. And **he sought** (וַיִּשְׁאַל) many wives for them. (NASB)

| בִּנְיָמִן | Benjamin | 168x |
|---|---|---|
| binyāmīn | | S1144 |

שָׁאַל ➤ DAY 266     בִּין ➤ DAY 272

וַיָּבֶן וַיִּפְרֹץ מִכָּל־בָּנָיו לְכָל־אַרְצוֹת יְהוּדָה וּבִנְיָמִן לְכֹל עָרֵי הַמְּצֻרוֹת
וַיִּתֵּן לָהֶם הַמָּזוֹן לָרֹב וַיִּשְׁאַל הֲמוֹן נָשִׁים:

| | |
|---|---|
| He acted wisely | וַיָּבֶן |
| and distributed | וַיִּפְרֹץ |
| some of his sons | מִכָּל־בָּנָיו |
| through all the territories of | לְכָל־אַרְצוֹת |
| Judah and **Benjamin** | יְהוּדָה וּבִנְיָמִן |
| to all the fortified cities | לְכֹל עָרֵי הַמְּצֻרוֹת |
| and he gave them | וַיִּתֵּן לָהֶם |
| food in abundance | הַמָּזוֹן לָרֹב |
| And **he sought** . . . for them | וַיִּשְׁאַל |
| many wives | הֲמוֹן נָשִׁים |

Then he took his staff in his hand, and **chose** (וַיִּבְחַר) five smooth stones from the wadi, and put them in his **shepherd's** (רֹעִים) **bag** (כְּלִי), in the pouch. (NRSV)

| | | |
|---|---|---|
| רעה | to shepherd, tend, graze | 167x |
| rāʿâ | | S7462 |

כְּלִי    ➤   DAY 156      בחר   ➤   DAY 269

וַיִּקַּח מַקְלוֹ בְּיָדוֹ וַיִּבְחַר־לוֹ חֲמִשָּׁה חַלֻּקֵי־אֲבָנִים מִן־הַנַּחַל וַיָּשֶׂם אֹתָם בִּכְלִי הָרֹעִים אֲשֶׁר־לוֹ וּבַיַּלְקוּט

| | |
|---|---|
| Then he took his staff | וַיִּקַּח מַקְלוֹ |
| in his hand | בְּיָדוֹ |
| and **chose** | וַיִּבְחַר־לוֹ |
| five | חֲמִשָּׁה |
| smooth stones | חַלֻּקֵי־אֲבָנִים |
| from the wadi | מִן־הַנַּחַל |
| and put them | וַיָּשֶׂם אֹתָם |
| in his **shepherd's bag** | בִּכְלִי הָרֹעִים אֲשֶׁר־לוֹ |
| in the pouch | וּבַיַּלְקוּט |

**It will** never **be inhabited** (תֵשֵׁב) or lived in from **generation** (דּוֹר) to **generation** (דּוֹר); a nomad will not pitch his tent there, and **shepherds** (רֹעִים) will not let their flocks rest there. (CSB)

| דּוֹר | generation | 167x |
|---|---|---|
| *dôr* | | S1755 |

יָשַׁב ▹ DAY 41      רעה ▹ DAY 275

לֹא־תֵשֵׁב לָנֶצַח וְלֹא תִשְׁכֹּן עַד־דּוֹר וָדוֹר וְלֹא־יַהֵל שָׁם עֲרָבִי וְרֹעִים
לֹא־יַרְבִּצוּ שָׁם׃

| | |
|---|---|
| **It will** never **be inhabited** | לֹא־תֵשֵׁב לָנֶצַח |
| or lived in | וְלֹא תִשְׁכֹּן |
| from **generation** to **generation** | עַד־דּוֹר וָדוֹר |
| a nomad | עֲרָבִי |
| will not pitch his tent | וְלֹא־יַהֵל |
| there | שָׁם |
| and **shepherds** | וְרֹעִים |
| will not let their flocks rest | לֹא־יַרְבִּצוּ |
| there | שָׁם |

The Chaldeans who **are fighting** (נִלְחָמִים) against this city shall come and set this city on **fire** (אֵשׁ) and burn it with the houses upon whose roofs incense has been offered to Baal and drink offerings have been poured out to **other** (אֲחֵרִים) gods. (MLB)

| | | |
|---|---|---|
| **אַחֵר** | another, other | 167x |
| ʾaḥēr | | S312 |

אֵשׁ   ➤   DAY 138          לחם   ➤   DAY 271

וּבָאוּ הַכַּשְׂדִּים הַנִּלְחָמִים עַל־הָעִיר הַזֹּאת וְהִצִּיתוּ אֶת־הָעִיר הַזֹּאת
בָּאֵשׁ וּשְׂרָפוּהָ וְאֵת הַבָּתִּים אֲשֶׁר קִטְּרוּ עַל־גַּגּוֹתֵיהֶם לַבַּעַל וְהִסִּכוּ
נְסָכִים לֵאלֹהִים אֲחֵרִים

| | |
|---|---|
| The Chaldeans . . . shall come | וּבָאוּ הַכַּשְׂדִּים |
| who **are fighting** | הַנִּלְחָמִים |
| against this city | עַל־הָעִיר הַזֹּאת |
| and set . . . on **fire** | וְהִצִּיתוּ . . . בָּאֵשׁ |
| this city | אֶת־הָעִיר הַזֹּאת |
| and burn it | וּשְׂרָפוּהָ |
| with the houses | וְאֵת הַבָּתִּים |
| upon whose roofs | אֲשֶׁר . . . עַל־גַּגּוֹתֵיהֶם |
| incense has been offered to Baal | קִטְּרוּ לַבַּעַל |
| and drink offerings have been poured out | וְהִסִּכוּ נְסָכִים |
| to **other** gods | לֵאלֹהִים אֲחֵרִים |

Adam **made love to** (וַיֵּדַע) his wife again, and she gave birth to a son and named him Seth, saying, "God has granted me **another** (אַחֵר) child in place of Abel, since Cain **killed** (הֲרָגוֹ) him." (NIV)

| הרג | to kill | | 167x |
| --- | --- | --- | --- |
| *hārag* | | | S2026 |

יָדַע   ➤   DAY 50      אַחֵר   ➤   DAY 277

וַיֵּדַע אָדָם עוֹד אֶת־אִשְׁתּוֹ וַתֵּלֶד בֵּן וַתִּקְרָא אֶת־שְׁמוֹ שֵׁת כִּי שָׁת־לִי אֱלֹהִים זֶרַע אַחֵר תַּחַת הֶבֶל כִּי הֲרָגוֹ קָיִן:

| | |
| --- | --- |
| Adam **made love to** his wife again | וַיֵּדַע אָדָם עוֹד אֶת־אִשְׁתּוֹ |
| and she gave birth to a son | וַתֵּלֶד בֵּן |
| and named him Seth | וַתִּקְרָא אֶת־שְׁמוֹ שֵׁת |
| saying | כִּי |
| God has granted me | שָׁת־לִי אֱלֹהִים |
| **another** child | זֶרַע אַחֵר |
| in place of Abel | תַּחַת הֶבֶל |
| since Cain **killed** him | כִּי הֲרָגוֹ קָיִן |

You shall not do any **work** (מְלָאכָה). It is a statute **forever** (עוֹלָם) throughout your **generations** (דֹרֹתֵיכֶם) in all your dwelling places. (ESV)

| מְלָאכָה | work, service | 167x |
| --- | --- | --- |
| mĕlāʾkâ | | S4399 |

עוֹלָם  ➤  DAY 119     דֹר  ➤  DAY 276

כָּל־מְלָאכָה לֹא תַעֲשׂוּ חֻקַּת עוֹלָם לְדֹרֹתֵיכֶם בְּכֹל מֹשְׁבֹתֵיכֶם׃

| You shall not do | לֹא תַעֲשׂוּ |
| --- | --- |
| any **work** | כָּל־מְלָאכָה |
| It is a statute **forever** | חֻקַּת עוֹלָם |
| throughout your **generations** | לְדֹרֹתֵיכֶם |
| in all your dwelling places | בְּכֹל מֹשְׁבֹתֵיכֶם |

And he went out to meet Asa, saying to him, "Listen to me, Asa and all Judah and **Benjamin** (בְנְיָמִן)! The LORD is with you while you are with Him; if **you seek** (תִּדְרְשֻׁהוּ) Him, He will be found by you; but if **you forsake** (תַעַזְבֻהוּ) Him, **He will forsake** (יַעֲזֹב) you." (MLB)

| דָּרַשׁ | to seek, demand | 165x |
|---|---|---|
| *dāraš* | | S1875 |

עָזַב ➤ DAY 227      בִּנְיָמִן ➤ DAY 274

וַיֵּצֵא לִפְנֵי אָסָא וַיֹּאמֶר לוֹ שְׁמָעוּנִי אָסָא וְכָל־יְהוּדָה וּבִנְיָמִן יְהוָה עִמָּכֶם בִּהְיוֹתְכֶם עִמּוֹ וְאִם־תִּדְרְשֻׁהוּ יִמָּצֵא לָכֶם וְאִם־תַּעַזְבֻהוּ יַעֲזֹב אֶתְכֶם:

| | |
|---|---|
| And he went out | וַיֵּצֵא |
| to meet Asa | לִפְנֵי אָסָא |
| saying to him | וַיֹּאמֶר לוֹ |
| Listen to me | שְׁמָעוּנִי |
| Asa and all Judah and **Benjamin**! | אָסָא וְכָל־יְהוּדָה וּבִנְיָמִן |
| The LORD is with you | יְהוָה עִמָּכֶם |
| while you are with Him | בִּהְיוֹתְכֶם עִמּוֹ |
| if **you seek** Him | וְאִם־תִּדְרְשֻׁהוּ |
| He will be found by you | יִמָּצֵא לָכֶם |
| but if **you forsake** Him | וְאִם־תַּעַזְבֻהוּ |
| **He will forsake** you | יַעֲזֹב אֶתְכֶם |

The LORD was with Jehoshaphat, because he walked in the **earlier** (רִאשֹׁנִים) ways of his father David. **He did** not **seek** (דָּרַשׁ) the **Baals** (בְּעָלִים). (ESV)

| בַּעַל | master, husband; Baal | 164x |
|---|---|---|
| *ba'al* | | S1167 |

רִאשׁוֹן ➤ DAY 259      דרשׁ ➤ DAY 280

וַיְהִי יְהוָה עִם־יְהוֹשָׁפָט כִּי הָלַךְ בְּדַרְכֵי דָּוִיד אָבִיו הָרִאשֹׁנִים וְלֹא דָרַשׁ לַבְּעָלִים׃

| The LORD was | וַיְהִי יְהוָה |
|---|---|
| with Jehoshaphat | עִם־יְהוֹשָׁפָט |
| because he walked | כִּי הָלַךְ |
| in the **earlier** ways of his father David | בְּדַרְכֵי דָּוִיד אָבִיו הָרִאשֹׁנִים |
| **He did** not **seek** | וְלֹא דָרַשׁ |
| the **Baals** | לַבְּעָלִים |

Prepare your **work** (מְלַאכְתְּךָ) **outside** (חוּץ) and get it ready for yourself in the **field** (שָׂדֶה); afterwards, then, build your house.
(MLB)

| חוּץ | outside | | 164x |
|---|---|---|---|
| ḥûṣ | | | S2351 |

שָׂדֶה ➤ DAY 158        מְלָאכָה ➤ DAY 279

הָכֵן בַּחוּץ מְלַאכְתֶּךָ וְעַתְּדָהּ בַּשָּׂדֶה לָךְ אַחַר וּבָנִיתָ בֵיתֶךָ׃

| Prepare | הָכֵן |
|---|---|
| your **work** | מְלַאכְתֶּךָ |
| **outside** | בַּחוּץ |
| and get it ready | וְעַתְּדָהּ |
| for yourself | לָךְ |
| in the **field** | בַּשָּׂדֶה |
| afterwards, then | אַחַר |
| build | וּבָנִיתָ |
| your house | בֵיתֶךָ |

It shall be a regular burnt offering throughout your **generations** (דֹרֹתֵיכֶם) at the **entrance** (פֶּתַח) of the tent of **meeting** (מוֹעֵד) before the LORD, where I will meet with you, to speak to you there. (NRSV)

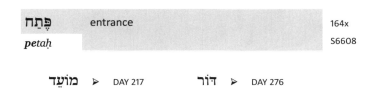

| | |
|---|---|
| פֶּתַח | entrance | 164x |
| *petaḥ* | | S6608 |

מוֹעֵד  ➤  DAY 217        דֹּוֹר  ➤  DAY 276

עֹלַת תָּמִיד לְדֹרֹתֵיכֶם פֶּתַח אֹהֶל־מוֹעֵד לִפְנֵי יְהוָה אֲשֶׁר אִוָּעֵד לָכֶם שָׁמָּה לְדַבֵּר אֵלֶיךָ שָׁם:

| It shall be a regular burnt offering | עֹלַת תָּמִיד |
|---|---|
| throughout your **generations** | לְדֹרֹתֵיכֶם |
| at the **entrance** of | פֶּתַח |
| the tent of **meeting** | אֹהֶל־מוֹעֵד |
| before the LORD | לִפְנֵי יְהוָה |
| where | אֲשֶׁר . . . שָׁמָּה |
| I will meet with you | אִוָּעֵד לָכֶם |
| to speak to you | לְדַבֵּר אֵלֶיךָ |
| there | שָׁם |

The **lords** (בַּעֲלֵי) of Gibeah rose up against me, and **surrounded**
(וַיָּסֹבּוּ) the house [against me] at night. They intended **to kill**
(הֲרֹג) me, and they raped my concubine until she died. (NRSV)

| | | | |
|---|---|---|---|
| **סבב** | to surround, make a circuit | | 163x |
| *sāvav* | | | S5437 |

הרג   ➤   DAY 278              בַּעַל   ➤   DAY 281

וַיָּקֻמוּ עָלַי בַּעֲלֵי הַגִּבְעָה וַיָּסֹבּוּ עָלַי אֶת־הַבַּיִת לַיְלָה אוֹתִי דִּמּוּ
לַהֲרֹג וְאֶת־פִּילַגְשִׁי עִנּוּ וַתָּמֹת:

| | |
|---|---|
| The **lords** of Gibeah | בַּעֲלֵי הַגִּבְעָה |
| rose up against me | וַיָּקֻמוּ עָלַי |
| and **surrounded** the house | וַיָּסֹבּוּ . . . אֶת־הַבַּיִת |
| [against me] at night | עָלַי . . . לַיְלָה |
| They intended **to kill** | דִּמּוּ לַהֲרֹג |
| me | אוֹתִי |
| and . . . my concubine | וְאֶת־פִּילַגְשִׁי |
| they raped | עִנּוּ |
| until she died | וַתָּמֹת |

**He shall remain unclean** (יִטְמָא) as long as he has the disease. He is unclean. He shall live alone. His dwelling shall be **outside** (חוּץ) the **camp** (מַחֲנֶה). (ESV)

| טמא | to be unclean, polluted, defiled | 162x |
|---|---|---|
| ṭāmēʾ | | S2930 |

מַחֲנֶה  ➤  DAY 228            חוּץ  ➤  DAY 282

כָּל־יְמֵי אֲשֶׁר הַנֶּגַע בּוֹ יִטְמָא טָמֵא הוּא בָּדָד יֵשֵׁב מִחוּץ לַמַּחֲנֶה מוֹשָׁבוֹ׃

| He shall remain unclean | יִטְמָא |
|---|---|
| as long as | כָּל־יְמֵי אֲשֶׁר |
| he has the disease | הַנֶּגַע בּוֹ |
| He is unclean | טָמֵא הוּא |
| He shall live alone | בָּדָד יֵשֵׁב |
| His dwelling | מוֹשָׁבוֹ |
| shall be **outside** | מִחוּץ |
| the **camp** | לַמַּחֲנֶה |

But as for you, speak to the sons of Israel, saying, "You shall **surely (אַךְ)** observe My sabbaths; for this is a sign between Me and you throughout your **generations (דֹרֹתֵיכֶם)**, that you may know that I am the LORD **who sanctifies (מְקַדִּשְׁכֶם)** you." (NASB)

| | | |
|---|---|---|
| **אַךְ** | surely, only, however | 161x |
| ʾak̲ | | S389 |

קדשׁ  ➤  DAY 273          דוֹר  ➤  DAY 276

וְאַתָּה דַּבֵּר אֶל־בְּנֵי יִשְׂרָאֵל לֵאמֹר אַךְ אֶת־שַׁבְּתֹתַי תִּשְׁמֹרוּ כִּי אוֹת הִוא בֵּינִי וּבֵינֵיכֶם לְדֹרֹתֵיכֶם לָדַעַת כִּי אֲנִי יְהוָה מְקַדִּשְׁכֶם:

| | |
|---|---|
| But as for you | וְאַתָּה |
| speak | דַּבֵּר |
| to the sons of Israel | אֶל־בְּנֵי יִשְׂרָאֵל |
| saying | לֵאמֹר |
| You shall **surely** observe | אַךְ . . . תִּשְׁמֹרוּ |
| My sabbaths | אֶת־שַׁבְּתֹתַי |
| for this is a sign | כִּי אוֹת הִוא |
| between Me and you | בֵּינִי וּבֵינֵיכֶם |
| throughout your **generations** | לְדֹרֹתֵיכֶם |
| that you may know that | לָדַעַת כִּי |
| I am the LORD | אֲנִי יְהוָה |
| **who sanctifies** you | מְקַדִּשְׁכֶם |

Though these three men were in it, as I **live** (חַי), **declares** (נְאֻם)
the Lord GOD, they would deliver neither sons nor daughters, but
they **alone** (לְבַדָּם) would be delivered. (ESV)

| לְבַד | apart, only, besides | 161x |
|---|---|---|
| *lĕvad* | | S905 |

נְאֻם ➤ DAY 141          חַי ➤ DAY 193

וּשְׁלֹשֶׁת הָאֲנָשִׁים הָאֵלֶּה בְּתוֹכָהּ חַי־אָנִי נְאֻם אֲדֹנָי יְהוִה לֹא יַצִּילוּ
בָּנִים וּבָנוֹת כִּי הֵם לְבַדָּם יִנָּצֵלוּ׃

| Though these three men | וּשְׁלֹשֶׁת הָאֲנָשִׁים הָאֵלֶּה |
|---|---|
| were in it | בְּתוֹכָהּ |
| as I **live** | חַי־אָנִי |
| **declares** the Lord GOD | נְאֻם אֲדֹנָי יְהוִה |
| they would deliver neither sons nor daughters | לֹא יַצִּילוּ בָּנִים וּבָנוֹת |
| but they **alone** | כִּי הֵם לְבַדָּם |
| would be delivered | יִנָּצֵלוּ |

And Zichri, a **mighty man** (גִּבּוֹר) of **Ephraim** (אֶפְרַיִם), **killed**
(וַיַּהֲרֹג) Maaseiah the king's son and Azrikam the commander of
the palace and Elkanah the next in authority to the king. (ESV)

| גִּבּוֹר | warrior, mighty man | 160x |
|---|---|---|
| *gibbôr* | | S1368 |

אֶפְרַיִם ➤ DAY 260　　　　　הרג ➤ DAY 278

וַיַּהֲרֹג זִכְרִי גִּבּוֹר אֶפְרַיִם אֶת־מַעֲשֵׂיָהוּ בֶן־הַמֶּלֶךְ וְאֶת־עַזְרִיקָם נְגִיד
הַבַּיִת וְאֶת־אֶלְקָנָה מִשְׁנֵה הַמֶּלֶךְ:

| And Zichri . . . **killed** | וַיַּהֲרֹג זִכְרִי |
|---|---|
| a **mighty man** of **Ephraim** | גִּבּוֹר אֶפְרַיִם |
| Maaseiah | אֶת־מַעֲשֵׂיָהוּ |
| the king's son | בֶן־הַמֶּלֶךְ |
| and Azrikam | וְאֶת־עַזְרִיקָם |
| the commander of the palace | נְגִיד הַבַּיִת |
| and Elkanah | וְאֶת־אֶלְקָנָה |
| the next in authority to the king | מִשְׁנֵה הַמֶּלֶךְ |

Then David ran and stood over the Philistine; he grasped his sword, drew it out of its sheath, and killed him; then **he cut off** (וַיִּכְרׇת) his head with it. When the Philistines saw that their **champion** (גִּבּוֹרָם) was dead, **they fled** (וַיָּנֻסוּ). (NRSV)

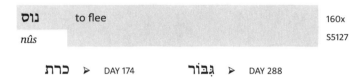

| נוּס | to flee | | 160x |
| nûs | | | S5127 |

כָּרַת ➤ DAY 174     גִּבּוֹר ➤ DAY 288

וַיָּרׇץ דָּוִד וַיַּעֲמֹד אֶל־הַפְּלִשְׁתִּי וַיִּקַּח אֶת־חַרְבּוֹ וַיִּשְׁלְפָהּ מִתַּעְרָהּ
וַיְמֹתְתֵהוּ **וַיִּכְרׇת־בָּהּ** אֶת־רֹאשׁוֹ וַיִּרְאוּ הַפְּלִשְׁתִּים כִּי־מֵת **גִּבּוֹרָם**
**וַיָּנֻסוּ:**

| Then David ran | וַיָּרׇץ דָּוִד |
| and stood over the Philistine | וַיַּעֲמֹד אֶל־הַפְּלִשְׁתִּי |
| he grasped his sword | וַיִּקַּח אֶת־חַרְבּוֹ |
| drew it out of its sheath | וַיִּשְׁלְפָהּ מִתַּעְרָהּ |
| and killed him | וַיְמֹתְתֵהוּ |
| then **he cut off** . . . with it | **וַיִּכְרׇת־בָּהּ** |
| his head | אֶת־רֹאשׁוֹ |
| When the Philistines saw | וַיִּרְאוּ הַפְּלִשְׁתִּים |
| that their **champion** was dead | כִּי־מֵת **גִּבּוֹרָם** |
| **they fled** | **וַיָּנֻסוּ** |

**Only** (אַךְ) in the LORD, it shall be said of me, are **righteousness** (צְדָקוֹת) and strength; to him **shall come** (יָבוֹא) and be ashamed all who were incensed against him. (ESV)

| צְדָקָה | righteousness, justice, virtue | 159x |
|---|---|---|
| ṣĕdāqâ | | S6666 |

בוֹא ➤ DAY 20　　　　　אַךְ ➤ DAY 286

אַךְ בַּיהוָה לִי אָמַר צְדָקוֹת וָעֹז עָדָיו יָבוֹא וְיֵבֹשׁוּ כֹּל הַנֶּחֱרִים בּוֹ׃

| | |
|---|---|
| **Only** in the LORD | אַךְ בַּיהוָה |
| it shall be said of me | לִי אָמַר |
| are **righteousness** and strength | צְדָקוֹת וָעֹז |
| to him | עָדָיו |
| **shall come** | יָבוֹא |
| and be ashamed | וְיֵבֹשׁוּ |
| all who were incensed | כֹּל הַנֶּחֱרִים |
| against him | בּוֹ |

The **name** (שֵׁם) of the **second** (שֵׁנִי) river is Gihon; it is the one **that flows around** (סוֹבֵב) the whole land of Cush. (NRSV)

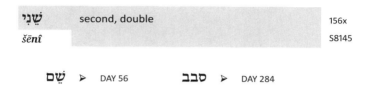

| שֵׁנִי | second, double | 156x |
|---|---|---|
| *šēnî* | | S8145 |

שֵׁם   ➤   DAY 56      סבב   ➤   DAY 284

וְשֵׁם־הַנָּהָר הַשֵּׁנִי גִּיחוֹן הוּא הַסּוֹבֵב אֵת כָּל־אֶרֶץ כּוּשׁ׃

| The **name** of | וְשֵׁם־ |
|---|---|
| the **second** river | הַנָּהָר הַשֵּׁנִי |
| is Gihon | גִּיחוֹן |
| it is | הוּא |
| the one **that flows around** | הַסּוֹבֵב |
| the whole land of Cush | אֵת כָּל־אֶרֶץ כּוּשׁ |

O children of Zion, be glad and **rejoice** (שִׂמְחוּ) in the Lᴏʀᴅ your God; for he has given the early rain for your **vindication** (צְדָקָה), he has poured down for you abundant rain, the early and the later rain, as **before** (רִאשׁוֹן). (NRSV)

| שׂמח<br>*śāmaḥ* | to rejoice | 156x<br>S8055 |
|---|---|---|

| רִאשׁוֹן | ➤ DAY 259 | צְדָקָה | ➤ DAY 290 |
|---|---|---|---|

וּבְנֵי צִיּוֹן גִּילוּ וְשִׂמְחוּ בַּיהוָה אֱלֹהֵיכֶם כִּי־נָתַן לָכֶם אֶת־הַמּוֹרֶה לִצְדָקָה וַיּוֹרֶד לָכֶם גֶּשֶׁם מוֹרֶה וּמַלְקוֹשׁ בָּרִאשׁוֹן:

| O children of Zion | וּבְנֵי צִיּוֹן |
|---|---|
| be glad and **rejoice** | גִּילוּ וְשִׂמְחוּ |
| in the Lᴏʀᴅ your God | בַּיהוָה אֱלֹהֵיכֶם |
| for he has given | כִּי־נָתַן |
| the early rain | אֶת־הַמּוֹרֶה |
| for your **vindication** | לָכֶם . . . לִצְדָקָה |
| he has poured down for you | וַיּוֹרֶד לָכֶם |
| abundant rain | גֶּשֶׁם |
| the early and the later rain | מוֹרֶה וּמַלְקוֹשׁ |
| as **before** | בָּרִאשׁוֹן |

Zion (צִיּוֹן) hears and **rejoices** (וַתִּשְׂמַח) and the villages [lit., daughters] of Judah are glad **because of** (לְמַעַן) your judgments, Lᴏʀᴅ. (NIV)

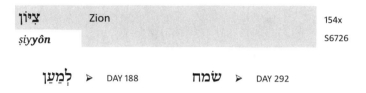

| צִיּוֹן | Zion | 154x |
| --- | --- | --- |
| ṣiyyôn | | S6726 |

לְמַעַן  ➤  DAY 188        שׂמח  ➤  DAY 292

שָׁמְעָה וַתִּשְׂמַח צִיּוֹן וַתָּגֵלְנָה בְּנוֹת יְהוּדָה לְמַעַן מִשְׁפָּטֶיךָ יְהוָה:

| | |
| --- | --- |
| **Zion** | צִיּוֹן |
| hears | שָׁמְעָה |
| and **rejoices** | וַתִּשְׂמַח |
| and . . . are glad | וַתָּגֵלְנָה |
| the villages [lit., daughters] of Judah | בְּנוֹת יְהוּדָה |
| **because of** | לְמַעַן |
| your judgments | מִשְׁפָּטֶיךָ |
| Lᴏʀᴅ | יְהוָה |

His holy mountain, beautiful in elevation, is the joy of all the earth, Mount **Zion** (צִיּוֹן), in the far **north** (צָפוֹן), the city of the **great** (רָב) King. (NRSV)

| צָפוֹן | north | 154x |
|---|---|---|
| ṣāfôn | | S6828 |

רָב ▸ DAY 127          צִיּוֹן ▸ DAY 293

הַר־קָדְשׁוֹ יְפֵה נוֹף מְשׂוֹשׂ כָּל־הָאָרֶץ הַר־צִיּוֹן יַרְכְּתֵי צָפוֹן קִרְיַת מֶלֶךְ רָב:

| His holy mountain | הַר־קָדְשׁוֹ |
|---|---|
| beautiful in elevation | יְפֵה נוֹף |
| is the joy of | מְשׂוֹשׂ |
| all the earth | כָּל־הָאָרֶץ |
| Mount **Zion** | הַר־צִיּוֹן |
| in the far **north** | יַרְכְּתֵי צָפוֹן |
| the city of | קִרְיַת |
| the **great** King | מֶלֶךְ רָב |

This is another [lit., **second (שֵׁנִית)**] thing you do. You are
**covering (כַּסּוֹת)** the Lord's altar with tears, with weeping and
groaning, because he no longer respects your **offerings (מִנְחָה)** or
receives them gladly from your hands. (CSB)

| | | | | |
|---|---|---|---|---|
| מִנְחָה | ➤ | DAY 235 | שֵׁנִי | ➤ DAY 291 |

וְזֹאת שֵׁנִית תַּעֲשׂוּ כַּסּוֹת דִּמְעָה אֶת־מִזְבַּח יְהוָה בְּכִי וַאֲנָקָה מֵאֵין
עוֹד פְּנוֹת אֶל־הַמִּנְחָה וְלָקַחַת רָצוֹן מִיֶּדְכֶם:

| | |
|---|---|
| This is another [lit., **second**] thing | וְזֹאת שֵׁנִית |
| you do | תַּעֲשׂוּ |
| You are **covering** . . . with tears | כַּסּוֹת דִּמְעָה |
| the Lord's altar | אֶת־מִזְבַּח יְהוָה |
| with weeping and groaning | בְּכִי וַאֲנָקָה |
| because he no longer respects | מֵאֵין עוֹד פְּנוֹת |
| your **offerings** | אֶל־הַמִּנְחָה |
| or receives them gladly | וְלָקַחַת רָצוֹן |
| from your hands | מִיֶּדְכֶם |

For **death** (מָוֶת) has come up into our windows; it has entered our palaces, **cutting off** (הַכְרִית) the children from the **streets** (חוּץ) and the young men from the squares. (ESV)

| מָוֶת | death | | 153x |
|---|---|---|---|
| *māvet* | | | S4194 |

כרת ➤ DAY 174         חוּץ ➤ DAY 282

כִּי־עָלָה מָוֶת בְּחַלּוֹנֵינוּ בָּא בְּאַרְמְנוֹתֵינוּ לְהַכְרִית עוֹלָל מִחוּץ בַּחוּרִים מֵרְחֹבוֹת:

| For | כִּי־ |
|---|---|
| **death** has come up | עָלָה מָוֶת |
| into our windows | בְּחַלּוֹנֵינוּ |
| it has entered our palaces | בָּא בְּאַרְמְנוֹתֵינוּ |
| **cutting off** the children | לְהַכְרִית עוֹלָל |
| from the **streets** | מִחוּץ |
| and the young men | בַּחוּרִים |
| from the squares | מֵרְחֹבוֹת |

The Almighty—**we can**not **find** (מְצָאנֻהוּ) him; he is great
in power; justice and abundant [lit., an **abundance** (רֹב) of]
**righteousness** (צְדָקָה) he will not violate. (ESV)

| רֹב | abundance, greatness | 152x |
|---|---|---|
| *rōv* | | S7230 |

מצא ➤ DAY 117            צְדָקָה ➤ DAY 290

שַׁדַּי לֹא־מְצָאנֻהוּ שַׂגִּיא־כֹחַ וּמִשְׁפָּט וְרֹב־צְדָקָה לֹא יְעַנֶּה:

| The Almighty | שַׁדַּי |
|---|---|
| **we can**not **find** him | לֹא־מְצָאנֻהוּ |
| he is great in power | שַׂגִּיא־כֹחַ |
| justice | וּמִשְׁפָּט |
| and abundant [lit., an **abundance** of] **righteousness** | וְרֹב־צְדָקָה |
| he will not violate | לֹא יְעַנֶּה |

Then all the people of **war** (מִלְחָמָה) who were with him went up
and drew near and arrived **in front of** (נֶגֶד) the city, and camped
on the **north side** (צָפוֹן) of Ai. Now there was a valley between
him and Ai. (NASB)

| נֶגֶד | before, in front of, opposite | 152x |
|---|---|---|
| *ne*ged | | S5048 |

מִלְחָמָה ▸ DAY 159          צָפוֹן ▸ DAY 294

וְכָל־הָעָם הַמִּלְחָמָה אֲשֶׁר אִתּוֹ עָלוּ וַיִּגְּשׁוּ וַיָּבֹאוּ נֶגֶד הָעִיר וַיַּחֲנוּ
מִצָּפוֹן לָעַי וְהַגַּי בֵּינָיו וּבֵין־הָעָי:

| | |
|---|---|
| Then all the people of **war** | וְכָל־הָעָם הַמִּלְחָמָה |
| who were with him | אֲשֶׁר אִתּוֹ |
| went up | עָלוּ |
| and drew near | וַיִּגְּשׁוּ |
| and arrived | וַיָּבֹאוּ |
| **in front of** the city | נֶגֶד הָעִיר |
| and camped | וַיַּחֲנוּ |
| on the **north side** of Ai | מִצָּפוֹן לָעַי |
| Now there was a valley | וְהַגַּי |
| between him and Ai | בֵּינָיו וּבֵין־הָעָי |

Therefore, the Lord G**OD** of Armies says this: "My people who dwell in **Zion** (צִיּוֹן), do not fear **Assyria** (אַשּׁוּר), though they strike you with a rod and raise their **staff** (מַטֵּהוּ) over you as the Egyptians did." (CSB)

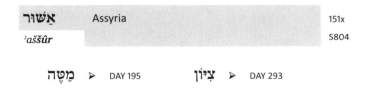

| אַשּׁוּר | Assyria | 151x |
| ʾaššûr | | S804 |

מַטֶּה   ➤   DAY 195       צִיּוֹן   ➤   DAY 293

לָכֵן כֹּה־אָמַר אֲדֹנָי יְהוִה צְבָאוֹת אַל־תִּירָא עַמִּי יֹשֵׁב **צִיּוֹן** מֵ**אַשּׁוּר** בַּשֵּׁבֶט יַכֶּכָּה וּ**מַטֵּהוּ** יִשָּׂא־עָלֶיךָ בְּדֶרֶךְ מִצְרָיִם:

| | |
|---|---|
| Therefore | לָכֵן |
| the Lord G**OD** of Armies | אֲדֹנָי יְהוִה צְבָאוֹת |
| says this | כֹּה־אָמַר |
| My people who dwell in **Zion** | עַמִּי יֹשֵׁב **צִיּוֹן** |
| do not fear **Assyria** | אַל־תִּירָא . . . מֵ**אַשּׁוּר** |
| though they strike you | יַכֶּכָּה |
| with a rod | בַּשֵּׁבֶט |
| and . . . their **staff** | וּ**מַטֵּהוּ** |
| raise . . . over you | יִשָּׂא־עָלֶיךָ |
| as the Egyptians did | בְּדֶרֶךְ מִצְרָיִם |

So the Lord brought against them the commanders of the army
of the king of **Assyria** (אַשּׁוּר). They seized **Manasseh** (מְנַשֶּׁה)
with hooks, binding him in double fetters, and carried him off to
**Babylon** (בָּבֶלָה). (MLB)

| מְנַשֶּׁה | Manasseh | 150x |
|---|---|---|
| *měnaššê* | | S4519 |

בָּבֶל  ➤  DAY 192          אַשּׁוּר  ➤  DAY 299

וַיָּבֵא יְהוָה עֲלֵיהֶם אֶת־שָׂרֵי הַצָּבָא אֲשֶׁר לְמֶלֶךְ **אַשּׁוּר** וַיִּלְכְּדוּ אֶת־
**מְנַשֶּׁה** בַּחֹחִים וַיַּאַסְרֻהוּ בַּנְחֻשְׁתַּיִם וַיּוֹלִיכֻהוּ **בָּבֶלָה**׃

| So the Lord brought against them | וַיָּבֵא יְהוָה עֲלֵיהֶם |
|---|---|
| the commanders of the army | אֶת־שָׂרֵי הַצָּבָא |
| of the king of **Assyria** | אֲשֶׁר לְמֶלֶךְ **אַשּׁוּר** |
| They seized | וַיִּלְכְּדוּ |
| **Manasseh** | אֶת־**מְנַשֶּׁה** |
| with hooks | בַּחֹחִים |
| binding him | וַיַּאַסְרֻהוּ |
| in double fetters | בַּנְחֻשְׁתַּיִם |
| and carried him off | וַיּוֹלִיכֻהוּ |
| to **Babylon** | **בָּבֶלָה** |

And behold, one who resembled a human being **was touching** (נֹגֵעַ) my **lips** (שְׂפָתָי); then I opened my mouth and spoke and said to him who was standing **before** (לְנֶגְדִּי) me, "O my lord, as a result of the vision anguish has come upon me, and I have retained no strength." (NASB)

| נגע | to touch, reach, strike | 150x |
|-----|-------------------------|------|
| *nāgaʿ* |  | S5060 |

| שָׂפָה | ➤ | DAY 263 | נֶגֶד | ➤ | DAY 298 |
|--------|---|---------|-------|---|---------|

וְהִנֵּה כִּדְמוּת בְּנֵי אָדָם נֹגֵעַ עַל־שְׂפָתָי וָאֶפְתַּח־פִּי וָאֲדַבְּרָה וָאֹמְרָה אֶל־הָעֹמֵד לְנֶגְדִּי אֲדֹנִי בַּמַּרְאָה נֶהֶפְכוּ צִירַי עָלַי וְלֹא עָצַרְתִּי כֹּחַ:

| And behold | וְהִנֵּה |
|---|---|
| one who resembled a human being | כִּדְמוּת בְּנֵי אָדָם |
| **was touching** my **lips** | נֹגֵעַ עַל־שְׂפָתָי |
| then I opened my mouth | וָאֶפְתַּח־פִּי |
| and spoke and said | וָאֲדַבְּרָה וָאֹמְרָה |
| to him who was standing | אֶל־הָעֹמֵד |
| **before** me | לְנֶגְדִּי |
| O my lord | אֲדֹנִי |
| as a result of the vision | בַּמַּרְאָה |
| anguish has come upon me | נֶהֶפְכוּ צִירַי עָלַי |
| and I have retained no strength | וְלֹא עָצַרְתִּי כֹּחַ |

He warned the **assembly** (עֵדָה), "Move back from the tents of these **wicked** (רְשָׁעִים) men! Do not **touch** (תִּגְּעוּ) anything belonging to them, or you will be swept away because of all their sins." (NIV)

| עֵדָה | assembly, congregation | 149x |
|---|---|---|
| ʿēdâ | | S5712 |

רָשָׁע ➤ DAY 191         נגע ➤ DAY 301

וַיְדַבֵּר אֶל־הָעֵדָה לֵאמֹר סוּרוּ נָא מֵעַל אָהֳלֵי הָאֲנָשִׁים הָרְשָׁעִים הָאֵלֶּה וְאַל־תִּגְּעוּ בְּכָל־אֲשֶׁר לָהֶם פֶּן־תִּסָּפוּ בְּכָל־חַטֹּאתָם:

| He warned the **assembly** | וַיְדַבֵּר אֶל־הָעֵדָה לֵאמֹר |
|---|---|
| Move back from | סוּרוּ נָא מֵעַל |
| the tents of | אָהֳלֵי |
| these **wicked** men! | הָאֲנָשִׁים הָרְשָׁעִים הָאֵלֶּה |
| Do not **touch** | וְאַל־תִּגְּעוּ |
| anything belonging to them | בְּכָל־אֲשֶׁר לָהֶם |
| or you will be swept away | פֶּן־תִּסָּפוּ |
| because of all their sins | בְּכָל־חַטֹּאתָם |

I thought, "Age [lit., days] should speak; advanced [lit., an
**abundance (רֹב)** of] years **should teach (יֹדִיעוּ) wisdom (חָכְמָה)**."
(NIV)

| חָכְמָה | wisdom | 149x |
|---|---|---|
| ḥokmâ | | S2451 |

| יָדַע | ➤ DAY 50 | רֹב | ➤ DAY 297 |
|---|---|---|---|

אָמַרְתִּי יָמִים יְדַבֵּרוּ וְרֹב שָׁנִים יֹדִיעוּ חָכְמָה:

| I thought | אָמַרְתִּי |
|---|---|
| Age [lit., days] | יָמִים |
| should speak | יְדַבֵּרוּ |
| advanced [lit., an **abundance** of] years | וְרֹב שָׁנִים |
| **should teach** | יֹדִיעוּ |
| **wisdom** | חָכְמָה |

At Tehaphnehes the day will become dark when I **break** (שִׁבְרִי) there the yoke of Egypt and when the pride of her power ceases. She **shall be covered** (יְכַסֶּנָּה) by a cloud, and her daughters **shall go** (תֵלַכְנָה) into captivity. (MLB)

| | | |
|---|---|---|
| שׁבר | to break, destroy | 148x |
| *šāvar* | | S7665 |

הלך ➤ DAY 31          כסה ➤ DAY 295

וּבִתְחַפְנְחֵס חָשַׂךְ הַיּוֹם בְּשִׁבְרִי־שָׁם אֶת־מֹטוֹת מִצְרַיִם וְנִשְׁבַּת־בָּהּ גְּאוֹן עֻזָּהּ הִיא עָנָן יְכַסֶּנָּה וּבְנוֹתֶיהָ בַּשְּׁבִי תֵלַכְנָה:

| | |
|---|---|
| At Tehaphnehes | וּבִתְחַפְנְחֵס |
| the day will become dark | חָשַׂךְ הַיּוֹם |
| when I **break** there | בְּשִׁבְרִי־שָׁם |
| the yoke of Egypt | אֶת־מֹטוֹת מִצְרַיִם |
| and when . . . ceases | וְנִשְׁבַּת־בָּהּ |
| the pride of her power | גְּאוֹן עֻזָּהּ |
| She **shall be covered** by a cloud | הִיא עָנָן יְכַסֶּנָּה |
| and her daughters | וּבְנוֹתֶיהָ |
| **shall go** into captivity | בַּשְּׁבִי תֵלַכְנָה |

Be gracious to me, O Lord, see what I suffer from **those who hate**
(שֹׂנְאָי) me, O Thou who dost lift me up from the **gates** (שַׁעֲרֵי) of
**death** (מָוֶת). (MLB)

| שׂנא | to hate | 148x |
|---|---|---|
| *śānā'* | | S8130 |

שַׁעַר ➤ DAY 142        מָוֶת ➤ DAY 296

חָנְנֵנִי יְהוָה רְאֵה עָנְיִי מִשֹּׂנְאָי מְרוֹמְמִי מִשַּׁעֲרֵי מָוֶת:

| Be gracious to me | חָנְנֵנִי |
|---|---|
| O Lord | יְהוָה |
| see | רְאֵה |
| what I suffer | עָנְיִי |
| from **those who hate** me | מִשֹּׂנְאָי |
| O Thou who dost lift me up | מְרוֹמְמִי |
| from the **gates** of **death** | מִשַּׁעֲרֵי מָוֶת |

For in the eighth year [lit., **eight** (שְׁמוֹנֶה) years] of his reign, while he was still a **boy** (נַעַר), he began **to seek** (דְרוֹשׁ) the God of his ancestor David. (NRSV)

| שְׁמוֹנֶה | eight | 147x |
|---|---|---|
| *šĕmōnê* | | S8083 |

נַעַר ➤ DAY 202     דרשׁ ➤ DAY 280

וּבִשְׁמוֹנֶה שָׁנִים לְמָלְכוֹ וְהוּא עוֹדֶנּוּ נַעַר הֵחֵל לִדְרוֹשׁ לֵאלֹהֵי דָּוִיד אָבִיו

| For in the eighth year [lit., **eight** years] | וּבִשְׁמוֹנֶה שָׁנִים |
|---|---|
| of his reign | לְמָלְכוֹ |
| while he was still a **boy** | וְהוּא עוֹדֶנּוּ נַעַר |
| he began | הֵחֵל |
| **to seek** | לִדְרוֹשׁ |
| the God of | לֵאלֹהֵי |
| his ancestor David | דָּוִיד אָבִיו |

**Praise** (הַלְלוּ) the LORD! I will give thanks to the LORD with my whole **heart** (לֵבָב), in the company of the upright, in the **congregation** (עֵדָה). (ESV)

| הָלַל | to praise, boast | 146x |
|---|---|---|
| *hālal* | | S1984 |

לֵבָב ➤ DAY 194         עֵדָה ➤ DAY 302

הַלְלוּ יָהּ אוֹדֶה יְהוָה בְּכָל־לֵבָב בְּסוֹד יְשָׁרִים וְעֵדָה׃

| | |
|---|---|
| **Praise** | הַלְלוּ |
| the LORD! | יָהּ |
| I will give thanks to | אוֹדֶה |
| the LORD | יְהוָה |
| with my whole **heart** | בְּכָל־לֵבָב |
| in the company of | בְּסוֹד |
| the upright | יְשָׁרִים |
| in the **congregation** | וְעֵדָה |

Whenever the ark **set out** (נְסֹעַ), Moses would say: Arise, LORD!
Let your **enemies** (אֹיְבֶיךָ) be scattered, and **those who hate**
(מְשַׂנְאֶיךָ) you flee from your presence. (CSB)

| נסע | to pull out, set out, journey | 146x |
|---|---|---|
| *nāsaʿ* | | S5265 |

| אֹיֵב | ➤ | DAY 178 | | שָׂנֵא | ➤ | DAY 305 |
|---|---|---|---|---|---|---|

וַיְהִי בִּנְסֹעַ הָאָרֹן וַיֹּאמֶר מֹשֶׁה קוּמָה יְהוָה וְיָפֻצוּ אֹיְבֶיךָ וְיָנֻסוּ
מְשַׂנְאֶיךָ מִפָּנֶיךָ׃

| Whenever the ark **set out** | וַיְהִי בִּנְסֹעַ הָאָרֹן |
|---|---|
| Moses would say | וַיֹּאמֶר מֹשֶׁה |
| Arise, LORD! | קוּמָה יְהוָה |
| Let your **enemies** be scattered | וְיָפֻצוּ אֹיְבֶיךָ |
| and . . . flee | וְיָנֻסוּ |
| **those who hate** you | מְשַׂנְאֶיךָ |
| from your presence | מִפָּנֶיךָ |

And **Joab** (יוֹאָב) gave the number of the registration of the people to the king; and there were in Israel **eight** (שְׁמֹנֶה) hundred **thousand** (אֶלֶף) valiant men who drew the sword, and the men of Judah were five hundred **thousand** (אֶלֶף) men. (NASB)

| | | |
|---|---|---|
| **יוֹאָב** | Joab | 145x |
| *yô'āv* | | S3097 |

אֶלֶף　＞　DAY 107　　　שְׁמֹנֶה　＞　DAY 306

וַיִּתֵּן יוֹאָב אֶת־מִסְפַּר מִפְקַד־הָעָם אֶל־הַמֶּלֶךְ וַתְּהִי יִשְׂרָאֵל שְׁמֹנֶה
מֵאוֹת אֶלֶף אִישׁ־חַיִל שֹׁלֵף חֶרֶב וְאִישׁ יְהוּדָה חֲמֵשׁ־מֵאוֹת אֶלֶף
אִישׁ:

| | |
|---|---|
| And **Joab** gave | וַיִּתֵּן יוֹאָב |
| the number of | אֶת־מִסְפַּר |
| the registration of the people | מִפְקַד־הָעָם |
| to the king | אֶל־הַמֶּלֶךְ |
| and there were in Israel | וַתְּהִי יִשְׂרָאֵל |
| **eight** hundred **thousand** | שְׁמֹנֶה מֵאוֹת אֶלֶף |
| valiant men | אִישׁ־חַיִל |
| who drew the sword | שֹׁלֵף חֶרֶב |
| and the men of Judah | וְאִישׁ יְהוּדָה |
| were five hundred **thousand** | חֲמֵשׁ־מֵאוֹת אֶלֶף |
| men | אִישׁ |

And they came, everyone whose heart stirred him, and everyone whose **spirit** (רוּחוֹ) moved him, and brought the LORD's contribution to be used for [lit., for the **work** (מְלֶאכֶת) of] the tent of meeting, and for all its **service** (עֲבֹדָתוֹ), and for the holy garments. (ESV)

| עֲבֹדָה | work, labor, service, worship | 145x |
|---|---|---|
| *ʿăvōdâ* | | S5656 |

רוּחַ  ➤  DAY 139      מְלָאכָה  ➤  DAY 279

וַיָּבֹאוּ כָּל־אִישׁ אֲשֶׁר־נְשָׂאוֹ לִבּוֹ וְכֹל אֲשֶׁר נָדְבָה רוּחוֹ אֹתוֹ הֵבִיאוּ
אֶת־תְּרוּמַת יְהוָה לִמְלֶאכֶת אֹהֶל מוֹעֵד וּלְכָל־עֲבֹדָתוֹ וּלְבִגְדֵי הַקֹּדֶשׁ:

| | |
|---|---|
| And they came | וַיָּבֹאוּ |
| everyone | כָּל־אִישׁ |
| whose heart stirred him | אֲשֶׁר־נְשָׂאוֹ לִבּוֹ |
| and everyone | וְכֹל |
| whose **spirit** moved him | אֲשֶׁר נָדְבָה רוּחוֹ אֹתוֹ |
| and brought | הֵבִיאוּ |
| the LORD's contribution | אֶת־תְּרוּמַת יְהוָה |
| to be used for [lit., for the **work** of] the tent of meeting | לִמְלֶאכֶת אֹהֶל מוֹעֵד |
| and for all its **service** | וּלְכָל־עֲבֹדָתוֹ |
| and for the holy garments | וּלְבִגְדֵי הַקֹּדֶשׁ |

So **Joab** (יוֹאָב) blew the trumpet; and all the people halted and **pursued** (יִרְדְּפוּ) Israel no longer, nor did they continue **to fight** (הִלָּחֵם) anymore. (NASB)

| | | |
|---|---|---|
| רדף | to pursue, persecute | 144x |
| rādaf | | S7291 |

לחם    ➤   DAY 271        יוֹאָב    ➤   DAY 309

וַיִּתְקַע **יוֹאָב** בַּשּׁוֹפָר וַיַּעַמְדוּ כָּל־הָעָם וְלֹא־**יִרְדְּפוּ** עוֹד אַחֲרֵי יִשְׂרָאֵל וְלֹא־יָסְפוּ עוֹד לְהִלָּחֵם:

| | |
|---|---|
| So **Joab** blew | וַיִּתְקַע **יוֹאָב** |
| the trumpet | בַּשּׁוֹפָר |
| and all the people halted | וַיַּעַמְדוּ כָּל־הָעָם |
| and **pursued** Israel no longer | וְלֹא־**יִרְדְּפוּ** עוֹד אַחֲרֵי יִשְׂרָאֵל |
| nor did they continue | וְלֹא־יָסְפוּ |
| **to fight** anymore | עוֹד לְהִלָּחֵם |

Then the Egyptians **chased** (וַיִּרְדְּפוּ) after them with all the horses and chariots of **Pharaoh** (פַּרְעֹה), his horsemen and his army, and they overtook them **camping** (חֹנִים) by the sea, beside Pi-hahiroth, in front of Baal-zephon. (NASB)

| חנה | to pitch a tent, encamp | 143x |
|-----|-------------------------|------|
| ḥānâ | | S2583 |

פַּרְעֹה    ➤    DAY 185         רדף    ➤    DAY 311

וַיִּרְדְּפוּ מִצְרַיִם אַחֲרֵיהֶם וַיַּשִּׂיגוּ אוֹתָם **חֹנִים** עַל־הַיָּם כָּל־סוּס רֶכֶב פַּרְעֹה וּפָרָשָׁיו וְחֵילוֹ עַל־פִּי הַחִירֹת לִפְנֵי בַּעַל צְפֹן:

| | |
|---|---|
| Then the Egyptians **chased** | וַיִּרְדְּפוּ מִצְרַיִם |
| after them | אַחֲרֵיהֶם |
| with all the horses | כָּל־סוּס |
| and chariots of **Pharaoh** | רֶכֶב פַּרְעֹה |
| his horsemen | וּפָרָשָׁיו |
| and his army | וְחֵילוֹ |
| and they overtook them | וַיַּשִּׂיגוּ אוֹתָם |
| **camping** | חֹנִים |
| by the sea | עַל־הַיָּם |
| beside Pi-hahiroth | עַל־פִּי הַחִירֹת |
| in front of Baal-zephon | לִפְנֵי בַּעַל צְפֹן |

So **I hated** (שָׂנֵאתִי) life, because the work **that** (שֶׁ) is done **under** (תַּחַת) the sun was grievous to me. All of it is meaningless, a chasing after the wind. (NIV)

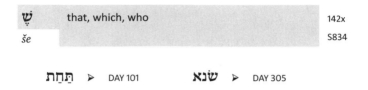

| | | |
|---|---|---|
| שֶׁ | that, which, who | 142x |
| še | | S834 |

תַּחַת　▷　DAY 101　　　　שנא　▷　DAY 305

וְשָׂנֵאתִי אֶת־הַחַיִּים כִּי רַע עָלַי הַמַּעֲשֶׂה שֶׁנַּעֲשָׂה תַּחַת הַשָּׁמֶשׁ כִּי־הַכֹּל הֶבֶל וּרְעוּת רוּחַ:

| So **I hated** | וְשָׂנֵאתִי |
|---|---|
| life | אֶת־הַחַיִּים |
| because | כִּי |
| the work | הַמַּעֲשֶׂה |
| **that** is done | שֶׁנַּעֲשָׂה |
| **under** the sun | תַּחַת הַשָּׁמֶשׁ |
| was grievous to me | רַע עָלַי |
| All of it | כִּי־הַכֹּל |
| is meaningless | הֶבֶל |
| a chasing after the wind | וּרְעוּת רוּחַ |

By his cunning he shall make deceit prosper under his hand, and in his own **mind** (לְבָבוֹ) he shall be great. Without warning **he shall destroy** (יַשְׁחִית) many and shall even rise up against the Prince of princes. But **he shall be broken** (יִשָּׁבֵר), and not by human hands. (NRSV)

| שׁחת | to ruin, corrupt, destroy | 142x |
|---|---|---|
| šāḥat | | S7843 |

לֵבָב ➤ DAY 194      שׁבר ➤ DAY 304

וְעַל־שִׂכְלוֹ וְהִצְלִיחַ מִרְמָה בְּיָדוֹ וּבִלְבָבוֹ יַגְדִּיל וּבְשַׁלְוָה יַשְׁחִית רַבִּים וְעַל־שַׂר־שָׂרִים יַעֲמֹד וּבְאֶפֶס יָד יִשָּׁבֵר:

| By his cunning | וְעַל־שִׂכְלוֹ |
|---|---|
| he shall make deceit prosper | וְהִצְלִיחַ מִרְמָה |
| under his hand | בְּיָדוֹ |
| and in his own **mind** | וּבִלְבָבוֹ |
| he shall be great | יַגְדִּיל |
| Without warning | וּבְשַׁלְוָה |
| **he shall destroy** many | יַשְׁחִית רַבִּים |
| and . . . against the Prince of princes | וְעַל־שַׂר־שָׂרִים |
| shall even rise up | יַעֲמֹד |
| But **he shall be broken** | יִשָּׁבֵר |
| and not by human hands | וּבְאֶפֶס יָד |

You have exalted the **right hand** (יְמִין) of his foes; **you have made** all his **enemies rejoice** (הִשְׂמַחְתָּ כָּל־אוֹיְבָיו). (NIV)

| יָמִין yāmîn | right hand; south | 141x S3225 |

אֹיֵב ➢ DAY 178       שׂמח ➢ DAY 292

הֲרִימוֹתָ יְמִין צָרָיו הִשְׂמַחְתָּ כָּל־אוֹיְבָיו:

| You have exalted | הֲרִימוֹתָ |
| the **right hand** of | יְמִין |
| his foes | צָרָיו |
| **you have made . . . rejoice** | הִשְׂמַחְתָּ |
| all his **enemies** | כָּל־אוֹיְבָיו |

"**Bad (רַע)! Bad (רַע)!**" says the buyer; but when he goes his way,
**then (אָז) he boasts (יִתְהַלָּל).** (MLB)

| אָז | at that time; therefore | 141x |
|---|---|---|
| ʾāz | | S227 |

רַע ◁ DAY 146          הלל ◁ DAY 307

רַע רַע יֹאמַר הַקּוֹנֶה וְאֹזֵל לוֹ אָז יִתְהַלָּל:

| Bad! Bad! | רַע רַע |
|---|---|
| says | יֹאמַר |
| the buyer | הַקּוֹנֶה |
| but when he goes his way | וְאֹזֵל לוֹ |
| **then** | אָז |
| **he boasts** | יִתְהַלָּל |

**wine** (יַיִן) that **makes** human hearts **glad** (יְשַׂמַּח)—making his face shine with oil—and **bread** (לֶחֶם) that sustains human hearts. (CSB)

| | | | |
|---|---|---|---|
| יַיִן | wine | | 141x |
| *yayin* | | | S3196 |

לֶחֶם   ➤   DAY 167      שׂמח   ➤   DAY 292

וְיַיִן יְשַׂמַּח לְבַב־אֱנוֹשׁ לְהַצְהִיל פָּנִים מִשָּׁמֶן וְלֶחֶם לְבַב־אֱנוֹשׁ יִסְעָד:

| | |
|---|---|
| **wine** | וְיַיִן |
| that **makes . . . glad** | יְשַׂמַּח |
| human hearts | לְבַב־אֱנוֹשׁ |
| making . . . shine | לְהַצְהִיל |
| his face | פָּנִים |
| with oil | מִשָּׁמֶן |
| and **bread** | וְלֶחֶם |
| that sustains | יִסְעָד |
| human hearts | לְבַב־אֱנוֹשׁ |

So there was hail, and fire flashing continually in the midst of the hail, **very (מְאֹד)** severe, such as [lit., which **like (כָּמֹהוּ)** it] had not been in all the land of Egypt since [lit., from **that time (אָז)** when] it became a nation. (NASB)

| כְּמוֹ | as, like | 141x |
|---|---|---|
| kěmō | | S3644 |

מְאֹד    ➤    DAY 166        אָז    ➤    DAY 316

וַיְהִי בָרָד וְאֵשׁ מִתְלַקַּחַת בְּתוֹךְ הַבָּרָד כָּבֵד מְאֹד אֲשֶׁר לֹא־הָיָה כָמֹהוּ בְּכָל־אֶרֶץ מִצְרַיִם מֵאָז הָיְתָה לְגוֹי:

| So there was hail | וַיְהִי בָרָד |
|---|---|
| and fire | וְאֵשׁ |
| flashing continually | מִתְלַקַּחַת |
| in the midst of the hail | בְּתוֹךְ הַבָּרָד |
| **very** severe | כָּבֵד מְאֹד |
| such as [lit., which **like** it] | אֲשֶׁר . . . כָמֹהוּ |
| had not been | לֹא־הָיָה |
| in all the land of Egypt | בְּכָל־אֶרֶץ מִצְרַיִם |
| since [lit., from **that time** when] | מֵאָז |
| it became a nation | הָיְתָה לְגוֹי |

And I heard the man clothed in linen, who was **above** (מַעַל) the waters of the stream; he raised his **right hand** (יְמִינוֹ) and his left hand toward heaven and swore by him who **lives** (חַי) forever . . . (ESV)

| | | |
|---|---|---|
| מַעַל | above | 140x |
| ma'al | | S4605 |

חַי  ➤  DAY 193          יָמִין  ➤  DAY 315

וָאֶשְׁמַע אֶת־הָאִישׁ לְבוּשׁ הַבַּדִּים אֲשֶׁר מִמַּעַל לְמֵימֵי הַיְאֹר וַיָּרֶם יְמִינוֹ וּשְׂמֹאלוֹ אֶל־הַשָּׁמַיִם וַיִּשָּׁבַע בְּחֵי הָעוֹלָם

| | |
|---|---|
| And I heard | וָאֶשְׁמַע |
| the man | אֶת־הָאִישׁ |
| clothed in linen | לְבוּשׁ הַבַּדִּים |
| who was **above** | אֲשֶׁר מִמַּעַל |
| the waters of the stream | לְמֵימֵי הַיְאֹר |
| he raised | וַיָּרֶם |
| his **right hand** | יְמִינוֹ |
| and his left hand | וּשְׂמֹאלוֹ |
| toward heaven | אֶל־הַשָּׁמַיִם |
| and swore | וַיִּשָּׁבַע |
| by him who **lives** forever | בְּחֵי הָעוֹלָם |

All the utensils of the tabernacle for every **use** (עֲבֹדָתוֹ), and all its pegs and all the pegs of the **court** (חָצֵר), shall be of **bronze** (נְחֹשֶׁת). (NRSV)

| נְחֹשֶׁת | copper, bronze | 140x |
|---|---|---|
| *něḥōšet* | | S5178 |

חָצֵר   ▷  DAY 248      עֲבֹדָה   ▷  DAY 310

לְכֹל כְּלֵי הַמִּשְׁכָּן בְּכֹל עֲבֹדָתוֹ וְכָל־יְתֵדֹתָיו וְכָל־יִתְדֹת הֶחָצֵר נְחֹשֶׁת׃

| | |
|---|---|
| All the utensils of | לְכֹל כְּלֵי |
| the tabernacle | הַמִּשְׁכָּן |
| for every **use** | בְּכֹל עֲבֹדָתוֹ |
| and all its pegs | וְכָל־יְתֵדֹתָיו |
| and all the pegs of | וְכָל־יִתְדֹת |
| the **court** | הֶחָצֵר |
| shall be of **bronze** | נְחֹשֶׁת |

Then **Samuel** (שְׁמוּאֵל) took the horn of **oil** (שֶׁמֶן) and anointed him in the midst of his brothers; and the Spirit of the LORD came mightily upon David from that day **forward** (מָעְלָה). And **Samuel** (שְׁמוּאֵל) arose and went to Ramah. (NASB)

| שְׁמוּאֵל | Samuel | 140x |
|---|---|---|
| šĕmûʾēl | | S8050 |

שֶׁמֶן ▷ DAY 246          מַעַל ▷ DAY 319

וַיִּקַּח שְׁמוּאֵל אֶת־קֶרֶן הַשֶּׁמֶן וַיִּמְשַׁח אֹתוֹ בְּקֶרֶב אֶחָיו וַתִּצְלַח רוּחַ־
יְהוָה אֶל־דָּוִד מֵהַיּוֹם הַהוּא וָמָעְלָה וַיָּקָם שְׁמוּאֵל וַיֵּלֶךְ הָרָמָתָה׃

| Then **Samuel** took | וַיִּקַּח שְׁמוּאֵל |
|---|---|
| the horn of **oil** | אֶת־קֶרֶן הַשֶּׁמֶן |
| and anointed him | וַיִּמְשַׁח אֹתוֹ |
| in the midst of his brothers | בְּקֶרֶב אֶחָיו |
| and . . . came mightily upon David | וַתִּצְלַח . . . אֶל־דָּוִד |
| the Spirit of the LORD | רוּחַ־יְהוָה |
| from that day **forward** | מֵהַיּוֹם הַהוּא וָמָעְלָה |
| And **Samuel** arose | וַיָּקָם שְׁמוּאֵל |
| and went to Ramah | וַיֵּלֶךְ הָרָמָתָה |

A feast is prepared for laughter, and **wine** (יַיִן) makes **life** (חַיִּים) happy, and **money** (כֶּסֶף) is the answer for everything. (CSB)

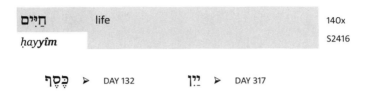

| חַיִּים | life | 140x |
|---|---|---|
| *ḥayyîm* | | S2416 |

כֶּסֶף    ➤   DAY 132       יַיִן    ➤   DAY 317

לִשְׂחוֹק עֹשִׂים לֶחֶם וְיַיִן יְשַׂמַּח **חַיִּים** וְהַכֶּסֶף יַעֲנֶה אֶת־הַכֹּל:

| A feast is prepared | עֹשִׂים לֶחֶם |
|---|---|
| for laughter | לִשְׂחוֹק |
| and **wine** | וְיַיִן |
| makes . . . happy | יְשַׂמַּח |
| **life** | חַיִּים |
| and **money** | וְהַכֶּסֶף |
| is the answer | יַעֲנֶה |
| for everything | אֶת־הַכֹּל |

And you said, "No! **We will flee** (נָנוּס) upon **horses** (סוּס)";
therefore **you shall flee away** (תְּנוּסוּן); and, "We will ride upon
swift steeds"; therefore your **pursuers** (רֹדְפֵיכֶם) shall be swift. (ESV)

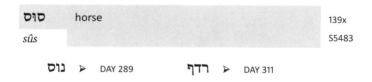

| סוּס | horse | | 139x |
| sûs | | | S5483 |

נוּס  ▷  DAY 289          רדף  ▷  DAY 311

וַתֹּאמְרוּ לֹא־כִי עַל־סוּס נָנוּס עַל־כֵּן תְּנוּסוּן וְעַל־קַל נִרְכָּב עַל־כֵּן
יִקַּלּוּ רֹדְפֵיכֶם:

| And you said | וַתֹּאמְרוּ |
| No! | לֹא־ |
| **We will flee** | כִּי . . . נָנוּס |
| upon **horses** | עַל־סוּס |
| therefore | עַל־כֵּן |
| **you shall flee away** | תְּנוּסוּן |
| and, . . . upon swift steeds | וְעַל־קַל |
| We will ride | נִרְכָּב |
| therefore | עַל־כֵּן |
| your **pursuers** | רֹדְפֵיכֶם |
| shall be swift | יִקַּלּוּ |

When the **tabernacle** (מִשְׁכָּן) is to set out, the Levites **shall take** it **down** (יוֹרִידוּ); and when the **tabernacle** (מִשְׁכָּן) **is to be pitched** (חֲנֹת), the Levites shall set it up. And any outsider who comes near shall be put to death. (NRSV)

| מִשְׁכָּן | dwelling, tabernacle | 139x |
|---|---|---|
| *miškān* | | S4908 |

יָרַד ▹ DAY 137        חנה ▹ DAY 312

וּבִנְסֹעַ הַמִּשְׁכָּן יוֹרִידוּ אֹתוֹ הַלְוִיִּם וּבַחֲנֹת הַמִּשְׁכָּן יָקִימוּ אֹתוֹ הַלְוִיִּם
וְהַזָּר הַקָּרֵב יוּמָת:

| When the **tabernacle** is to set out | וּבִנְסֹעַ הַמִּשְׁכָּן |
|---|---|
| the Levites | הַלְוִיִּם |
| **shall take** it **down** | יוֹרִידוּ אֹתוֹ |
| and when the **tabernacle is to be pitched** | וּבַחֲנֹת הַמִּשְׁכָּן |
| the Levites | הַלְוִיִּם |
| shall set it up | יָקִימוּ אֹתוֹ |
| And any outsider | וְהַזָּר |
| who comes near | הַקָּרֵב |
| shall be put to death | יוּמָת |

My brothers are as treacherous **as** (כְּמוֹ) a **wadi** (נָחַל), as seasonal streams [lit., as a channel of **wadis** (נְחָלִים)] that **overflow** (יַעֲבֹרוּ).
(CSB)

| נַחַל | stream, wadi | 138x |
|---|---|---|
| *naḥal* | | S5158 |

עבר  ➤  DAY 97          כְּמוֹ  ➤  DAY 318

אַחַי בָּגְדוּ כְמוֹ־נָחַל כַּאֲפִיק נְחָלִים יַעֲבֹרוּ:

| My brothers | אַחַי |
|---|---|
| are as treacherous **as** | בָּגְדוּ כְמוֹ־ |
| a **wadi** | נָחַל |
| as seasonal streams [lit., as a channel of **wadis**] | כַּאֲפִיק נְחָלִים |
| that **overflow** | יַעֲבֹרוּ |

The teaching of the **wise** (חָכָם) is a fountain of **life** (חַיִּים), that one may turn away from the snares of **death** (מָוֶת). (ESV)

| | | | |
|---|---|---|---|
| **חָכָם**<br>ḥāḵām | wise | | 138x<br>S2450 |

מָוֶת ➤ DAY 296      חַיִּים ➤ DAY 322

תּוֹרַת חָכָם מְקוֹר חַיִּים לָסוּר מִמֹּקְשֵׁי מָוֶת:

| | |
|---|---|
| The teaching of the **wise** | תּוֹרַת חָכָם |
| is a fountain of **life** | מְקוֹר חַיִּים |
| that one may turn away | לָסוּר |
| from the snares of **death** | מִמֹּקְשֵׁי מָוֶת |

There is (יֵשׁ) a vanity that takes place on earth, that **there are**
(יֵשׁ) righteous people to whom **it happens** (מַגִּיעַ) according to
the deeds of the wicked, and **there are** (יֵשׁ) wicked people to
whom [lit., **that** (שֶׁ) to them] **it happens** (מַגִּיעַ) according to the
deeds of the righteous. I said **that** (שֶׁ) this also is vanity. (ESV)

| יֵשׁ | there is/are | 138x |
|---|---|---|
| yēš | | S3426 |

נגע ➤ DAY 301        שֶׁ ➤ DAY 313

יֵשׁ־הֶבֶל אֲשֶׁר נַעֲשָׂה עַל־הָאָרֶץ אֲשֶׁר יֵשׁ צַדִּיקִים אֲשֶׁר מַגִּיעַ
אֲלֵהֶם כְּמַעֲשֵׂה הָרְשָׁעִים וְיֵשׁ רְשָׁעִים שֶׁמַּגִּיעַ אֲלֵהֶם כְּמַעֲשֵׂה
הַצַּדִּיקִים אָמַרְתִּי שֶׁגַּם־זֶה הָבֶל:

| There is a vanity that | יֵשׁ־הֶבֶל אֲשֶׁר |
|---|---|
| takes place on earth | נַעֲשָׂה עַל־הָאָרֶץ |
| that **there are** righteous people | אֲשֶׁר יֵשׁ צַדִּיקִים |
| to whom **it happens** | אֲשֶׁר מַגִּיעַ אֲלֵהֶם |
| according to the deeds of the wicked | כְּמַעֲשֵׂה הָרְשָׁעִים |
| and **there are** wicked people | וְיֵשׁ רְשָׁעִים |
| to whom [lit., **that** to them] **it happens** | שֶׁמַּגִּיעַ אֲלֵהֶם |
| according to the deeds of the righteous | כְּמַעֲשֵׂה הַצַּדִּיקִים |
| I said | אָמַרְתִּי |
| **that** this also is vanity | זֶה הָבֶל |

So **Samuel** (שְׁמוּאֵל) lay down until morning. Then **he opened** (וַיִּפְתַּח) the doors of the house of the LORD. But **Samuel** (שְׁמוּאֵל) was afraid **to tell** (הַגִּיד) the vision to Eli. (NASB)

| פתח | to open | 136x |
|---|---|---|
| *pātaḥ* | | S6605 |

| נגד | ➤ DAY 143 | שְׁמוּאֵל | ➤ DAY 321 |
|---|---|---|---|

וַיִּשְׁכַּב שְׁמוּאֵל עַד־הַבֹּקֶר וַיִּפְתַּח אֶת־דַּלְתוֹת בֵּית־יְהוָה וּשְׁמוּאֵל
יָרֵא מֵהַגִּיד אֶת־הַמַּרְאָה אֶל־עֵלִי:

| So **Samuel** lay down | וַיִּשְׁכַּב שְׁמוּאֵל |
|---|---|
| until morning | עַד־הַבֹּקֶר |
| Then **he opened** | וַיִּפְתַּח |
| the doors of | אֶת־דַּלְתוֹת |
| the house of the LORD | בֵּית־יְהוָה |
| But **Samuel** was afraid | וּשְׁמוּאֵל יָרֵא |
| **to tell** | מֵהַגִּיד |
| the vision | אֶת־הַמַּרְאָה |
| to Eli | אֶל־עֵלִי |

Then David came to the **two hundred** (מָאתַיִם) men who had
been too exhausted to follow David, and who had been left at the
**Wadi** (נַחַל) Besor. They went out **to meet** (קְרַאת) David and **to
meet** (קְרַאת) the people who were with him. (NRSV)

| קרא | to meet, encounter, happen | 136x |
|---|---|---|
| qārā' | | S7122 |

מֵאָה ► DAY 91　　נַחַל ► DAY 325

וַיָּבֹא דָוִד אֶל־מָאתַיִם הָאֲנָשִׁים אֲשֶׁר־פִּגְּרוּ מִלֶּכֶת אַחֲרֵי דָוִד
וַיֹּשִׁיבֵם בְּנַחַל הַבְּשׂוֹר וַיֵּצְאוּ לִקְרַאת דָוִד וְלִקְרַאת הָעָם אֲשֶׁר־אִתּוֹ

| Then David came to | וַיָּבֹא דָוִד אֶל־ |
|---|---|
| the **two hundred** men | מָאתַיִם הָאֲנָשִׁים |
| who had been too exhausted to follow David | אֲשֶׁר־פִּגְּרוּ מִלֶּכֶת אַחֲרֵי דָוִד |
| and who had been left | וַיֹּשִׁיבֵם |
| at the **Wadi** Besor | בְּנַחַל הַבְּשׂוֹר |
| They went out | וַיֵּצְאוּ |
| **to meet** David | לִקְרַאת דָוִד |
| and **to meet** the people | וְלִקְרַאת הָעָם |
| who were with him | אֲשֶׁר־אִתּוֹ |

They set your sanctuary on **fire** (אֵשׁ); **they profaned** (חִלְּלוּ) the **dwelling place** (מִשְׁכַּן) of your name, bringing it down to the ground. (ESV)

| חלל | to be defiled; profane; begin | 135x |
|---|---|---|
| ḥālal | | S2490 |

אֵשׁ ➤ DAY 138     מִשְׁכַּן ➤ DAY 324

שִׁלְחוּ בָאֵשׁ מִקְדָּשֶׁךָ לָאָרֶץ חִלְּלוּ מִשְׁכַּן־שְׁמֶךָ:

| They set | שִׁלְחוּ |
|---|---|
| your sanctuary | מִקְדָּשֶׁךָ |
| on **fire** | בָאֵשׁ |
| **they profaned** | חִלְּלוּ |
| the **dwelling place** of | מִשְׁכַּן־ |
| your name | שְׁמֶךָ |
| bringing it down to the ground | לָאָרֶץ |

The two angels arrived in Sodom at **evening** (עֶרֶב) as Lot was sitting in the gate of Sodom. When Lot noticed them, he got up **to meet** (קְרָאתָם) them; **he bowed** (וַיִּשְׁתַּחוּ) his face to the ground. (MLB)

| עֶרֶב | evening | 135x |
|---|---|---|
| ʿerev | | S6153 |

| חוה | ▷ DAY 268 | קרא | ▷ DAY 329 |
|---|---|---|---|

וַיָּבֹאוּ שְׁנֵי הַמַּלְאָכִים סְדֹמָה בָּעֶרֶב וְלוֹט יֹשֵׁב בְּשַׁעַר־סְדֹם וַיַּרְא־
לוֹט וַיָּקָם לִקְרָאתָם וַיִּשְׁתַּחוּ אַפַּיִם אָרְצָה:

| The two angels arrived | וַיָּבֹאוּ שְׁנֵי הַמַּלְאָכִים |
|---|---|
| in Sodom | סְדֹמָה |
| at **evening** | בָּעֶרֶב |
| as Lot was sitting | וְלוֹט יֹשֵׁב |
| in the gate of Sodom | בְּשַׁעַר־סְדֹם |
| When Lot noticed them | וַיַּרְא־לוֹט |
| he got up | וַיָּקָם |
| **to meet** them | לִקְרָאתָם |
| **he bowed** his face | וַיִּשְׁתַּחוּ אַפַּיִם |
| to the ground | ־צָה |

"Therefore," he said, "Listen to the word of the Lord. I saw the Lord seated upon His **throne** (כִּסְאוֹ) with all the **host** (צְבָא) of heaven standing beside Him on His **right** (מִימִינוֹ) and on His left." (MLB)

| | seat, throne | 135x |
|---|---|---|
| כִּסֵּא | | |
| kissē' | | S3678 |

צְבָא ➤ DAY 114     יָמִין ➤ DAY 315

וַיֹּאמֶר לָכֵן שְׁמַע דְּבַר־יְהוָה רָאִיתִי אֶת־יְהוָה יֹשֵׁב עַל־כִּסְאוֹ וְכָל־צְבָא הַשָּׁמַיִם עֹמֵד עָלָיו מִימִינוֹ וּמִשְּׂמֹאלוֹ:

| Therefore | לָכֵן |
|---|---|
| he said | וַיֹּאמֶר |
| Listen to | שְׁמַע |
| the word of the Lord | דְּבַר־יְהוָה |
| I saw | רָאִיתִי |
| the Lord | אֶת־יְהוָה |
| seated | יֹשֵׁב |
| upon His **throne** | עַל־כִּסְאוֹ |
| with all the **host** of heaven | וְכָל־צְבָא הַשָּׁמַיִם |
| standing beside Him | עֹמֵד עָלָיו |
| on His **right** | מִימִינוֹ |
| and on His left | וּמִשְּׂמֹאלוֹ |

If sometimes [lit., And **it was (יְשׁ)** that] the cloud remained a
**few (מִסְפָּר)** days over the tabernacle, according to the command
of the LORD they remained camped. Then according to the
command of the LORD **they set out (יִסָּעוּ)**. (NASB)

| מִסְפָּר | number, few | 135x |
|---|---|---|
| *mispār* | | S4557 |

נָסַע ▷ DAY 308        יְשׁ ▷ DAY 327

וְיֵשׁ אֲשֶׁר יִהְיֶה הֶעָנָן יָמִים מִסְפָּר עַל־הַמִּשְׁכָּן עַל־פִּי יְהוָה יַחֲנוּ
וְעַל־פִּי יְהוָה יִסָּעוּ:

| If sometimes [lit., And **it was that**] | וְיֵשׁ אֲשֶׁר |
|---|---|
| the cloud remained | יִהְיֶה הֶעָנָן |
| a **few** days | יָמִים מִסְפָּר |
| over the tabernacle | עַל־הַמִּשְׁכָּן |
| according to the command of the LORD | עַל־פִּי יְהוָה |
| they remained camped | יַחֲנוּ |
| Then according to the command of the LORD | וְעַל־פִּי יְהוָה |
| **they set out** | יִסָּעוּ |

They took up twelve stones out of the middle of the **Jordan** (יַרְדֵּן),
according to the **number** (מִסְפַּר) of the tribes of the Israelites, as
the Lᴏʀᴅ told Joshua, carried them over with them to the place
where they camped, and **laid** them **down** (וַיַּנִּחוּם) there. (NRSV)

| נוּחַ | to rest | | 135x |
| *nûaḥ* | | | S5117 |

| יַרְדֵּן | ▷ | DAY 258 | מִסְפַּר | ▷ | DAY 333 |

וַיִּשְׂאוּ שְׁתֵּי־עֶשְׂרֵה אֲבָנִים מִתּוֹךְ הַיַּרְדֵּן כַּאֲשֶׁר דִּבֶּר יְהוָה אֶל־
יְהוֹשֻׁעַ לְמִסְפַּר שִׁבְטֵי בְנֵי־יִשְׂרָאֵל וַיַּעֲבִרוּם עִמָּם אֶל־הַמָּלוֹן וַיַּנִּחוּם
שָׁם:

| They took up | וַיִּשְׂאוּ |
| twelve stones | שְׁתֵּי־עֶשְׂרֵה אֲבָנִים |
| out of the middle of the **Jordan** | מִתּוֹךְ הַיַּרְדֵּן |
| according to the **number** of | לְמִסְפַּר |
| the tribes of the Israelites | שִׁבְטֵי בְנֵי־יִשְׂרָאֵל |
| as the Lᴏʀᴅ told | כַּאֲשֶׁר דִּבֶּר יְהוָה |
| Joshua | אֶל־יְהוֹשֻׁעַ |
| carried them over with them | וַיַּעֲבִרוּם עִמָּם |
| to the place where they camped | אֶל־הַמָּלוֹן |
| and **laid** them **down** there | וַיַּנִּחוּם שָׁם |

Behold, what I have seen to be good and fitting is to eat and **drink** (שְׁתּוֹת) and find enjoyment in all the toil with which one toils under the **sun** (שֶׁמֶשׁ) the few days of his **life** (חַיָּיו) that God has given him, for this is his lot. (ESV)

| | | |
|---|---|---|
| שֶׁמֶשׁ | sun | 135x |
| šemeš | | S8121 |

שׁתה ➤ DAY 225      חַיִּים ➤ DAY 322

הִנֵּה אֲשֶׁר־רָאִיתִי אָנִי טוֹב אֲשֶׁר־יָפֶה לֶאֱכוֹל־וְלִשְׁתּוֹת וְלִרְאוֹת טוֹבָה בְּכָל־עֲמָלוֹ שֶׁיַּעֲמֹל תַּחַת־הַשֶּׁמֶשׁ מִסְפַּר יְמֵי־חַיָּיו אֲשֶׁר־נָתַן־לוֹ הָאֱלֹהִים כִּי־הוּא חֶלְקוֹ:

| | |
|---|---|
| Behold | הִנֵּה |
| what I have seen | אֲשֶׁר־רָאִיתִי אָנִי |
| to be good and fitting | טוֹב אֲשֶׁר־יָפֶה |
| is to eat and **drink** | לֶאֱכוֹל־וְלִשְׁתּוֹת |
| and find enjoyment | וְלִרְאוֹת טוֹבָה |
| in all the toil | בְּכָל־עֲמָלוֹ |
| with which one toils | שֶׁיַּעֲמֹל |
| under the **sun** | תַּחַת־הַשֶּׁמֶשׁ |
| the few days of his **life** | מִסְפַּר יְמֵי־חַיָּיו |
| that God has given him | אֲשֶׁר־נָתַן־לוֹ הָאֱלֹהִים |
| for this is his lot | כִּי־הוּא חֶלְקוֹ |

But at the place that the LORD your God will choose as a dwelling for his name, only there **shall you offer** (תִּזְבַּח) the passover sacrifice, in the **evening** (עֶרֶב) at sunset [lit., the entering of the **sun** (שֶׁמֶשׁ)], the time of day when you departed from Egypt. (NRSV)

| זבח | to sacrifice | 134x |
|-----|--------------|------|
| *zāvaḥ* | | S2076 |

עֶרֶב ➤ DAY 331      שֶׁמֶשׁ ➤ DAY 335

כִּי אִם־אֶל־הַמָּקוֹם אֲשֶׁר־יִבְחַר יְהוָה אֱלֹהֶיךָ לְשַׁכֵּן שְׁמוֹ שָׁם תִּזְבַּח
אֶת־הַפֶּסַח בָּעָרֶב כְּבוֹא הַשֶּׁמֶשׁ מוֹעֵד צֵאתְךָ מִמִּצְרָיִם:

| But at the place | כִּי אִם־אֶל־הַמָּקוֹם |
|---|---|
| that . . . will choose | אֲשֶׁר־יִבְחַר |
| the LORD your God | יְהוָה אֱלֹהֶיךָ |
| as a dwelling for his name | לְשַׁכֵּן שְׁמוֹ |
| only there **shall you offer** | שָׁם תִּזְבַּח |
| the passover sacrifice | אֶת־הַפֶּסַח |
| in the **evening** | בָּעָרֶב |
| at sunset [lit., the entering of the **sun**] | כְּבוֹא הַשֶּׁמֶשׁ |
| the time of day when | מוֹעֵד |
| you departed from Egypt | צֵאתְךָ מִמִּצְרָיִם |

And now the LORD your God **has given rest** (הֵנִיחַ) to your brothers, as He spoke to them; therefore **turn** (פְּנוּ) now and go to your tents, to the land of your possession, . . . beyond the **Jordan** (יַרְדֵּן). (NASB)

| פנה | to turn | 134x |
|---|---|---|
| *pānâ* | | S6437 |

יַרְדֵּן　▷　DAY 258　　　　נוח　▷　DAY 334

וְעַתָּה הֵנִיחַ יְהוָה אֱלֹהֵיכֶם לַאֲחֵיכֶם כַּאֲשֶׁר דִּבֶּר לָהֶם וְעַתָּה פְּנוּ
וּלְכוּ לָכֶם לְאָהֳלֵיכֶם אֶל־אֶרֶץ אֲחֻזַּתְכֶם . . . בְּעֵבֶר הַיַּרְדֵּן:

| And now | וְעַתָּה |
|---|---|
| the LORD your God | יְהוָה אֱלֹהֵיכֶם |
| **has given rest** | **הֵנִיחַ** |
| to your brothers | לַאֲחֵיכֶם |
| as He spoke to them | כַּאֲשֶׁר דִּבֶּר לָהֶם |
| therefore **turn** now | וְעַתָּה **פְּנוּ** |
| and go to your tents | וּלְכוּ לָכֶם לְאָהֳלֵיכֶם |
| to the land of your possession, . . . | אֶל־אֶרֶץ אֲחֻזַּתְכֶם . . . |
| beyond the **Jordan** | בְּעֵבֶר הַ**יַּרְדֵּן** |

All the **princes** (נְשִׂיאֵי) of the sea will descend from their
**thrones** (כִּסְאוֹתָם), **remove** (וְהֵסִירוּ) their robes, and strip off
their embroidered garments. They will clothe themselves with
trembling; they will sit on the ground, tremble continually, and be
appalled at you. (CSB)

| נָשִׂיא | prince, ruler, chief | 133x |
|---|---|---|
| nāśîʾ | | S5387 |

סוּר ▷ DAY 169     כִּסֵּא ▷ DAY 332

וְיָרְדוּ מֵעַל כִּסְאוֹתָם כֹּל נְשִׂיאֵי הַיָּם וְהֵסִירוּ אֶת־מְעִילֵיהֶם וְאֶת־
בִּגְדֵי רִקְמָתָם יִפְשֹׁטוּ חֲרָדוֹת יִלְבָּשׁוּ עַל־הָאָרֶץ יֵשֵׁבוּ וְחָרְדוּ
לִרְגָעִים וְשָׁמְמוּ עָלָיִךְ:

| All the **princes** of the sea | כֹּל נְשִׂיאֵי הַיָּם |
|---|---|
| will descend from their **thrones** | וְיָרְדוּ מֵעַל כִּסְאוֹתָם |
| **remove** their robes | וְהֵסִירוּ אֶת־מְעִילֵיהֶם |
| and . . . their embroidered garments | וְאֶת־בִּגְדֵי רִקְמָתָם |
| strip off | יִפְשֹׁטוּ |
| They will clothe themselves with trembling | חֲרָדוֹת יִלְבָּשׁוּ |
| they will sit on the ground | עַל־הָאָרֶץ יֵשֵׁבוּ |
| tremble continually | וְחָרְדוּ לִרְגָעִים |
| and be appalled at you | וְשָׁמְמוּ עָלָיִךְ |

Their heart cried to the Lord. O **wall** (חוֹמַת) of the daughter of
**Zion** (צִיּוֹן), let tears stream down like a **torrent** (נַחַל) day and
night! Give yourself no rest, your eyes no respite! (ESV)

| חוֹמָה | wall | 133x |
|---|---|---|
| ḥômâ | | S2346 |

צִיּוֹן ➤ DAY 293     נַחַל ➤ DAY 325

צָעַק לִבָּם אֶל־אֲדֹנָי חוֹמַת בַּת־צִיּוֹן הוֹרִידִי כַנַּחַל דִּמְעָה יוֹמָם
וָלַיְלָה אַל־תִּתְּנִי פוּגַת לָךְ אַל־תִּדֹּם בַּת־עֵינֵךְ:

| Their heart cried | צָעַק לִבָּם |
|---|---|
| to the Lord | אֶל־אֲדֹנָי |
| O **wall** of | חוֹמַת |
| the daughter of **Zion** | בַּת־צִיּוֹן |
| let tears stream down | הוֹרִידִי . . . דִּמְעָה |
| like a **torrent** | כַנַּחַל |
| day and night! | יוֹמָם וָלַיְלָה |
| Give yourself no rest | אַל־תִּתְּנִי פוּגַת לָךְ |
| your eyes no respite! | אַל־תִּדֹּם בַּת־עֵינֵךְ |

Then they said, "The God of the Hebrews **has met** (נִקְרָא) with us. Please let us go a three days' journey into the wilderness that **we may sacrifice** (וְנִזְבְּחָה) to the LORD our God, **lest** (פֶּן) he fall upon us with pestilence or with the sword." (ESV)

| פֶּן | lest, so that . . . not | | 133x |
|------|-------------------------|--|------|
| *pen* | | | S6435 |

קרא ➤ DAY 329            זבח ➤ DAY 336

וַיֹּאמְרוּ אֱלֹהֵי הָעִבְרִים נִקְרָא עָלֵינוּ נֵלֲכָה נָּא דֶרֶךְ שְׁלֹשֶׁת יָמִים בַּמִּדְבָּר וְנִזְבְּחָה לַיהוָה אֱלֹהֵינוּ פֶּן־יִפְגָּעֵנוּ בַּדֶּבֶר אוֹ בֶחָרֶב:

| Then they said | וַיֹּאמְרוּ |
|----------------|-------------|
| The God of the Hebrews | אֱלֹהֵי הָעִבְרִים |
| **has met** with us | נִקְרָא עָלֵינוּ |
| Please let us go | נֵלֲכָה נָּא |
| a three days' journey | דֶרֶךְ שְׁלֹשֶׁת יָמִים |
| into the wilderness | בַּמִּדְבָּר |
| that **we may sacrifice** | וְנִזְבְּחָה |
| to the LORD our God | לַיהוָה אֱלֹהֵינוּ |
| **lest** he fall upon us | פֶּן־יִפְגָּעֵנוּ |
| with pestilence | בַּדֶּבֶר |
| or with the sword | אוֹ בֶחָרֶב |

You shall eat the flesh of the mighty, and drink the blood of the **princes** (נְשִׂיאֵי) of the earth—of **rams** (אֵילִים), of lambs, and of goats, of **bulls** (פָּרִים), all of them fatlings of Bashan. (NRSV)

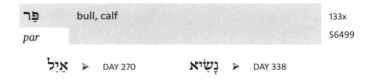

| | | | |
|---|---|---|---|
| פַּר | bull, calf | | 133x |
| *par* | | | S6499 |

אַיִל ▷ DAY 270　　　נָשִׂיא ▷ DAY 338

בְּשַׂר גִּבּוֹרִים תֹּאכֵלוּ וְדַם־נְשִׂיאֵי הָאָרֶץ תִּשְׁתּוּ אֵילִים כָּרִים וְעַתּוּדִים פָּרִים מְרִיאֵי בָשָׁן כֻּלָּם:

| | |
|---|---|
| You shall eat | תֹּאכֵלוּ |
| the flesh of the mighty | בְּשַׂר גִּבּוֹרִים |
| and . . . the blood of | וְדַם־ |
| the **princes** of the earth | נְשִׂיאֵי הָאָרֶץ |
| drink | תִּשְׁתּוּ |
| of **rams** | אֵילִים |
| of lambs | כָּרִים |
| and of goats | וְעַתּוּדִים |
| of **bulls** | פָּרִים |
| all of them | כֻּלָּם |
| fatlings of Bashan | מְרִיאֵי בָשָׁן |

So the prophet **took up** (וַיִּשָּׂא) the body of the man of God and **laid** (וַיַּנִּחֵהוּ) it on the donkey and brought it back, and he came to the city of the old prophet to mourn and **to bury** (קָבְרוֹ) him. (NASB)

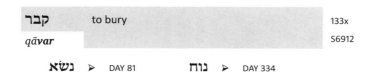

| קָבַר | to bury | 133x |
|---|---|---|
| qāvar | | S6912 |

נָשָׂא   ➤   DAY 81        נוּחַ   ➤   DAY 334

וַיִּשָּׂא הַנָּבִיא אֶת־נִבְלַת אִישׁ־הָאֱלֹהִים וַיַּנִּחֵהוּ אֶל־הַחֲמוֹר וַיְשִׁיבֵהוּ
וַיָּבֹא אֶל־עִיר הַנָּבִיא הַזָּקֵן לִסְפֹּד וּלְקָבְרוֹ:

| So the prophet **took up** | וַיִּשָּׂא הַנָּבִיא |
|---|---|
| the body of | אֶת־נִבְלַת |
| the man of God | אִישׁ־הָאֱלֹהִים |
| and **laid** it | וַיַּנִּחֵהוּ |
| on the donkey | אֶל־הַחֲמוֹר |
| and brought it back | וַיְשִׁיבֵהוּ |
| and he came | וַיָּבֹא |
| to the city of | אֶל־עִיר |
| the old prophet | הַנָּבִיא הַזָּקֵן |
| to mourn | לִסְפֹּד |
| and **to bury** him | וּלְקָבְרוֹ |

They said to me, "The **remnant** (נִשְׁאָרִים) there in the province who **survived** (נִשְׁאֲרוּ) the captivity are in great distress and reproach, and the **wall** (חוֹמַת) of Jerusalem is broken down and its gates are burned with **fire** (אֵשׁ)." (NASB)

| שָׁאַר | to remain, be left over | 133x |
|---|---|---|
| *šāʾar* | | S7604 |

אֵשׁ   ➤   DAY 138          חוֹמָה   ➤   DAY 339

וַיֹּאמְרוּ לִי הַנִּשְׁאָרִים אֲשֶׁר־נִשְׁאֲרוּ מִן־הַשְּׁבִי שָׁם בַּמְּדִינָה בְּרָעָה גְדֹלָה וּבְחֶרְפָּה וְחוֹמַת יְרוּשָׁלַ͏ִם מְפֹרָצֶת וּשְׁעָרֶיהָ נִצְּתוּ בָאֵשׁ:

| They said to me | וַיֹּאמְרוּ לִי |
|---|---|
| The **remnant** | הַנִּשְׁאָרִים |
| there in the province | שָׁם בַּמְּדִינָה |
| who **survived** | אֲשֶׁר־נִשְׁאֲרוּ |
| the captivity | מִן־הַשְּׁבִי |
| are in great distress | בְּרָעָה גְדֹלָה |
| and reproach | וּבְחֶרְפָּה |
| and the **wall** of Jerusalem | וְחוֹמַת יְרוּשָׁלַ͏ִם |
| is broken down | מְפֹרָצֶת |
| and its gates | וּשְׁעָרֶיהָ |
| are burned with **fire** | נִצְּתוּ בָאֵשׁ |

And those of you **who are left** (נִשְׁאָרִים) shall rot away in your enemies' lands because of their **iniquity** (עֲוֹנָם), and **also** (אַף) because of the **iniquities** (עֲוֹנֹת) of their fathers they shall rot away like [lit., with] them. (ESV)

| | | |
|---|---|---|
| **אַף** | also, even, yet | 133x |
| ʾaf | | S637 |

עָוֺן   ▷   DAY 207      שׁאר   ▷   DAY 343

וְהַנִּשְׁאָרִים בָּכֶם יִמַּקּוּ בַּעֲוֹנָם בְּאַרְצֹת אֹיְבֵיכֶם וְאַף בַּעֲוֹנֹת אֲבֹתָם אִתָּם יִמָּקּוּ׃

| And those of you **who are left** | וְהַנִּשְׁאָרִים בָּכֶם |
|---|---|
| shall rot away | יִמַּקּוּ |
| in your enemies' lands | בְּאַרְצֹת אֹיְבֵיכֶם |
| because of their **iniquity** | בַּעֲוֹנָם |
| and **also** | וְאַף |
| because of the **iniquities** of their fathers | בַּעֲוֹנֹת אֲבֹתָם |
| they shall rot away | יִמָּקּוּ |
| like [lit., with] them | אִתָּם |

Now Ezra **had determined** (הֵכִין) in his heart to study [lit., **seek** (דְּרוֹשׁ)] the law of the LORD, obey it, and teach its **statutes** (חֹק) and ordinances in Israel. (CSB)

| חֹק | statute, portion, limit | 131x |
| --- | --- | --- |
| ḥōq | | S2706 |

| כון | ▷ DAY 221 | | דרשׁ | ▷ DAY 280 |
| --- | --- | --- | --- | --- |

כִּי עֶזְרָא הֵכִין לְבָבוֹ לִדְרוֹשׁ אֶת־תּוֹרַת יְהוָה וְלַעֲשֹׂת וּלְלַמֵּד בְּיִשְׂרָאֵל חֹק וּמִשְׁפָּט:

| Now Ezra | כִּי עֶזְרָא |
| --- | --- |
| **had determined** | הֵכִין |
| in his heart | לְבָבוֹ |
| to study [lit., **seek**] | לִדְרוֹשׁ |
| the law of the LORD | אֶת־תּוֹרַת יְהוָה |
| obey it | וְלַעֲשֹׂת |
| and teach | וּלְלַמֵּד |
| its **statutes** and ordinances | חֹק וּמִשְׁפָּט |
| in Israel | בְּיִשְׂרָאֵל |

Therefore my heart **was glad** (שָׂמַח) and my glory rejoiced; my
body **too** (אַף) **shall dwell** (יִשְׁכֹּן) securely. (MLB)

| | | |
|---|---|---|
| שׁכן | to dwell | 130x |
| *šāḵan* | | S7931 |

שׂמח    ➢  DAY 292          אַף   ➢   DAY 344

לָכֵן **שָׂמַח** לִבִּי וַיָּגֶל כְּבוֹדִי **אַף**־בְּשָׂרִי **יִשְׁכֹּן** לָבֶטַח:

| | |
|---|---|
| Therefore | לָכֵן |
| my heart **was glad** | שָׂמַח לִבִּי |
| and my glory rejoiced | וַיָּגֶל כְּבוֹדִי |
| my body **too** | אַף־בְּשָׂרִי |
| **shall dwell** | יִשְׁכֹּן |
| securely | לָבֶטַח |

**Jeremiah** (יִרְמְיָהוּ) also uttered a lament for Josiah, and all the singing men and singing women have spoken of Josiah in their laments to this day. They made these a **custom** (חֹק) in Israel; they are **recorded** (כְּתוּבִים) in the Laments. (NRSV)

| יִרְמְיָהוּ | Jeremiah | 129x |
|---|---|---|
| *yirmĕyāhû* | | S3414 |

כתב  ▷  DAY 215     חֹק  ▷  DAY 345

וַיְקוֹנֵן יִרְמְיָהוּ עַל־יֹאשִׁיָּהוּ וַיֹּאמְרוּ כָל־הַשָּׁרִים וְהַשָּׁרוֹת בְּקִינוֹתֵיהֶם עַל־יֹאשִׁיָּהוּ עַד־הַיּוֹם וַיִּתְּנוּם לְחֹק עַל־יִשְׂרָאֵל וְהִנָּם כְּתוּבִים עַל־הַקִּינוֹת:

| **Jeremiah** also uttered a lament | וַיְקוֹנֵן יִרְמְיָהוּ |
|---|---|
| for Josiah | עַל־יֹאשִׁיָּהוּ |
| and . . . have spoken of Josiah | וַיֹּאמְרוּ . . . עַל־יֹאשִׁיָּהוּ |
| all the singing men | כָל־הַשָּׁרִים |
| and singing women | וְהַשָּׁרוֹת |
| in their laments | בְּקִינוֹתֵיהֶם |
| to this day | עַד־הַיּוֹם |
| They made these a **custom** | וַיִּתְּנוּם לְחֹק |
| in Israel | עַל־יִשְׂרָאֵל |
| they are **recorded** | וְהִנָּם כְּתוּבִים |
| in the Laments | עַל־הַקִּינוֹת |

So they waited until they were **embarrassed** (בּוֹשׁ). When he still **did** not **open** (פָּתַח) the doors of the roof chamber, they took the key and **opened** (וַיִּפְתָּחוּ) them. There was their **lord** (אֲדֹנֵיהֶם) lying dead on the floor. (NRSV)

| בּוֹשׁ | to be ashamed | 127x |
|---|---|---|
| *bôš* | | S954 |

אָדוֹן  ▷  DAY 65       **פתח**  ▷  DAY 328

וַיָּחִילוּ עַד־**בּוֹשׁ** וְהִנֵּה אֵינֶנּוּ **פֹתֵחַ** דַּלְתוֹת הָעֲלִיָּה וַיִּקְחוּ אֶת־הַמַּפְתֵּחַ
**וַיִּפְתָּחוּ** וְהִנֵּה **אֲדֹנֵיהֶם** נֹפֵל אַרְצָה מֵת׃

| So they waited | וַיָּחִילוּ |
|---|---|
| until they were **embarrassed** | עַד־**בּוֹשׁ** |
| When he still **did** not **open** | וְהִנֵּה אֵינֶנּוּ **פֹתֵחַ** |
| the doors of the roof chamber | דַּלְתוֹת הָעֲלִיָּה |
| they took the key | וַיִּקְחוּ אֶת־הַמַּפְתֵּחַ |
| and **opened** them | **וַיִּפְתָּחוּ** |
| There was their **lord** | וְהִנֵּה **אֲדֹנֵיהֶם** |
| lying dead | נֹפֵל . . . מֵת |
| on the floor | אַרְצָה |

Thus says the Lord: **I have returned** (שַׁבְתִּי) to Zion, and **I will dwell** (וְשָׁכַנְתִּי) in the midst of Jerusalem. Jerusalem shall be called the city of **truth** (אֱמֶת), and the mountain of the Lord of hosts, the holy mountain. (MLB)

| | | |
|---|---|---|
| אֱמֶת | truth, faithfulness | 127x |
| ʾĕmet | | S571 |

שׁוּב   ➤   DAY 44      שׁכן   ➤   DAY 346

כֹּה אָמַר יְהוָה שַׁבְתִּי אֶל־צִיּוֹן וְשָׁכַנְתִּי בְּתוֹךְ יְרוּשָׁלָ͏ִם וְנִקְרְאָה יְרוּשָׁלַ͏ִם עִיר־הָאֱמֶת וְהַר־יְהוָה צְבָאוֹת הַר הַקֹּדֶשׁ:

| | |
|---|---|
| Thus says the Lord | כֹּה אָמַר יְהוָה |
| **I have returned** | שַׁבְתִּי |
| to Zion | אֶל־צִיּוֹן |
| and **I will dwell** | וְשָׁכַנְתִּי |
| in the midst of Jerusalem | בְּתוֹךְ יְרוּשָׁלָ͏ִם |
| Jerusalem shall be called | וְנִקְרְאָה יְרוּשָׁלַ͏ִם |
| the city of **truth** | עִיר־הָאֱמֶת |
| and the mountain of the Lord of hosts | וְהַר־יְהוָה צְבָאוֹת |
| the holy mountain | הַר הַקֹּדֶשׁ |

And the Lᴏʀᴅ **turned** (וַיִּפֶן) to him and said, "Go in this **might** (בְּכֹחֲךָ) of yours and save Israel from the **hand** (כַּף) of Midian; do not I send you?" (ESV)

| כֹּחַ | strength | 127x |
|---|---|---|
| *kōaḥ* | | S3581 |

כַּף ➤ DAY 244            פנה ➤ DAY 337

וַיִּפֶן אֵלָיו יְהוָה וַיֹּאמֶר לֵךְ בְּכֹחֲךָ זֶה וְהוֹשַׁעְתָּ אֶת־יִשְׂרָאֵל מִכַּף מִדְיָן הֲלֹא שְׁלַחְתִּיךָ׃

| And the Lᴏʀᴅ **turned** to him | וַיִּפֶן אֵלָיו יְהוָה |
|---|---|
| and said | וַיֹּאמֶר |
| Go | לֵךְ |
| in this **might** of yours | בְּכֹחֲךָ זֶה |
| and save | וְהוֹשַׁעְתָּ |
| Israel | אֶת־יִשְׂרָאֵל |
| from the **hand** of Midian | מִכַּף מִדְיָן |
| do not I send you? | הֲלֹא שְׁלַחְתִּיךָ |

**Let** all the nations **gather** (נִקְבְּצוּ) together, and **let** the peoples **assemble** (יֵאָסְפוּ). . . . Let them bring their witnesses to justify them, and let them hear and say, "It is **true** (אֱמֶת)." (NRSV)

| קבץ | to gather, assemble | 127x |
|---|---|---|
| qāvaṣ | | S6908 |

אסף  ▷  DAY 241      אֱמֶת  ▷  DAY 349

כָּל־הַגּוֹיִם נִקְבְּצוּ יַחְדָּו וְיֵאָסְפוּ לְאֻמִּים . . . יִתְּנוּ עֵדֵיהֶם וְיִצְדָּקוּ וְיִשְׁמְעוּ וְיֹאמְרוּ אֱמֶת:

| **Let** . . . **gather** together | נִקְבְּצוּ יַחְדָּו |
|---|---|
| all the nations | כָּל־הַגּוֹיִם |
| and **let** . . . **assemble**. . . . | . . . וְיֵאָסְפוּ |
| the peoples | לְאֻמִּים |
| Let them bring | יִתְּנוּ |
| their witnesses | עֵדֵיהֶם |
| to justify them | וְיִצְדָּקוּ |
| and let them hear | וְיִשְׁמְעוּ |
| and say | וְיֹאמְרוּ |
| It is **true** | אֱמֶת |

Indeed, my life **is consumed** (כָּלוּ) with grief and my years with groaning; my **strength** (כֹחִי) has failed because of my iniquity, and my **bones** (עֲצָמַי) waste away. (CSB)

| עֶצֶם | bone, strength | 126x |
| ---- | ---- | ---- |
| ʿeṣem | | S6106 |

**כלה** ➤ DAY 236     **כֹּחַ** ➤ DAY 350

כִּי כָלוּ בְיָגוֹן חַיַּי וּשְׁנוֹתַי בַּאֲנָחָה כָּשַׁל בַּעֲוֺנִי כֹחִי וַעֲצָמַי עָשֵׁשׁוּ׃

| Indeed | כִּי |
| --- | --- |
| my life | חַיַּי |
| **is consumed** | כָלוּ |
| with grief | בְיָגוֹן |
| and my years | וּשְׁנוֹתַי |
| with groaning | בַּאֲנָחָה |
| my **strength** | כֹחִי |
| has failed | כָּשַׁל |
| because of my iniquity | בַּעֲוֺנִי |
| and my **bones** | וַעֲצָמַי |
| waste away | עָשֵׁשׁוּ |

Some time later, Ben-Hadad king of **Aram (אֲרָם) mobilized**
(וַיִּקְבֹּץ) his entire **army** (מַחֲנֵהוּ) and marched up and laid siege to
Samaria. (NIV)

| אֲרָם | Aram | 125x |
|---|---|---|
| *ʾărām* | | S758 |

מַחֲנֶה  ▷  DAY 228          קבץ  ▷  DAY 351

וַיְהִי אַחֲרֵי־כֵן וַיִּקְבֹּץ בֶּן־הֲדַד מֶלֶךְ־אֲרָם אֶת־כָּל־מַחֲנֵהוּ וַיַּעַל וַיָּצַר
עַל־שֹׁמְרוֹן:

| Some time later | וַיְהִי אַחֲרֵי־כֵן |
|---|---|
| Ben-Hadad | בֶּן־הֲדַד |
| king of **Aram** | מֶלֶךְ־אֲרָם |
| **mobilized** | וַיִּקְבֹּץ |
| his entire **army** | אֶת־כָּל־מַחֲנֵהוּ |
| and marched up | וַיַּעַל |
| and laid siege | וַיָּצַר |
| to Samaria | עַל־שֹׁמְרוֹן |

The one who is far off will die by plague; the one who is near will fall by the sword; and the one **who remains** (נִשְׁאָר) and is spared will die of famine. In this way **I will exhaust** (וְכִלֵּיתִי) my **wrath** (חֲמָתִי) on them. (CSB)

| חֵמָה | heat, anger, poison | 125x |
|---|---|---|
| ḥēmâ | | S2534 |

כלה   ➤   DAY 236        שאר   ➤   DAY 343

הָרָחוֹק בַּדֶּבֶר יָמוּת וְהַקָּרוֹב בַּחֶרֶב יִפּוֹל וְהַנִּשְׁאָר וְהַנָּצוּר בָּרָעָב יָמוּת וְכִלֵּיתִי חֲמָתִי בָּם:

| The one who is far off | הָרָחוֹק |
|---|---|
| will die by plague | בַּדֶּבֶר יָמוּת |
| the one who is near | וְהַקָּרוֹב |
| will fall by the sword | בַּחֶרֶב יִפּוֹל |
| and the one **who remains** | וְהַנִּשְׁאָר |
| and is spared | וְהַנָּצוּר |
| will die of famine | בָּרָעָב יָמוּת |
| In this way **I will exhaust** | וְכִלֵּיתִי |
| my **wrath** | חֲמָתִי |
| on them | בָּם |

So we labored at the **work** (מְלָאכָה), and **half** (חֲצָיִם) of them held the spears from break of dawn until the stars **came out** (צֵאת). (NRSV)

| חֲצִי | half, middle | 125x |
| --- | --- | --- |
| ḥăṣî | | S2677 |

**יצא**  ➤  DAY 43     **מְלָאכָה**  ➤  DAY 279

וַאֲנַחְנוּ עֹשִׂים בַּמְּלָאכָה וְחֶצְיָם מַחֲזִיקִים בָּרְמָחִים מֵעֲלוֹת הַשַּׁחַר עַד צֵאת הַכּוֹכָבִים:

| So we | וַאֲנַחְנוּ |
| --- | --- |
| labored | עֹשִׂים |
| at the **work** | בַּמְּלָאכָה |
| and **half** of them | וְחֶצְיָם |
| held | מַחֲזִיקִים |
| the spears | בָּרְמָחִים |
| from break of | מֵעֲלוֹת |
| dawn | הַשַּׁחַר |
| until | עַד |
| the stars **came out** | צֵאת הַכּוֹכָבִים |

Then, if the king's **anger** (חֲמַת) rises, and if he says to you, "Why **did you go** so **near** (נִגַּשְׁתֶּם) the city to fight? Did you not know that they would shoot from the **wall** (חוֹמָה)? . . ." (ESV)

| | | |
|---|---|---|
| **נגשׁ** | to approach; present | 125x |
| *nāgaš* | | S5066 |

| **חוֹמָה** | ➤ DAY 339 | **חֵמָה** | ➤ DAY 354 |
|---|---|---|---|

וְהָיָה אִם־תַּעֲלֶה חֲמַת הַמֶּלֶךְ וְאָמַר לְךָ מַדּוּעַ נִגַּשְׁתֶּם אֶל־הָעִיר לְהִלָּחֵם הֲלוֹא יְדַעְתֶּם אֵת אֲשֶׁר־יֹרוּ מֵעַל הַחוֹמָה:

| | |
|---|---|
| Then, if | וְהָיָה אִם־ |
| the king's **anger** | חֲמַת הַמֶּלֶךְ |
| rises | תַּעֲלֶה |
| and if he says to you | וְאָמַר לְךָ |
| Why | מַדּוּעַ |
| **did you go** so **near** | נִגַּשְׁתֶּם |
| the city | אֶל־הָעִיר |
| to fight? | לְהִלָּחֵם |
| Did you not know | הֲלוֹא יְדַעְתֶּם |
| that they would shoot | אֵת אֲשֶׁר־יֹרוּ |
| from the **wall**? | מֵעַל הַחוֹמָה |

So they followed them as far as the Jordan. They saw that the whole way was littered with clothes and equipment the **Arameans** (אֲרָם) **had thrown off** (הִשְׁלִיכוּ) in their haste. The **messengers** (מַלְאָכִים) returned and told the king. (CSB)

| | | |
|---|---|---|
| שׁלך | to throw, cast | 125x |
| *šālak* | | S7993 |

מַלְאָךְ ➤ DAY 232　　　אֲרָם ➤ DAY 353

וַיֵּלְכוּ אַחֲרֵיהֶם עַד־הַיַּרְדֵּן וְהִנֵּה כָל־הַדֶּרֶךְ מְלֵאָה בְגָדִים וְכֵלִים אֲשֶׁר־הִשְׁלִיכוּ אֲרָם בְּחָפְזָם וַיָּשֻׁבוּ הַמַּלְאָכִים וַיַּגִּדוּ לַמֶּלֶךְ:

| So they followed them | וַיֵּלְכוּ אַחֲרֵיהֶם |
|---|---|
| as far as the Jordan | עַד־הַיַּרְדֵּן |
| They saw that | וְהִנֵּה |
| the whole way | כָל־הַדֶּרֶךְ |
| was littered | מְלֵאָה |
| with clothes and equipment | בְגָדִים וְכֵלִים |
| the **Arameans** | אֲשֶׁר־ . . . אֲרָם |
| **had thrown off** | הִשְׁלִיכוּ |
| in their haste | בְּחָפְזָם |
| The **messengers** returned | וַיָּשֻׁבוּ הַמַּלְאָכִים |
| and told the king | וַיַּגִּדוּ לַמֶּלֶךְ |

They told him, "This is what **Hezekiah** (חִזְקִיָּהוּ) says: This day
is a day of distress and rebuke and disgrace, as when **children**
(בָּנִים) come to the moment of birth and there is no **strength** (כֹּחַ)
to deliver them." (NIV)

| חִזְקִיָּהוּ / חִזְקִיָּה | Hezekiah | 125x |
|---|---|---|
| ḥizqiyyāhû / ḥizqiyyâ | | S2396 |

בֵּן ➤ DAY 14    כֹּחַ ➤ DAY 350

וַיֹּאמְרוּ אֵלָיו כֹּה אָמַר חִזְקִיָּהוּ יוֹם־צָרָה וְתוֹכֵחָה וּנְאָצָה הַיּוֹם הַזֶּה
כִּי בָאוּ בָנִים עַד־מַשְׁבֵּר וְכֹחַ אַיִן לְלֵדָה:

| They told him | וַיֹּאמְרוּ אֵלָיו |
|---|---|
| This is what **Hezekiah** says | כֹּה אָמַר חִזְקִיָּהוּ |
| This day | הַיּוֹם הַזֶּה |
| is a day of distress | יוֹם־צָרָה |
| and rebuke | וְתוֹכֵחָה |
| and disgrace | וּנְאָצָה |
| as when | כִּי |
| **children** come | בָאוּ בָנִים |
| to the moment of birth | עַד־מַשְׁבֵּר |
| and there is no **strength** | וְכֹחַ אַיִן |
| to deliver them | לְלֵדָה |

Then they said, "Come, and **let us devise** (נַחְשְׁבָה) schemes
against **Jeremiah** (יִרְמְיָהוּ); for direction shall not perish from the
priest, nor counsel from the **wise** (חָכָם), nor the word from the
prophet." (MLB)

| חשֹׁב | to think, plan | 124x |
|---|---|---|
| ḥāšav | | S2803 |

חָכָם   ▷   DAY 326          יִרְמְיָהוּ   ▷   DAY 347

וַיֹּאמְרוּ לְכוּ וְנַחְשְׁבָה עַל־יִרְמְיָהוּ מַחֲשָׁבוֹת כִּי לֹא־תֹאבַד תּוֹרָה
מִכֹּהֵן וְעֵצָה מֵחָכָם וְדָבָר מִנָּבִיא

| Then they said | וַיֹּאמְרוּ |
|---|---|
| Come | לְכוּ |
| and **let us devise** schemes | וְנַחְשְׁבָה . . . מַחֲשָׁבוֹת |
| against **Jeremiah** | עַל־יִרְמְיָהוּ |
| for direction . . . from the priest | כִּי . . . תּוֹרָה מִכֹּהֵן |
| shall not perish | לֹא־תֹאבַד |
| nor counsel from the **wise** | וְעֵצָה מֵחָכָם |
| nor the word from the prophet | וְדָבָר מִנָּבִיא |

For King **Hezekiah** (חִזְקִיָּהוּ) of Judah gave the **assembly** (קָהָל) a thousand **bulls** (פָּרִים) and seven thousand sheep for offerings, and the officials gave the **assembly** (קָהָל) a thousand **bulls** (פָּרִים) and ten thousand sheep. The priests sanctified themselves in great numbers. (NRSV)

| קָהָל | assembly, congregation | 123x |
|---|---|---|
| *qāhāl* | | S6951 |

פַּר    ➤    DAY 341        חִזְקִיָּהוּ / חִזְקִיָּה    ➤    DAY 358

כִּי חִזְקִיָּהוּ מֶלֶךְ־יְהוּדָה הֵרִים לַקָּהָל אֶלֶף פָּרִים וְשִׁבְעַת אֲלָפִים צֹאן וְהַשָּׂרִים הֵרִימוּ לַקָּהָל פָּרִים אֶלֶף וְצֹאן עֲשֶׂרֶת אֲלָפִים וַיִּתְקַדְּשׁוּ כֹהֲנִים לָרֹב:

| For King **Hezekiah** of Judah | כִּי חִזְקִיָּהוּ מֶלֶךְ־יְהוּדָה |
|---|---|
| gave the **assembly** . . . for offerings | הֵרִים לַקָּהָל |
| a thousand **bulls** | אֶלֶף פָּרִים |
| and seven thousand sheep | וְשִׁבְעַת אֲלָפִים צֹאן |
| and the officials | וְהַשָּׂרִים |
| gave the **assembly** | הֵרִימוּ לַקָּהָל |
| a thousand **bulls** | פָּרִים אֶלֶף |
| and ten thousand sheep | וְצֹאן עֲשֶׂרֶת אֲלָפִים |
| The priests sanctified themselves | וַיִּתְקַדְּשׁוּ כֹהֲנִים |
| in great numbers | לָרֹב |

The goat **became** very **great** (הִגְדִּיל), but at the height of its
**power** (עָצְמוֹ) the large horn **was broken off** (נִשְׁבְּרָה), and in its
place four prominent horns grew up toward the four winds of
heaven. (NIV)

| גדל | | to be(come) great | | 121x |
|---|---|---|---|---|
| *gādal* | | | | S1431 |

**שׁבר** ▷ DAY 304　　　　**עָצֵם** ▷ DAY 352

וּצְפִיר הָעִזִּים הִגְדִּיל עַד־מְאֹד וּכְעָצְמוֹ נִשְׁבְּרָה הַקֶּרֶן הַגְּדוֹלָה
וַתַּעֲלֶנָה חָזוּת אַרְבַּע תַּחְתֶּיהָ לְאַרְבַּע רוּחוֹת הַשָּׁמָיִם:

| The goat | וּצְפִיר הָעִזִּים |
|---|---|
| **became** very **great** | הִגְדִּיל עַד־מְאֹד |
| but at the height of its **power** | וּכְעָצְמוֹ |
| the large horn | הַקֶּרֶן הַגְּדוֹלָה |
| **was broken off** | נִשְׁבְּרָה |
| and . . . grew up | וַתַּעֲלֶנָה |
| in its place | תַּחְתֶּיהָ |
| four prominent horns | חָזוּת אַרְבַּע |
| toward the four | לְאַרְבַּע |
| winds of heaven | רוּחוֹת הַשָּׁמָיִם |

Woe to **them that plan** (חֹשְׁבֵי) iniquity, that scheme wickedness upon their beds; in the morning **light** (אוֹר) they act on it; for **it is** (יֶשׁ) in the power of their hands. (MLB)

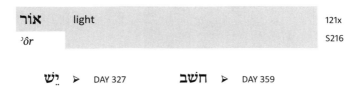

| | | |
|---|---|---|
| **אוֹר** | light | 121x |
| ʾôr | | S216 |

יֶשׁ ➤ DAY 327      חָשַׁב ➤ DAY 359

הוֹי חֹשְׁבֵי־אָוֶן וּפֹעֲלֵי רָע עַל־מִשְׁכְּבוֹתָם בְּאוֹר הַבֹּקֶר יַעֲשׂוּהָ כִּי יֶשׁ־לְאֵל יָדָם:

| | |
|---|---|
| Woe to | הוֹי |
| **them that plan** iniquity | חֹשְׁבֵי־אָוֶן |
| that scheme wickedness | וּפֹעֲלֵי רָע |
| upon their beds | עַל־מִשְׁכְּבוֹתָם |
| in the morning **light** | בְּאוֹר הַבֹּקֶר |
| they act on it | יַעֲשׂוּהָ |
| for **it is** | כִּי יֶשׁ־ |
| in the power of their hands | לְאֵל יָדָם |

At midnight [lit., the **middle** (חֲצִי) of the night] the LORD struck
down all the **firstborn** (בְּכוֹר) in the land of Egypt, from the
**firstborn** (בְּכֹר) of Pharaoh who sat on his **throne** (כִּסְאוֹ) to the
**firstborn** (בְּכוֹר) of the prisoner who was in the dungeon, and all
the **firstborn** (בְּכוֹר) of the livestock. (NRSV)

| בְּכֹר | firstborn | 121x |
|---|---|---|
| *bĕkōr* | | S1060 |

כִּסֵּא  ➤  DAY 332          חֲצִי  ➤  DAY 355

וַיְהִי בַּחֲצִי הַלַּיְלָה וַיהוָה הִכָּה כָל־בְּכוֹר בְּאֶרֶץ מִצְרַיִם מִבְּכֹר פַּרְעֹה
הַיֹּשֵׁב עַל־כִּסְאוֹ עַד בְּכוֹר הַשְּׁבִי אֲשֶׁר בְּבֵית הַבּוֹר וְכֹל בְּכוֹר
בְּהֵמָה:

| At midnight [lit., the **middle** of the night] | וַיְהִי בַּחֲצִי הַלַּיְלָה |
|---|---|
| the LORD struck down | וַיהוָה הִכָּה |
| all the **firstborn** | כָל־בְּכוֹר |
| in the land of Egypt | בְּאֶרֶץ מִצְרַיִם |
| from the **firstborn** of Pharaoh | מִבְּכֹר פַּרְעֹה |
| who sat on his **throne** | הַיֹּשֵׁב עַל־כִּסְאוֹ |
| to the **firstborn** of the prisoner | עַד בְּכוֹר הַשְּׁבִי |
| who was in the dungeon | אֲשֶׁר בְּבֵית הַבּוֹר |
| and all the **firstborn** of the livestock | וְכֹל בְּכוֹר בְּהֵמָה |

For **we** (אֲנַחְנוּ) **are about to destroy** (מַשְׁחִתִים) this place,
because their outcry **has become** so **great** (גָדְלָה) before the Lord
that the Lord has sent us **to destroy** (שַׁחֲתָהּ) it. (NASB)

| אֲנַחְנוּ | we | 121x |
|---|---|---|
| ʾănaḥnû | | S587 |

שׁחת　▷　DAY 314　　　　גדל׳　▷　DAY 361

כִּי־מַשְׁחִתִים אֲנַחְנוּ אֶת־הַמָּקוֹם הַזֶּה כִּי־גָדְלָה צַעֲקָתָם אֶת־פְּנֵי
יְהוָה וַיְשַׁלְּחֵנוּ יְהוָה לְשַׁחֲתָהּ:

| For **we** | כִּי־ . . . אֲנַחְנוּ |
|---|---|
| **are about to destroy** | מַשְׁחִתִים |
| this place | אֶת־הַמָּקוֹם הַזֶּה |
| because their outcry | כִּי־ . . . צַעֲקָתָם |
| **has become** so **great** | גָדְלָה |
| before the Lord | אֶת־פְּנֵי יְהוָה |
| that the Lord has sent us | וַיְשַׁלְּחֵנוּ יְהוָה |
| **to destroy** it | לְשַׁחֲתָהּ |

Now then **gather** the rest of the people **together** (אֱסֹף) and encamp against the city and **take** (לְכָדָה) it, **lest** (פֶּן) I **take** (אֶלְכֹּד) the city and it be called by my name. (ESV)

| לכד | to catch, capture | 121x |
|---|---|---|
| lā<u>k</u>ad | | S3920 |

אסף ➤ DAY 241　　　פֶּן ➤ DAY 340

וְעַתָּה אֱסֹף אֶת־יֶתֶר הָעָם וַחֲנֵה עַל־הָעִיר וְלָכְדָהּ פֶּן־אֶלְכֹּד אֲנִי אֶת־הָעִיר וְנִקְרָא שְׁמִי עָלֶיהָ:

| Now then | וְעַתָּה |
|---|---|
| **gather . . . together** | אֱסֹף |
| the rest of the people | אֶת־יֶתֶר הָעָם |
| and encamp | וַחֲנֵה |
| against the city | עַל־הָעִיר |
| and **take** it | וְלָכְדָהּ |
| **lest** I **take** | פֶּן־אֶלְכֹּד אֲנִי |
| the city | אֶת־הָעִיר |
| and it be called by my name | וְנִקְרָא שְׁמִי עָלֶיהָ |

# INDEX OF SCRIPTURE REFERENCES

| | | | | | |
|---|---|---|---|---|---|
| 10:16 | DAY 301 | 7:12 | DAY 61 | 2:19 | DAY 155 |
| 12:7 | DAY 319 | 9:11 | DAY 120 | | |
| | | | | **Zechariah** | |
| **Hosea** | | **Obadiah** | | 1:4 | DAY 78 |
| 2:1[1:10] | DAY 135 | 1:16 | DAY 96 | 1:16 | DAY 141 |
| 2:19[17] | DAY 6 | | | 2:15[11] | DAY 127 |
| 2:20[18] | DAY 159 | **Jonah** | | 3:3 | DAY 223 |
| 7:1 | DAY 260 | 1:14 | DAY 77 | 3:8 | DAY 72 |
| | | | | 8:3 | DAY 349 |
| **Joel** | | **Micah** | | 9:9 | DAY 238 |
| 2:11 | DAY 103 | 2:1 | DAY 362 | 14:5 | DAY 21 |
| 2:23 | DAY 292 | 2:3 | DAY 164 | | |
| | | | | **Malachi** | |
| **Amos** | | **Habakkuk** | | 1:14 | DAY 56 |
| 1:8 | DAY 255 | 3:10 | DAY 97 | 2:13 | DAY 295 |
| 2:8 | DAY 226 | | | 3:23[4:5] | DAY 161 |
| 3:1 | DAY 39 | **Haggai** | | | |
| 3:2 | DAY 165 | 1:14 | DAY 20 | | |
| 5:19 | DAY 27 | 2:3 | DAY 122 | | |